Dennis A. Mahony

The Four Acts of Despotism

Comprising I. The tax bill, with all the amendments. II. The finance bill. III. The

conscription act. IV. The indemnity bill. With introductions and comments

Dennis A. Mahony

The Four Acts of Despotism
Comprising I. The tax bill, with all the amendments. II. The finance bill. III. The conscription act. IV. The indemnity bill. With introductions and comments

ISBN/EAN: 9783337402792

Printed in Europe, USA, Canada, Australia, Japan

Cover: Foto ©Suzi / pixelio.de

More available books at **www.hansebooks.com**

THE

FOUR ACTS OF DESPOTISM:

COMPRISING

I.
THE TAX BILL,
WITH ALL THE AMENDMENTS.

II.
THE FINANCE BILL.

III.
THE CONSCRIPTION ACT.

IV.
THE INDEMNITY BILL.

WITH

INTRODUCTIONS AND COMMENTS.

BY

D. A. MAHONY,

AUTHOR OF "THE PRISONER OF STATE."

"An *elective despotism* was not the government we fought for; but one which should not only be founded on free principles, but in which the powers of government should be so divided and balanced among several bodies of magistracy, as that no one could transcend their legal limits without being effectually checked and restrained by the others." THOMAS JEFFERSON.

"The legitimate authority of the Constitution is abundantly sufficient for all the purposes for which it was created; and its powers being expressly enumerated, there can be no justification of doing anything beyond them. That every attempt to exercise powers beyond those limits, should be promptly and firmly opposed." ANDREW JACKSON.

NEW YORK:

VAN EVRIE, HORTON & CO.,

No. 162 NASSAU STREET.

1863.

TABLE OF CONTENTS.

	PAGE
INTRODUCTION	5
INTRODUCTION TO THE TAX BILL	10
" " FINANCE ACT	14
" " CONSCRIPTION ACT	19
" " INDEMNITY BILL	25
THE TAX BILL, JULY 1, 1862	33
AMENDMENTS	105
THE FINANCE ACT	124
THE CONSCRIPTION ACT	129
THE INDEMNITY BILL	137
ALPHABETICAL RECAPITULATION	141

INTRODUCTION.

THE history of legislation in any age or country does not relate parallel instances of the arbitrary exercise of authority and power by a legislative body over a people to the four acts passed by the late Congress of the United States on taxation, finance, conscription, and indemnity for acts of Executive usurpation. No four acts ever passed by any legislative body equal these in despotic exaction, in tyrannic oppression, in ruthless disregard for popular rights and the interests of the community, and in doing violence to the principles of free government.

Taxation, which is but a necessary evil at best, is made almost intolerable to the people of the United States by the so-called Revenue Law, passed by the Thirty-seventh Congress. The currency, which should always, so far as governments are concerned, be made the measure of value, is converted by the financial acts of Congress into a means for driving the precious metals out of circulation, and for unsettling the value of every commodity of use in the community. For the first time in the history, not only of Anglo-Americans, but of Anglo-Saxons, an act to conscript citizens into the army is passed by the Federal Congress, following in this respect the example of absolute monarchies, and abandoning by this act the precedents in principle and the examples of policy set not only by our immediate ancestors, but those also of the constitutional monarchy of Great Britain, of which our system of government has been regarded to be an improvement. This, to say nothing of the constitutional checks and balances by which the respective sovereignties of the States and Federal Government are attempted to be restrained and poised, so that they shall not conflict with each other, is a sign of evil omen to the liberties of the American people. Not that it is not the right of the Federal Government to make a demand on the people for their services, when, in the opinion of the Government, these services should be rendered—for the Government is invested with the authority to do this—but this authority must be exercised, when it is needed to be done, in accordance with the terms on which the authority is given.

The Federal Government can not reach the people on a demand for their services except by a requisition made on the authorities of the respective States. Such, at least, is the theory of the Constitution—the compact between the people and the Federal Government, or, rather, the compact among the people which is attempted to be enforced by the means of the Federal Government.

No such organization as a National or Federal militia is contemplated by the Constitution. The militia referred to by the Constitution are State forces, until mustered into the service of the Federal Government. When, therefore, the Federal Government, by means of its executive and legislative branches, undertakes to conscript American citizens into the Federal army without regard to State authority and State laws, and without regard, too, of the Constitution of the United States, these branches of the Government, and by their means the Government itself, undertake to do an act for which there is not only no warrant of authority whatever, but which is contrary to the evident intent and meaning of the Constitution, and violative not only of that compact, but of the rights of individuals and the sovereignty of States.

The fourth act, which will be cited in all time to come as a reproach, not only on the Federal Government, but on the American people, is that which attempts to indemnify the President for his acts, violative both of the Constitution which he is sworn to support as a condition of his being invested with executive functions, and of the rights of American citizens whom he is specially chosen to protect in the enjoyment of their rights and liberties. The Constitution provides that the President shall be impeached for malfeasance in office, and if found guilty, removed in disgrace; but the Thirty-seventh Congress, under the influence of fanatical partisans, who care more for power and plunder than they do for the rights, liberties, or interests of the people, ignore and disregard the Constitution, and even willfully violate it, by making those acts of the President virtues which the Constitution and the laws had previously made criminal, triable by impeachment, and punishable by removal from office, stigmatized by disgrace.

These four acts of Congressional and Executive despotism may be thus briefly characterized:

I. The Tax Bill, by which the necessaries of life, the implements of mechanical and agricultural labor, the multifarious commercial, legal, and financial transactions of the people are subjected to onerous exactions, while capital invested in Government securities is specially exempted by law from bearing any share of the burden imposed by the hundred million upon the industry, labor, and absolute necessities of the people at large.

II. The Conscription Bill, by which a price—three hundred dollars—is set upon the body and life of a white man, and by which those who can not afford to redeem themselves at that price are conscripted into the Federal army, and compelled to do such service as the President may order by proclamation, regardless of the Constitution of the United States, to which, and not to the President, the allegiance of citizens is due.

III. The Finance Act, by which all the property of the country, real and personal, except such as is invested in Government securities, is mortgaged as security for the payment of the debt created by this and other acts of Congress, and which debts amount, in the aggregate, to as much as a third of the whole value of all the property in the States adhering to the Federal Government, and which, with semi-annual interest, must be paid out of the profits of this property and out of the labor, industry, and by a tax on the necessaries of life of the people for ages to come, and in consequence of which debt the American people will be subjected while it exists to all the exactions, oppressions, grievances, and evils of bad government which the down-trodden people of Europe experience from similar causes.

IV. The Indemnity Act, which nullifies and violates the Constitution by exempting the President from trial or punishment for any illegal act of despotism and tyranny which he might commit, and which protects him and his subordinates from prosecution, no matter how flagrant may be his or their acts against the constitutional rights of the people of the United States, and which places in his power—a power to be exercised according to his own will, since not restrained by law—the person of every citizen of the United States who may venture to exercise his rights as such, as these rights are prescribed in the Constitution of the United States, and of every individual State in the Union ; and which vests in the President not only the power to deprive every citizen of his constitutional rights, but also the power to subject every citizen to such indignities, outrages, and torments, as he or any of his subordinates choose to inflict, and to deprive citizens of their lives without the judgment of any court except of such a one as the President may choose to constitute, and which, if constituted, will be but an instrument of his will and malevolence.

These four acts are linked together in this place with such comments as present them to the reader in their true colors, both as regard their effects and the objects designed to be accomplished by those who enacted them. They are such acts of folly, wickedness, despotism, and tyranny as no people ever endured complacently, and as were never imposed with impunity upon a people, even by governments which did not depend upon the popular will for their power, or on the popular judgment for authority. It remains to be seen whether the American people are more tolerant than those of all other nations of acts of government flagrantly violative of their personal rights, manifestly subversive of their political liberty, and evidently designed to bring them under the subjection of arbitrary power exercised over them by a partisan faction, which, by the accident of division among conservative people and by the calamity of war provoked against the South by Northern fanatics, have acquired control of the Government and of its armed power and moral authority. If the American people submit to all this, history will have it to say for the first time that a nation of freemen became voluntarily the slaves of their public servants; that a people who prided themselves on their personal independence, and made a boast of their control over the Government of their country, became, by the mere enactment of a few statutes, the most subservient to arbitrary power, the most servile adulators of despotic masters, all of whose power and authority were derived originally from those who voluntarily conferred it, and became subjects without rights in place of sovereigns with all the attributes and dignity of freemen. The whole form and system of our Government have been changed by the Administration. The powers withheld by the Constitution have been assumed and exercised by it, and the rights and privileges declared to be sacred to the people it has ruthlessly violated. By the operations of this Finance Act the people are, indirectly, subjected to the will and pleasure of the Secretary of the Treasury. While their persons are subjected to the control of the President by means of the Conscript Act, their property is subjected to the will of the President, through the Secretary of the Treasury, by the Finance and Tax Acts.

Thus in person and property are the American people made as much the subjects of one man's will as are any people on the face of the globe reduced to the servitude of a ruler. Where is there in the civilized world a parallel case in which the persons and property of the people are placed so much under the control of a ruler as are the persons and property of the American people placed at the disposal of the President of the United States and of his subordinates? Not only are the purse and sword, the money and property of the people and their person (with the exceptional cases of those who can purchase exemption for three hundred dollars), placed under the control of the President by the Conscript Act, Tax Bill, and Finance Bill, but their liberty, their right to act as freemen, are also taken away by the Indemnity Bill. In vain does the Constitution interpose itself as a restraint upon Executive usurpations of power. In vain does it define and prescribe the duties of the Executive and Congress. In vain does it stipulate on behalf of the people with the Government created by it that the reserved rights of the people shall be respected inviolate by the Government, and protected if assailed from any source. In vain, indeed, was it that a Constitution was given to the Federal Government as its rule of action. As well might the Constitution have said, in a few words, that there shall be a President and Congress, and that their joint powers and authority shall be unlimited in extent and unrestrained in their exercise over the persons and property of the people of the United States. This is practically what the Constitution has become in relation to the people under the Administration of Abraham Lincoln. No more proof of this allegation is needed to convince the people of its truth than the enactment by Congress and the approval by the President of these four acts of despotism—the Tax Bill, the Conscript Bill, the Indemnity Bill, and the Finance Bill. These acts will stand on record as imperishable proofs of the despotism and tyranny of the Administration of Abraham Lincoln, and of the subserviency of its partisan supporters in these and other acts subversive of the constitutional Government of the United States.

THE TAX BILL.

IF the ingenuity of those who own among them the wealth of the country were put to the test of devising a measure by which the burdens of supporting the Federal Government might be placed upon the comparatively poor, the result could not be more perfect than the Tax Bill passed by Congress, and approved by the President on the 1st of July, 1862, and the amendments thereto passed and approved on the 3d of March, 1863.

It is estimated that by these acts $150,000,000 will be drawn from the people by direct taxation, besides some $50,000,000 by duties upon imported commodities, making in all not less than $200,000,000 per annum, the people will be required and obliged to pay for the wickedness of a fanatical party, and for the folly of having suffered this party to acquire the control of the Federal Government. Of this two hundred millions, the greater portion of it is ingeniously imposed upon the comparatively poor. It is assessed upon necessaries of life and implements of labor, rather than upon luxuries indulged in only by those who could afford to pay a tax upon such luxurious indulgence. A cup of coffee is as necessary to the health, strength, and comfort of a poor man as it is to a rich man, and more so, and a poor man uses, or should be able to use, as much coffee as a rich man. Yet this necessary of a poor man's life is taxed more, according to its value, than many of the luxuries of the rich man. And so of various other commodities. The tax is made to bear upon what is most universally used, by poor as well as by rich, and by this means the poor man, whose wages and means of procuring the necessaries of life are scarcely sufficient for that purpose, is required to pay as much taxes as the rich man for the necessaries of life? Is not this fair? some one might inquire. Ought not taxes to be equal? Personal taxes ought, perhaps, to be equal, because the protection given to one person by the Government is the same generally as it gives to another; but taxes upon property, whether of consumption or otherwise, should be in proportion to the ability of the possessor to pay them, and to the expense it is to the Government to afford protection and security to this property. A poor man who has no property requires no other protection from the Government than for his person. A rich man does require such protection in proportion to the amount or value of his property, and in that proportion estimating also his ability, he should be required to pay for the security and protection given him by the Government. These tax bills are formed upon a different principle. The weight of the exactions fall upon the people at large in nearly the proportion of their numbers. It is true that the incomes of the wealthy are subjected to a share of the tax burden, but it bears no just proportion to the amount of tax which a poor man is required to pay indirectly upon almost every commodity which contributes to his subsistence.

It will require the reader's examination of the tax bills to become well informed of the injustice of the discriminations made in favor of the comparatively wealthy and against the comparatively poor, and this unjust discrimination is carried out among dealers in merchandise, as will be seen by reference to paragraph numbered 42, of Amendments made by the act of the 3d of March, 1863, to the act of July 1st, 1862.

In this amendment it is provided that " Wholesale dealers, whose annual sales do not exceed $50,000," shall pay a license of $25, while a dealer whose sales amount to $2,000,000 per annum is required to pay only $500 for his license. Now, one would suppose that the more sales a dealer made, the more he could afford to pay a license tax, not only in comparative proportion to the amount of his sales, but in relative proportion to his ability. But the framers of these tax bills have proceeded throughout on the principle, that the more able a person is to pay taxes, the less he shall be required to pay in proportion. If it be a proper amount to charge $25 to a wholesale dealer whose sales per annum reach $50,000, what propriety is there in letting off the dealer whose sales may reach $2,000,000 with a tax of only $500 ? Two millions is forty times fifty thousand. Why, then, not tax the two-million dealer forty times as much as the fifty-thousand dealer ? For no other reason than to favor the rich, and to impose the greater portion of tax burden upon the comparatively poor.

And so it is throughout these tax bills. Even in cases where a tax is imposed apparently upon wealthy persons, it is imposed in such a manner as to fall indirectly upon the mass of the people. The dollar a barrel imposed upon malt liquors, though imposed apparently upon the brewer, is really a tax upon the glass of beer, or ale, or porter drank by the million. It would not have been so had the tax been imposed upon luxuries used and consumed almost exclusively by wealthy persons. The license taxes of all kinds required to be paid by dealers in the necessaries, conveniences, and comforts of life, might as well be imposed directly upon the consumers and users of these necessaries, conveniences, and comforts, for all the difference it makes to them as to how they have to pay, or for any advantage it is to them to pay to the merchant a higher price for their necessaries of life instead of paying the Government directly. Indeed, it would be better for the people to pay directly to the Government instead of indirectly to the merchant, for it so happens that for every dollar license the merchant is required to pay, and for every dollar of tax charged to him on his income profits, his customers are obliged to pay two, at least, in the increased price of the goods, so that these tax laws will not affect merchants and others who furnish commodities of necessary con-' sumption and use, except as the consumers might be reduced in circumstances and unable to buy. Were the means of the people at large equal to what they have been in prosperous times, no matter how onerously taxation may fall upon them, it would not affect the class who live upon the industry of the people, for the reason that the taxes are so imposed as to fall indirectly upon the masses, although an attempt is made to deceive the public by levying a considerable portion of the taxes apparently upon the more wealthy class. Had the Tax Bill exempted from taxation, direct and indirect, the actual necessaries of life, and imposed exactions only upon the luxuries, comforts, and conveniences which most people could do without, onerous as the large amount of tax required to be levied will be under any circumstances, it could be borne without subjecting the masses of the people to that species of despotism which is crushing out the life of the people in other countries subject to similar exactions. It is in vain that Ireland, and Poland, and Venetia are prolific of the necessaries of life, and these countries produce more than double what is necessary to feed the resident population. They are so burdened with taxation that they can not use the common necessaries of life, much less any of the comforts and luxuries which contribute to man's rational enjoyment. What different will we American people be, if it be required of us to pay interest by taxation on a Federal debt of at least two billions of dollars, and to support the Government by taxation of at least a hundred millions of dollars besides? What means have we to do this that is not possessed by the people of other countries? Taxation grinds them down to the dust, deprives them of the necessaries of life, to say nothing of comforts and conveniences. Will it not subject us to a similar condition? What is there to exempt us or protect us from the fate of the subjected people of other nations ? We have nothing to depend on if we once suffer ourselves to be subjected to despotism. The people who will hold out their hands to be manacled, and thank the despot for subjecting them to his will, are not likely to rise to the dignity of freemen and shake off the yoke of the despot ; nor will they be in such a condition to re-acquire their lost birthright, if they once suffer themselves to be despoiled of this God-given inheritance.

There can be no better evidence of a people being subjected to government control than the imposition on them of onerous taxation. Great Britain, indeed, may be pointed to as an exception to this hypothesis, but it is not an exception, for there are no people on the face of the earth oppressed more by a government than the people of Ireland are by the British Government. England, a portion of the British empire, may be regarded, to some extent, as an exception to the hypothesis ; but even in England, millions of the populace are sorely oppressed by taxation.

But it has taken Great Britain hundreds of years to become subject to the burdens which weigh so heavily upon her people ; and there were in many cases unavoidable circumstances which compelled the nation to increase its burdens. This has not been the case with the American people. *Our* difficulties are all of a domestic nature, and might have been all avoided, and no debt incurred to make the future life of the people uncomfortable and unhappy.

Is there no remedy for the evils which are manifestly imposed upon the people by these tax bills ? There are none but violent ones for the burden, as it is required to be imposed in consequence of suffering the Federal Government to involve the people in debt. Congress, if the people could only elect representatives of their interests and sentiments, could so change these tax bills as that the burden of taxation would fall where it properly belongs, on the wealthy classes.

As the laws stand now, wealth alone, as it may exist in Government securities, is exempt from taxation. The man who may own a million or ten millions of dollars in Government securities is exempt from taxation, except what he may have to pay, like the poorest individual, on the necessaries of life. The burdens are all taken off such a fortunate individual as may have investments in Government interest-bearing stocks, and placed upon those who have the misfortune to own nothing but such powers of muscle as Providence vouchsafes to them from day to day.

THE FINANCE ACT.

ONE of the most despotic acts of the Lincoln Administration is that which places it in the power of the Secretary of the Treasury to mortgage, for an indefinite period of time, the capital, labor, and enterprise of the American people, for a sum equal in the aggregate to one third of the value of all the property, *real* and personal, in the States remaining in the Union.

The Secretary of the Treasury may sell the credit of the United States for any sum or at any price he pleases ; he may make, and, no doubt, from his antecedents and course while Secretary of the Treasury, will make, bargains among his personal and political friends, which will give them the control of the United States bonds at such price as they and he may choose to agree upon.

The power placed by this act in the hands of the Secretary of the Treasury is such as was never before in the control of man; it is a power which enables him, at his mere whim, caprice, or will, to change the price of every merchantable commodity, to change the price of every species of property, to enrich his friends, to derange business, to inflict injury, and bring disaster on manufactures and commerce, and finally, as the ultimate effect of this monstrous delegation of power, to ruin the American people, by subjecting them for years interminable to the burden of a debt the interest on which will be more for them to pay than any other people are oppressed by, not excepting those of Great Britain. It is true that the British debt is more than ours in the aggregate, but the interest on that debt is not half as much per cent. as ours is. The British people can, therefore, carry twice as much debt as we of the United States can without feeling the burden of interest more than we would.

The taxable property of Great Britain is of more value than our taxable property ; hence the British people can afford to pay more taxes than we can.

It was the boast, not long since, of the American people, that we were comparatively exempt from taxation. It was a favorite argument of ours, that the comparative exemption of the American people from taxation was an evidence of the beneficence of republican forms of government. Indeed, the superiority of republicanism over monarchism was rested on the fact, that the people of the United States were taxed less to support their Government than were the people living under monarchical forms of government. What becomes now of this theory, when in two years the Federal Government, under an Administration which boasts of the purity of its republicanism, has become involved in more debt than any nation in Europe has incurred in a hundred years? There is no parallel in the world's known history to the monstrous use and abuse of power by the Administration of Abraham Lincoln. No people which ever existed were subjected so much to the rule and caprice of a despot as the people of the United States are to the will and caprice of the Secretary of the Treasury. The whole money power of the country is placed under his control by this Finance Act, and by means of this power he can at will expand or contract the circulating medium of the country, and keep the whole people in a feverish uncertainty about the value of their property and the condition of their business.

The power vested by the Constitution in Congress only is transferred by Congress to this one man, thus defeating the object of the framers of the Constitution in placing power under restraint, and dividing it among several departments and many persons, instead of centering it in one individual, and leaving him unchecked in its exercise.

Of what use is it for the American people to have adopted a constitutional rule of government, and to have established by that rule a government republican in form, if Congress may, notwithstanding the Constitution, vest despotic powers of government in one person, divesting itself of vested powers given to it as a legislative body, and transferring these vested powers to an officer not known to the Constitution ?

The assessed value of real and personal property in all the States and Territories, according to the census of 1860, amounted to $12,084,660,005, but it is estimated that the real value of this property is $16,159,616,068. Admitting this estimated value to be more correct than the assessed value of property, and that all of the property of the Union will become subject to the incumbrance of the national debt, even in this respect the debt authorized by the Finance Act, added to the obligations already incurred, will be equal in amount to one eighth, at least, of the highest estimated value of all the property in the country.

But if it should happen that the Southern States should acquire a

separate independence, and that all the debt created by the Lincoln
Administration should fall upon the people of the States adhering to
the old Union, the comparative amount of the Federal debt to the
assessed value of the property, real and personal, which the people
will have to meet, this debt obligation will be about as one is to two
and a half. In other words, of every two and a half dollars' worth of
property which the people of the States adhering to the Union may
own, a portion equal to one dollar of every two and a half will be required to meet the obligations of debt incurred by the Lincoln Administration. And this estimate goes no further than to include debt
authorized by existing acts and obligations already incurred.

By a reference to the Finance Act now under consideration, it will
be seen that the Secretary of the Treasury is authorized by the first
section of that act to incur a bonded debt of $900,000,000, and with-
out obtaining for such bonds an equal amount in money. He may
sell the bonds for what they will bring in the market. And what
might this be? Not more than seventy cents in greenbacks on the
dollar, if as much, which would be about equal to fifty cents on the
dollar in specie.

The second section of the Finance Act authorizes the issue of
$400,000,000 in Treasury notes, making with the $900,000,000 in
bonds, $1,300,000,000. The third section authorizes a further
issue of $150,000,000 in other Treasury notes, if so much should
be needed, as it of course will be, and more too, making in all
$1,450,000,000. This added to the debt already incurred will make
over two billions four hundred and fifty millions (2,450,000,000)
of dollars. To pay this debt there was assessed property, real and
personal together in 1860, in the non-slaveholding States, of the
value of $5,579,692,449. Or adding to this the assessed value of
property in such doubtful States as Maryland, Delaware, Missouri,
Kentucky, and Tennessee, and we have in round numbers $8,000,-
000,000 worth of assessed property. But as that portion of personal
property which is invested in United States debt is exempt from
taxation, the remaining property, equal in a round sum to $5,500,000,-
000, will be made responsible for the whole debt. According to this
estimate, the debt will be, as it stands now incurred and authorized, in
the proportion of one dollar of debt to less than three dollars' worth of
taxable property, including the property, real and personal, of all the
States adhering to the Union, Delaware, Maryland, Missouri, Kentucky, and Tennessee not excepted. This burden, it will not be too
much to say, is intolerable. It will become unendurable, and the act
of legislation by which it has been imposed, one of the most despotic

character, for despotism in government is nothing else than the imposition of burdens and taxation on the governed which they are not able to bear without suffering privations which mankind should not be required to endure by any acts of their public servants or rulers.

But the debts incurred already, and authorized to be incurred by this Finance Act, are not all that will be required in consequence of the existing war. The future annual expenses of the Government, should the American people adhere to each other under a government, will not be less than $100,000,000, without including anything but very ordinary expenses. To this must be added the interest on the public debt, which, if no more debt should be created than is already incurred and authorized, will amount to $2,450,000,000, the interest on this amount of debt at an average of six per cent. will be an annual sum of $147,000,000. This added to the lowest estimate that can be made of the ordinary expenditures of the Government will swell the amount required to be raised to carry on the Government and pay interest on its debt, to $247,000,000 annually.

Onerous as the existing Tax Law and Tariff Act are, these two means of raising revenue will not produce more than $200,000,000 in the aggregate by the most liberal estimates that can be made of these resources. This will fall $47,000,000 a year short of meeting the requirements of the Government, and this amount must be raised either by extra taxation or by adding that amount to the public debt, as is done usually by the governments of Europe. In either case the prospect is not flattering to a people who thought they were free, in the liberal sense of the term.

It is to be also taken into consideration that the estimate of $100,000,000 to meet the ordinary expenditures of the Government is far too low. The expenditures will be really nearly double that sum, unless there be a reform in our system of government. It must not be forgotten, in estimating future requirements of the Government, that the widows and orphans of soldiers who die in the existing war must be provided for, nor that the surviving soldiers who may be disabled by wounds or disease from making a livelihood, must be supported at the expense of the Government. The surviving soldiers will form a strong element in election contests, and their whole influence will be brought to bear, if necessary to secure that object, to compel the Government to support and pension themselves and families. Those among them who were demagogues before entering the army will not be the less so when they are obliged to return to civil life, nor will their appetite for public pap have become satiated by the pay and plunder which they will have received and secured in return

2

for their patriotic efforts to preserve the Union. Fifty millions a year for some time to come will not be too large an estimate of what will be required to support and pension the widows and orphans of deceased soldiers and the survivors of the existing war. Add this to the $247,-000,000 which will be required to carry on the Government and pay interest on its debt, and the annual aggregate required to be raised by taxation or by new loans amounts to $297,000,000. It will be impossible to raise this amount by taxation. The alternative must be re-sorted to of raising a portion of it by loans, and thus will the burdens upon the people be increased from year to year, until it becomes so exacting that it will require all the surplus accumulations of labor, industry, and capital to meet its requirements, and leave the great mass of the people no more on which to eke out their existence than have the over-burdened, misgoverned, down-trodden people of Europe. Such will be the effects of some of the Acts of the Thirty-seventh Congress, and of the Administration of Abraham Lincoln. Reader, if you doubt it, bear in mind the reflections placed before you for consideration; if you have the discernment to perceive the prospective reality, does it not become you as a true American to aid in restraining our rulers in their mad career?

THE CONSCRIPTION ACT.

THE preamble to the Conscription Act sets out with the declaration, " that there exists an insurrection or rebellion in the United States, and that it is the duty of the Government to suppress it, to guarantee to each State a republican form of government, and to preserve the domestic tranquillity." But it does not follow from these assertions that the Federal Government, or rather the constitutional authorities who administer that Government, become vested with any new power or authority on that account which they did not possess before. It is the duty of the Government to suppress insurrection, but it is also a requirement of the supreme law that the Government conform itself in the performance of that duty to certain rules prescribed for its conduct. As Government is but a creature of law, it must conform itself to the will of the law, which in this country is presumed to be the will of the people. Now the law which is above the Government says that the authority of training the militia and of appointing officers of the militia shall be reserved to the States respectively. This reservation of State rights is disregarded and violated by this Conscription Act, which takes no notice of States but acts directly on individuals, and subjects them to the immediate domination of Federal powers instead of securing to each State a republican form of government. The President and Congress by this Conscription Act reduce the States to subjection and deprive them of the power of government. State authority is entirely ignored by this act, and not only ignored in the States, but usurped by the Federal Government.

It is a provision of the Federal Constitution, that " a well-regulated militia" is necessary to the security of a free State, and that the right of the people to keep and bear arms shall not be infringed, but the President and Congress by the Conscription Act put the State militia out of existence, or take no notice of this constitutional security of a free State, and make conscripts of American citizens instead of State militia. This the Federal authorities have no right to do. They have a right to call out the militia, when organized and officered, in accordance with State laws, but they have no right to call out the people against their will to perform military service in any other manner than in accordance with the Constitution and acts of legislation which conform to the Constitution.

As an act in antagonism to the Constitution and to the sovereignty of States, this Conscription Act is manifestly of no binding effect upon the people of the United States; but admitting that it were constitutional, it is so repugnant in some of its provisions to the rights of persons, that it will not be endured otherwise than under the duress of armed force. When any government assumes this relation to the people, it becomes, *ipso facto*, a despotism, for despotism is nothing more than subjecting the people to a domination of power against their will. It is not the name or form of government that makes it a despotism, but the relation it holds to the people who are governed. If the people of a country choose the form of absolute monarchy for their government, it is not a despotism in relation to those people; while, on the other hand, if a government chosen by a free people becomes different in its relations to the form which they instituted it to be, and it becomes in its relations absolute and despotic, such a government, whatever be its name or form, is really a despotism. So that despotic governments may exist under the name and form of Democracy or Republicanism, as well as under the name and form of Monarchy or Absolutism. It is not the name nor the form of a government that gives it the character of despotism, but the relation it assumes to the people governed. People may be as free under absolute monarchies as they are under democratic or republican forms of government; for in absolute monarchies the government may conform itself to the popular judgment and will, as nearly as do republican governments, if not more so. It is the conformity of government to the popular will that makes the people free, as it is the non-conformity of acts of government to the will of the people that makes a government despotic.

Applying this hypothesis to the existing relations of the Federal Government to the people of the United States, it can not be said of the Government, in truth, that it is what is understood by a free Government, nor can it be assumed with propriety or truth that the American people are any longer a free people.

None but a despotic government would attempt to divest the people of their constitutional rights, and put a price upon their lives as the Federal Government does by this act of the President and Congress. This Conscript Act exempts a millionaire from giving his personal service to the country on the payment of three hundred dollars, and places him on an equality, in his relations to the Government, with a another citizen whose whole wealth might consist of just enough to purchase his exemption. This is an unjust discrimination in favor of the rich man and against the comparatively poor.

A more just discrimination would subject persons to exemption penalties in proportion to their ability in means to pay for their exemption. As, for instance, if a person worth, say, one thousand dollars, might purchase exemption from personal service for three hundred dollars, it should be required of a person worth ten thousand dollars, that he pay in proportion. Why not? Because, it may be answered, that one man's three hundred dollars is as good as another's. But to this the poor man will be apt to reply, " So is my life as valuable as the rich man's life; and if I, who own nothing, be required to give my life for the salvation of the country, why should these rich men be exempt from giving their lives? or are these three hundred dollars of a rich man's money as valuable as my life?"

No more despotic act was ever attempted to be committed on a people than this Conscript Act in the feature of it which values a poor man's life at the price of a rich man's three hundred dollars. Had Congress and the President subjected rich as well as poor to conscription, without the privilege of purchasing exemptions or procuring substitutes, there would soon be an end of the war. This would have been the fairest way to raise conscripts, because the privilege to purchase exemptions and to procure substitutes is one which can be taken advantage of by the rich only. This leaves the poor man without an alternative but to give his life, while the rich man can save his life by paying three hundred dollars. Was there ever so monstrous an act of despotism attempted to be inflicted by Government upon a people? If so, where or when was it?

"Three hundred dollars, or your life," exclaim the President and Congress. The rich man can pay the penalty, and save his life. The poor man has but one alternative, and that is, to sacrifice all—his life.

Services of citizens ought to bear some proportion to the protection and security given to persons and property by the Government. Why, if this be true, should a poor man be obliged to give his life for the services of the Government, while a rich man is obligated to give only three hundred dollars? Does the poor man owe more to the Government than the rich man, that he should be compelled to give his life, while the rich man is required to give but a portion of his superabundant wealth? In proportion to his wealth does the rich man owe to the Government for its protection of his wealth. Why not, then, require the rich man to give at least as much as the poor man to support and sustain the Government? If a poor man, who has nothing but his life, be compelled to give that to maintain the supremacy of the Government, should not a rich man, who owes more to the Government for the protection it affords him in person and property, be required to give both his life and a portion also of his wealth? Why not? Is a rich man's life, in a government of equals, more valuable than a poor man's life? And if a poor man be required to give all to maintain the Government, why should a rich man be exempt from giving as much? Why should there not be some more equitable discrimination made between rich and poor in their relations to the Government, than to require a poor man to give his life in the service of the Government, and to exempt a rich man from this service by paying the paltry sum of three hundred dollars? What are three hundred dollars to a millionaire? Is it, indeed, equal to the value of a poor man's life? The Federal Congress makes it so, and the infamous act is approved by Abraham Lincoln.

This Conscription Act violates not only the Constitution of the United States, but the Constitution of every State in the Union. And not only that, but it subjects every poor man who can not purchase his exemption from conscription, to military slavery. It places the same estimate upon the life of a white freeman that the same Congress and President did on the black slaves in the District of Columbia; three hundred dollars was made the price of a slave's liberty, and for want of three hundred dollars white freemen are to be enslaved and conscripted into military service, and offered in sacrifice to the demon of war. To this condition of degradation, of servitude, of despotism are the American people reduced by the President and Congress, the Constitution violated, the Government subverted, the rights of the people torn from them, the masses of the people treated like serfs; this is the condition to which America and Americans are reduced by the despotism of arbitrary power wielded by Abraham Lincoln and by his fellow-partisans of the Thirty-seventh Congress.

But, some one will inquire, has not the Government a right to call upon citizens to preserve its existence? That depends upon circumstances. If the Government be one of the people's choice, and that they have invested it with this attribute of sovereignty, it has the right to call upon the citizens for their services. Now what are the facts and circumstances, or, in other words, the relations between the Federal Government and citizens of the United States? The Government, as formed by the Constitution, is of their choice; hence, according to our hypothesis, while it conforms itself to the Constitution, it has a right to the services of citizens to perform its constitutional duties.

Does it conform itself to the Constitution—the law of its creators—in the enactment of this Conscription Bill? Palpably not, for while the Constitution says that its demands upon the citizens as militia shall be made through State authority, this act ignores the States entirely and assumes for the Federal Executive the authority reserved to themselves by the States, both in their own constitutions and in the Constitution of the United States. 'Hence the Government does not conform itself to the conditions on which it was invested with power, and on which it exists as a government.

But if its existence be in danger, has it not the right to assume extraordinary power to preserve itself from extinction? It has the right to preserve its existence legitimately, not otherwise. The Government has no right to exist by sacrificing the lives of the people in an illegitimate manner. The rights of the people to life are superior to that of the Government for existence. Like an individual, Government has to some extent, but not to the same degree as an individual, the right of self-defense. The right of a human being to self-defense, whether assailed unlawfully by another individual or by a government, is absolute, while that of a government is qualified by law. Government exists by the will of the people, not people by the will of the Government. Hence the popular will is superior to that of the Government will, and when these wills come in conflict with each other, that of the Government is generally arbitrary, despotic, tyrannical, and should yield to the will of the people.

If citizens do not choose to preserve the Government, what right has the Government to compel them to do so against their will? If Government has this power, its existence does not depend on the will of the people, nor have they the right to alter, much less abolish it. The very fact that the Federal Government has manifested a determination to compel the people to sustain it, is the assumption of a position that the Government, and not the people, is the supreme power; that government does not derive its existence from the people, and that despite what they may do to the contrary, it will not only exist, but exist in that form it chooses to assume, and for such purposes as it designs to have in view.

Is this the Government instituted by the Federal Constitution, or is it not a new form and system of Government unknown to the Constitution, and antagonistic to that which till recently gave security and protection to person and property, and repose and prosperity to our beloved country? As an emanation of this new Government, the Conscription Act is one of the questions to which the people will have to reply and determine whether or not the Government as it is, or as it was, is the Government of the Constitution—the Government of their choice—the legitimate Government, to which they owe allegiance and loyalty, if such a relation be consistent between a free people and their Government, and which has a legitimate right to demand of them, in the manner of this Conscription Act, the services of their person and the sacrifice of their lives. This question is put to the people by this Conscription Act. As they will hold themselves in relation to it, depends the existence and perpetuity of free Government in these States, or, in all human probability, its extinction forever among mankind.

THE INDEMNITY BILL.

ITS UNCONSTITUTIONALITY.

CONGRESS, by its act of legislation known as the Indemnity Bill, seemed to have forgotten the fact that it was merely a legislative body acting under the restraints and obligations of the Federal Constitution. It assumed the powers of a convention of a people in the enactment of this statute, instead of conforming itself to the rule by which it was created and became vested with authority.

In the first section of the Indemnity Bill, Congress delegates a power to the President which is only delegated to itself, thus disregarding the maxim and principle, that a delegated power can not be delegated by the agent on whom the power is first conferred. If Congress has the power to delegate to the President one portion of its authority, it has the same legitimate power to delegate to him all of its authority, and if it has not the power to delegate all the authority the Constitution gave it, Congress has not the power to delegate any portion of that authority.

So, if Congress has the power to delegate any portion, or all of its authority to the President, it has the power to delegate all or as much as it pleases of its authority to any one else; to a citizen of the United States, or to a person who is not a citizen, as well as to the President, or any other official. If Congress has the power or the right, which in the light the subject is considered is one and the same, to divest itself of a portion of its power or authority, it has the right to divest itself of all power and authority and become extinct, and transfer all legislative power to the Executive, or to any person whom it may choose to designate as the depositary of this power.

It would not be surprising if in these days of political latitudinarianism there be politicians, and lawyers even, who may be induced to contend for the right of Congress to transfer all its constitutional authority to the President, or to any one else, who may happen to be thought the "man for the times." Such things were done in ancient times, when the whole power of government was united in a dictator; but it was well understood that the legislative bodies which thus invested magistrates with dictatorial powers had the right to do so;

hence the doing of it was no wrong. The Federal Congress has no such right conferred on it—Congress alone is invested with legislative powers. It alone can enact laws ; it can not transfer the right to enact them either to the President or any one else, and in assuming to do so it commits a flagrant wrong, a violation of the Constitution, a breach of trust.

It is the right of Congress itself to suspend the privileges of the writ of *habeas corpus.* This is unquestioned; and although the contingencies on which this authority should be exercised are prescribed to Congress, that body is, of course, the judge of the fact, whether or not the state of things may exist on which it is warranted and authorized to suspend the *habeas corpus ;* this much must be conceded. But in no contingency is it contemplated that Congress shall or may delegate to another branch of the Government any of its functions. A man may as well undertake to delegate to another the right of his own existence and the performance of his moral duties, as for Congress to assume the right to delegate powers which are conferred exclusively upon itself.

Hence, Congress having no power, no right to delegate to the President the legislative power to suspend the writ of *habeas corpus*, the act by which it is attempted to confer this power upon the President must be null and void. For if Congress could not constitutionally divest itself of the legislative power to suspend the privileges of the writ of *habeas corpus* and invest the President with that power, it follows, of course, that the act by which Congress attempted to do so is unconstitutional.

The second section of the Indemnity Bill is, at least, onerous and arbitrary, if it be not unconstitutional. It provides that after a suspected person is found not guilty, he shall, nevertheless, be subjected to the reproach of disloyalty, and be compelled to take an oath administered only to persons who are presumed to have forfeited their allegiance by the commission of a crime or an offense against the Government. This, to a free man, is both degrading and humiliating ; and it is a subjection to arbitrary power which should not be attempted to be enforced on one side, nor can it be submitted to on the other without a surrender of our liberties. It is time enough to punish a person when found guilty, and to impose degrading conditions of release from imprisonment when the imprisonment itself may be found on trial of the charge against the subject of it to have been warranted. The American people, unless they have lost all sense of their rights and liberty, will never assent to the degrading exactions of the second section of this Indemnity Bill.

The third section of this bill imposes upon an imprisoned person against whom one indictment may be found, a grievous condition before he can be released from custody, viz., the taking of an oath to purge himself of the charge or accusation against him. It is not enough, according to this bill, that a grand jury finds no cause against the accused either to indict or present him; he must, nevertheless, testify under oath that he has been guiltless, contrary to every principle of law in similar cases. And after subjecting the accused to this humiliation, he is still held as a prisoner if the judge chooses to disbelieve him.

The fourth section of this Indemnity Bill is not probably known to the American people. This section undertakes to interpose the President's order for the arrest of any person, not only subsequent to the passage of the Indemnity Bill, but previous to it, in case of any suit brought, or which may be brought by any person aggrieved in consequence of such order. If this section of the Indemnity Bill should be sustained by the courts, no person who has been arrested arbitrarily and imprisoned illegally can have any redress whatever by law. The President's order, this section of the act says, "shall be a defense in all courts to any action, civil or criminal, pending, or to be commenced for any search, seizure, arrest, or imprisonment made, done, or committed." This is sweeping. Can Congress thus deprive American citizens of their right? Those who passed this Indemnity Bill must have thought so. But there are no rights if this act be legitimate, for rights can not be thus taken away, if they exist. If the President of the United States may, by a mere order of his, deprive a person of liberty and property, why not of his life? and if of life, liberty, and property, what becomes of one's rights? The Constitution of the United States wisely and prudently provided for the impeachment of the President, as well as for the impeachment of other officers of the Government who might fail to discharge their duties, or who might be influenced by venal considerations in their official acts; but Congress, by this Indemnity Bill, relieves the President from this constitutional restraint, and gives him full power to disregard the Constitution entirely, and the rights of his fellow-citizens, which the Constitution makes it his duty to protect and defend.

No monarch in the world is invested with more power over the lives, liberty, and property of the people than this Indemnity Bill vests in the President of the United States. His mere order to do an unlawful act is made a defense in all courts to an action for damages, and thus is redress for injuries not only denied, but provided against by this act of despotism. The President's will is thus made the permanent law. The Constitution, which is the will of the people, is superseded by the will of the President, and he is made as absolute and arbitrary a dictator as ever ruled over a subject people. What more does it need to constitute a dictator of the most absolute type than to make his will the law, as this Indemnity Bill makes the will of the President the law. Read the fourth section of this act again and again. Read it till you understand its meaning and feel its force, American citizen, and then, if you have concluded to be a slave, submit to it; but if you have determined to be still a freeman, assert your constitutional rights, and demand that this act, violative of both the Constitution and your personal rights, be left a dead letter, a memento to future ages of what fanaticism and partisanship dare to attempt when they acquire power, even in a country whose government is an institution of the people's will.

The fifth section of this Indemnity Bill is violative of State sovereignty. It takes away from the State courts authority which they have ever held, and transfers it to the Federal courts. It was not contemplated by the founders of the Federal Government that that Government should redress injuries to persons, nor afford security or protection to persons or property, except in specified cases. Wrongs to persons and injuries to property were designed to be redressed by State courts, and it is scarcely questionable whether Congress has the power to invest the Federal courts with authority to inquire into acts committed by one citizen upon the person and property of another except in the cases specified by the Constitution. If the Federal courts can be invested with the authority attempted to be conferred by this Indemnity Bill, Congress has the virtual authority to abolish or abrogate the State courts altogether, because such would be the effect of an act of Congress which would transfer to the Federal courts cases which might be commenced in the State courts.

The judicial power of the Federal Government does not extend to criminal cases of any other kind than violations of Federal laws. Wrongs inflicted upon persons and injuries done to property do not come within the scope of the Federal courts except in the cases prescribed by the Constitution, and the Constitution makes no provision for such cases as those embraced in the Indemnity Bill. The State courts are very properly the tribunals in which to seek redress for personal injuries, and to inflict punishment upon wrong-doers to person and property. The object of this Indemnity Bill is not to afford redress for injuries, not to provide with more authority than the laws did before for the punishment of offenses, but to make it difficult, if not impossible, to obtain redress, and to shield evil-doers in their violations of law and of personal rights.

One of the principal, if not the primary, objects of Government is to secure and protect the people individually from each other, and collectively from external aggressions, in the enjoyment of their rights, and when these rights are trespassed on, to punish the aggressor; but the Congress of the United States by this Indemnity Bill changes the purposes of Government, and makes it a party participant in the evil deeds which it is the duty of the Government to prevent, or, failing in the performance of that duty, to avenge by the punishment of the offender. Government, under the control of the Federal Congress and of the President of the United States, is made the means by which wrongs are inflicted on the people, and when committed, by which the wrong-doer is protected from the just and legal consequences of his crime. Thus is the Federal Government subverted and made an instrument of tyranny and despotism in place of being what it was designed, a protection and security of the people in the enjoyment of their rights of person and property. Instead of being as it was instituted to be, a terror to evil-doers, Congress and the President have made the Government the protector of criminals, ay, the protector of traitors who day by day are sapping the foundations of the Government itself, and who design to overthrow it entirely on the first favorable opportunity.

The reader will not fail to notice that, in the fifth section of the Indemnity Bill, if a plaintiff, under all the difficulties placed in his way of obtaining a verdict, should fail in his suit, he is subjected to the penalty of double costs for having the temerity to seek redress of his grievances. This, of course, is done for the purpose of deterring any aggrieved person from suing for redress. It was not enough that the President and Congress took away from citizens the right to sue the violators of their persons and property in the State courts, and to deprive these courts of their legitimate powers over offenders. Lest that even under such discouraging and disadvantageous circumstances redress might be sought for, this deterring clause is placed menacingly before the eyes of the victim of arbitrary power.

If the object of the appeal to the Supreme Court provided in the sixth section of the Indemnity Bill were to do justice to parties concerned, it would be commendable; but such is not its object. On the contrary, it is only another provision whose object and intent is to defeat the ends of justice, and to prevent any punishment being inflicted on a person who acts in the name and by authority of the

President of the United States in the commission of acts of arbitrary power. The limitation to two years within which suits may be brought for illegal arrests and imprisonments, or other wrongs done to persons who may subject themselves to the displeasure of the Federal Executive, is another evidence of the evil design of this Indemnity Bill. From first to last this bill bears the palpable impress of partisanship, of arrogant assumption of despotic power over those who venture to exercise their constitutional rights, or who, being deprived of these rights illegally and arbitrarily, attempt to obtain redress, as it is the right of even the basest serf under despotic governments to do—much more one would suppose is it the right of American citizens to invoke their Government for security and protection, and, when need be, for satisfaction of injuries which the Government may suffer to be inflicted.

This Indemnity Bill will live in history an eternal reproach to the American people ; for although the people may disclaim having had anything to do with its enactment, the judgment of the world will be, that if they did not approve of such an act, the Federal Congress nor the President would have had the temerity to put it in the form of law. Acquiescence in such acts as this Indemnity Bill is, commits the people to it as much as if they participated in its enactment ; and it is a fact of history, that the people have not only acquiesced in the enactment of this despotic statute, but many of them approve of it, although it places the people in total subjection to arbitrary power. This is the effect of this act, if it were not the design of those who inflicted it on the American people.

THE TAX BILL.

THE TAX BILL.

APPROVED JULY 1, 1862.

AN ACT

TO PROVIDE INTERNAL REVENUE TO SUPPORT THE GOVERNMENT AND TO PAY INTEREST ON THE PUBLIC DEBT.

Be it enacted by the Senate and House of Representatives of the United States of America in Congress assembled, That, for the purpose of superintending the collection of internal duties, stamp duties, licenses, or taxes imposed by this act, or which may be hereafter imposed, and of assessing the same, an office is hereby created in the Treasury Department, to be called the Office of the Commissioner of Internal Revenue; and the President of the United States is hereby authorized to nominate, and, with the advice and consent of the Senate, to appoint a Commissioner of Internal Revenue, with an annual salary of four thousand dollars, who shall be charged, and hereby is charged, under the direction of the Secretary of the Treasury, with preparing all the instructions, regulations, directions, forms, blanks, stamps, and licenses, and distributing the same, or any part thereof, and all other matters pertaining to the assessment and collection of the duties, stamp duties, licenses, and taxes which may be necessary to carry this act into effect, and with the general superintendence of his office, as aforesaid, and shall have authority, and hereby is authorized and required, to provide proper and sufficient stamps or dies for expressing and denoting the several stamp duties, or the amount thereof, in the case of per-centage duties, imposed by this act, and to alter and renew, or replace such stamps from time to time, as occasion shall require; and the Secretary of the Treasury may assign to the office of the Commissioner of Internal Revenue such number of clerks as he may deem necessary, or the exigencies of the public service may require, and the privilege of franking all letters and documents pertaining to the duties of his office, and of receiving, free of postage, all such letters and documents, is hereby extended to said Commissioner.

• GENERAL PROVISIONS.

SEC. 2. *And be it further enacted,* That, for the purpose of assessing, levying, and collecting the duties or taxes hereinafter prescribed by this act, the President of the United States be, and he is hereby, authorized to divide, respectively, the States and Territories of the

United States and District of Columbia into convenient collection districts, and to nominate, and, by and with the advice and consent of the Senate, to appoint an assessor and a collector for each such district, who shall be residents within the same : *Provided*, That any of said States and Territories and the District of Columbia may, if the President shall deem it proper, be erected into and included in one district : *Provided*, That the number of districts in any State shall not exceed the number of representatives to which such State shall be entitled in the present Congress, except in such States as are entitled to an increased representation in the Thirty-eighth Congress, in which States the number of districts shall not exceed the number of representatives to which any such State may be so entitled : *And provided, further*, That in the State of California the President may establish a number of districts not exceeding the number of senators and representatives to which said State is entitled in the present Congress.

SEC. 3. *And be it further enacted*, That each of the assessors shall divide his district into a convenient number of assessment districts, subject to such regulations and limitations as may be imposed by the Commissioner of Internal Revenue, within each of which he shall appoint one assistant assessor, who shall be resident therein ; and each assessor and assistant assessor so appointed, and accepting the appointment, shall, before he enters on the duties of his appointment, take and subscribe, before some competent magistrate, or some collector, to be appointed by virtue of this act (who is hereby empowered to administer the same), the following oath or affirmation, to wit: " I, A B, do swear, or affirm (as the case may be), that I will bear true faith and allegiance to the United States of America, and will support the Constitution thereof, and that I will, to the best of my knowledge, skill, and judgment, diligently and faithfully execute the office and duties of assessor for (naming the assessment district), without favor or partiality, and that I will do equal right and justice in every case in which I shall act as assessor." And a certificate of such oath or affirmation shall be delivered to the collector of the district for which such assessor or assistant assessor shall be appointed. And every assessor or assistant assessor acting in the said office, without having taken the said oath or affirmation, shall forfeit and pay one hundred dollars, one moiety thereof to the use of the United States, and the other moiety thereof to him who shall first sue for the same, with costs of suit.

SEC. 4. *And be it further enacted*, That before any such collector shall enter upon the duties of his office, he shall execute a bond for such amount as shall be prescribed by the Commissioner of Internal Revenue, under the direction of the Secretary of the Treasury, with not less than five sureties, to be approved as sufficient by the Solicitor of the Treasury, containing the condition that said collector shall faithfully perform the duties of his office according to law, and shall justly and faithfully account for and pay over to the United States, in compliance with the order or regulations of the Secretary of the Treasury, all public moneys which may come into his hands or possession; which bond shall be filed in the office of the First Comptroller of the Treasury. And such collectors shall, from time to time, renew, strengthen, and increase their official bond, as the Secretary of the Treasury may direct.

SEC. 5. *And be it further enacted,* That each collector shall be authorized to appoint, by an instrument of writing under his hand, as many deputies as he may think proper, to be by him compensated for their services, and also to revoke any such appointment, giving such notice thereof as the Commissioner of Internal Revenue shall prescribe; and may require bonds or other securities, and accept the same from such deputy; and each such deputy shall have the like authority, in every respect, to collect the duties and taxes levied or assessed within the portion of the district assigned to him, which is by this act vested in the collector himself; but each collector shall, in every respect, be responsible both to the United States and to individuals, as the case may be, for all moneys collected, and for every act done as deputy collector by any of his deputies while acting as such, and for every omission of duty: *Provided,* That nothing herein contained shall prevent any collector from collecting himself the whole or any part of the duties and taxes so assessed and payable in his district.

SEC. 6. *And be it further enacted,* That it shall be the duty of any person or persons, partnerships, firms, associations, or corporations, made liable to any duty, license, stamp, or tax imposed by this act, when not otherwise and differently provided for, on or before the first day of August, eighteen hundred and sixty-two, and on or before the first Monday of May in each year thereafter, and in all other cases before the day of levy, to make a list or return to the assistant assessor of the district where located, of the amount of annual income, the articles or objects charged with a special duty or tax, the quantity of goods, wares, and merchandise made or sold, and charged with a specific or ad valorem duty or tax, the several rates and aggregate amount according to the respective provisions of this act, and according to the forms and regulations to be prescribed by the Commissioner of Internal Revenue, under the direction of the Secretary of the Treasury, for which such person or persons, partnerships, firms, associations, or corporations are liable to be assessed under and by virtue of the provisions of this act.

SEC. 7. *And be it further enacted,* That the instructions, regulations, and directions, as hereinbefore mentioned, shall be binding on each assessor and his assistants, and on each collector and his deputies, in the performance of the duties enjoined by or under this act; pursuant to which instructions the said assessors shall, on the first day of August, eighteen hundred and sixty-two, and on the first Monday of May in each succeeding year, and from time to time thereafter, in accordance with this act, direct and cause the several assistant assessors to proceed through every part of their respective districts, and inquire after and concerning all persons being within the assessment districts where they respectively reside, owning, possessing, or having the care or management of any property, goods, wares, and

merchandise, articles or objects liable to pay any duty, stamp or tax,
including all persons liable to pay a license duty, under the provisions of this act (by reference as well to any lists of assessment
or collection taken under the laws of the respective States, as to any
other records or documents, and by all other lawful ways and means,
especially to the written list, schedule, or return required to be made
out and delivered to the assistant assessor by all persons owning, possessing, or having the care or management of any property, as aforesaid, liable to duty or taxation), and to value and enumerate the said
objects of taxation, respectively, in the manner prescribed by this
act, and in conformity with the regulations and instructions before
mentioned.

SEC. 8. *And be it further enacted,* That if any person owning,
possessing, or having the care or management of property, goods,
wares, and merchandise, articles or objects liable to pay any duty,
tax, or license, shall fail to make and exhibit a written list when required, as aforesaid, and shall consent to disclose the particulars of
any and all the property, goods, wares, and merchandise, articles and
objects liable to pay any duty or tax, or any business or occupation
liable to pay any license, as aforesaid, then, and in that case, it shall
be the duty of the officer to make such list, which, being distinctly
read, consented to, and signed, by the person so owning, possessing,
or having the care and management as aforesaid, shall be received as
the list of such person.

SEC. 9. *And be it further enacted,* That if any such person shall
deliver or disclose to any assessor or assistant assessor appointed in
pursuance of this act, and requiring a list or lists, as aforesaid, any
false or fraudulent list or statement, with intent to defeat or evade the
valuation or enumeration hereby intended to be made, such person
so offending, and being thereof convicted on indictment found therefor in any circuit or district court of the United States, held in the
district in which such offense may be committed, shall be fined in a
sum not exceeding five hundred dollars, at the discretion of the court,
and shall pay all costs and charges of prosecution; and the valuation
and enumeration required by this act shall, in all such cases, and in all
cases of under-valuation or under-statement in such lists or statements, be made, as aforesaid, upon lists, according to the form prescribed, to be made out by the assessors and assistant assessors,
respectively; which lists the said assessors and assistant assessors
are hereby authorized and required to make according to the best information they can obtain, and for the purpose of making which they
are hereby authorized to enter into and upon all and singular the
premises respectively; and from the valuation and enumeration so
made there shall be no appeal.

SEC. 10. *And be it further enacted,* That in case any person shall
be absent from his or her place of residence at the time an assistant
assessor shall call to receive the list of such person, it shall be the
duty of such assistant assessor to leave at the place of residence of
such person, with some person of suitable age and discretion, if such
be present, otherwise to deposit in the nearest post-office, a written

note or memorandum, addressed to such person, requiring him or her to present to such assessor the list or lists required by this act within ten days from the date of such note or memorandum. SEC. 11. *And be it further enacted*, That if any person, on being notified or required, as aforesaid, shall refuse or neglect to give such list or lists within the time required, as aforesaid, it shall be the duty of the assessor, for the assessment district within which such person shall reside, and he is hereby authorized and required, to enter into and upon the premises, if it be necessary, of such persons so refusing or neglecting, and to make, according to the best information which he can obtain, and on his own view and information, such lists of property, goods, wares, and merchandise, and all articles or objects liable to duty or taxation, owned or possessed, or under the care or management of such person, as are required by this act, including the amount, if any, due for license; and in case of refusal or neglect to make such lists, except in cases of sickness, the assessors shall thereupon add fifty per centum to the amount of the items thereof; and the lists, so made and subscribed by such assessor, shall be taken and reputed as good and sufficient lists of the persons and property for which such person is to be taxed for the purposes of this act; and the person so failing or neglecting, unless in case of sickness or failure to receive the notice, shall, moreover, forfeit and pay the sum of one hundred dollars, except where otherwise provided for, to be recovered for the use of the United States, with costs of suit.

SEC. 12. *And be it further enacted*, That whenever there shall be in any assessment district any property, goods, wares, and merchandise, articles or objects, not owned or possessed by, or under the care or management of, any person or persons within such district, and liable to be taxed as aforesaid, and no list of which shall have been transmitted to the assistant assessor in the manner provided by this act, it shall be the duty of the assistant assessor for such district, and he is hereby authorized and required, to enter into and upon the premises where such property is situated, and take such view thereof as may be necessary, and to make lists of the same, according to the form prescribed, which lists, being subscribed by the said assessor, shall be taken and reputed as good and sufficient lists of such property, goods, wares, and merchandise, articles or objects, as aforesaid, under and for the purposes of this act.

SEC. 13. *And be it further enacted*, That the owners, possessors, or persons having the care or management of property, goods, wares, and merchandise, articles or objects, not lying or being within the assessment district in which they reside, shall be permitted to make out and deliver the lists thereof required by this act (provided the assessment district in which the said objects of duty or taxation are situated is therein distinctly stated) at the time and in the manner prescribed to the assistant assessor of the assessment district wherein such persons reside. And it shall be the duty of the assistant assessor who receives any such list to transmit the same to the assistant assessor where such objects of taxation are situate, who shall examine such list; and if he approves the same, he shall return it to the assistant assessor from whom he received it, with his approval thereof; and if he fails to approve the same, he shall make such alterations therein as he may deem to be just and proper, and shall then return the said list, with such alterations therein or additions thereto, to the assistant assessor from whom he received the said list; and the assistant assessor, where the person liable to pay such tax resides, shall proceed in making the assessment of the tax upon the list by him so received, in all respects as if the said list had been made out by himself.

SEC. 14. *And be it further enacted,* That the lists aforesaid shall, where not otherwise specially provided for, be taken with reference to the day fixed for that purpose by this act, as aforesaid, and where duties accrue at other and different times, the lists shall be taken with reference to the time when said duties become due; and the assistant assessors, respectively, after collecting the said lists, shall proceed to arrange the same, and to make two general lists—the first of which shall exhibit, in alphabetical order, the names of all persons liable to pay any duty, tax, or license, under this act, residing within the assessment district, together with the value and assessment, or enumeration, as the case may require, of the objects liable to duty or taxation within such district for which each such person is liable, or for which any firm, company, or corporation is liable, with the amount of duty or tax payable thereon; and the second list shall exhibit, in alphabetical order, the names of all persons residing out of the collection district, owners of property within the district, together with the value and assessment or enumeration thereof, as the case may be, with the amount of duty or tax payable thereon as aforesaid. The forms of the said general list shall be devised and prescribed by the assessor, under the direction of the Commissioner of Internal Revenue, and lists taken according to such forms shall be made out by the assistant assessors and delivered to the assessor within thirty days after the day fixed by this act as aforesaid, requiring lists from individuals; or where duties, licenses, or taxes accrue at other and different times, the lists shall be delivered from time to time as they become due. And if any assistant assessor shall fail to perform any duty assigned by this act within the time prescribed by his precept, warrant, or other legal instructions, not being prevented therefrom by sickness or other unavoidable accident, every such assistant assessor shall be discharged from office, and shall, moreover, forfeit and pay two hundred dollars, to be recovered for the use of the United States, with costs of suit.

SEC. 15. *And be it further enacted,* That the assessors for each collection district shall, by advertisement in some public newspaper published in each county within said district, if any such there be, and by written or printed notifications, to be posted up in at least four public places within each assessment district, advertise all persons concerned of the time and place within said county when and where the lists, valuations, and enumerations made and taken within said county may be examined; and said lists shall remain open for examination for the space of fifteen days after notice shall have been given as aforesaid. And said notifications shall also state when and where within said county, after the expiration of said fifteen days, appeals will be received and determined relative to any erroneous or excessive valuations or enumerations by the assistant assessors. And it shall be the duty of the assessor for each collection district, at the time fixed for hearing such appeal as aforesaid, to submit the proceedings of the assistant assessors, and the lists taken and returned as aforesaid, to the inspection of any and all persons who may apply for that purpose. And the said assessor for each collection district is hereby authorized, at any time within fifteen days from and after the expiration of the time allowed for notification as aforesaid, to hear and determine, in a summary way, according to law and right, upon any and all appeals which may be exhibited against the proceedings of the said assistant assessors: *Provided*, That the question to be determined by the assessor, on an appeal respecting the valuation or enumeration of property, or objects liable to duty or taxation, shall be, whether the valuation complained of be or be not in a just relation or proportion to other valuations in the same assessment district, and whether the enumeration be or be not correct. And all appeals to the assessor, as aforesaid, shall be made in writing, and shall specify the particular cause, matter, or thing respecting which a decision is requested; and shall, moreover, state the ground or principle of inequality or error complained of. And the assessor shall have power to re-examine and equalize the valuations as shall appear just and equitable; but no valuation or enumeration shall be increased without a previous notice, of at least five days, to the party interested, to appear and object to the same, if he judge proper; which notice shall be given by a note in writing, to be left at the dwelling-house, office, or place of business of the party by such assessor or an assistant assessor.

Sec. 16. *And be it further enacted*, That the said assessors of each collection district, respectively, shall, immediately after the expiration of the time for hearing appeals, and, from time to time, as duties, taxes, or licenses become liable to be assessed, make out lists containing the sums payable according to the provisions of this act upon every object of duty or taxation in and for each collection district, which lists shall contain the name of each person residing within the said district, owning or having the care or superintendence of property lying within the said district which is liable to the said tax, or engaged in any business or pursuit requiring a license, when such person or persons are known, together with the sums payable by each; and where there is any property within any collection district liable to the payment of the said duty or tax, not owned or occupied by or under the superintendence of any person resident therein, there shall be a separate list of such property, specifying the sum payable, and the names of the respective proprietors, where known. And the assistant assessor making out any such separate list shall transmit therefrom to the assistant assessor, where the persons liable to pay such tax reside, or shall have their principal place of business, copies of the list of property held by persons so liable to pay such tax, to

the end that the taxes assessed under the provisions of this act may
be paid within the collection district where the persons liable to pay
the same reside, or may have their principal place of business.   And
in all other cases the said assessor shall furnish to the collectors of
the several collection districts, respectively, within ten days after the
time of hearing appeals, and from time to time thereafter as required,
a certified copy of such list or lists for their proper collection districts; and in default of performance of the duties enjoined upon assessors by this section they shall severally and individually forfeit and
pay the sum of five hundred dollars to the use of the United States,
and, moreover, shall forfeit their compensation as assessors: *Provided*,
That it shall be in the power of the Commissioner of Internal Revenue to exonerate any assessor as aforesaid from such forfeitures, in
whole or in part, as to him shall appear just and equitable.

   SEC. 17. *And be it further enacted*, That there shall be allowed
and paid to the several assessors and assistant assessors, for their
services under this act—to each assessor three dollars per day for
every day employed in making the necessary arrangements and giving the necessary instructions to the assistant assessors for the valuation; and five dollars per day for every day employed in hearing appeals, revising valuations, and making out lists agreeably to the provisions of this act; and one dollar for every hundred taxable persons
contained in the tax list, as delivered by him to said collectors, and
forwarded to the Commissioner of Internal Revenue; to each assistant assessor three dollars for every day actually employed in collecting lists and making valuations, the number of days necessary for
that purpose to be certified by the assessor, and approved by the
Commissioner of Internal Revenue; and one dollar for every hundred taxable persons contained in the tax list, as completed and delivered by him to the assessor.   And the said assessors and assistant
assessors, respectively, shall also be allowed their necessary and
reasonable charges for stationery and blank books used in the execution of their duties, and the compensation herein specified shall be in
full for all expenses not otherwise particularly authorized: *Provided*,
The Secretary of the Treasury shall be, and he is hereby, authorized
to fix such additional rates of compensation to be made to assessors
and assistant assessors in the States of California and Oregon and
the Territories, as may appear to him to be just and equitable, in
consequence of the greater cost of living and traveling in those
States and Territories, and as may, in his judgment, be necessary to
secure the services of competent and efficient men, provided the rates
of compensation thus allowed shall not exceed the rates paid to similar officers in such States and Territories respectively.   In cases
where a collection district embraces more than a single congressional
district the Secretary of the Treasury may allow the assessor such
compensation as he may deem necessary.

   SEC. 18. *And be it further enacted*, That each collector, on receiving a list, as aforesaid, and from time to time as such lists may be
received from the said assessors, respectively, shall subscribe three
receipts; one of which shall be given on a full and correct copy of

such list, which list shall be delivered by him to, and shall remain with, the assessor of his collection district, and shall be open to the inspection of any person who may apply to inspect the same; and the other two receipts shall be given on aggregate statements of the lists aforesaid, exhibiting the gross amount of taxes to be collected in his collection district, one of which aggregate statements and receipts shall be transmitted to the Commissioner of Internal Revenue, and the other to the First Comptroller of the Treasury; and all lists received from time to time, as aforesaid, shall be in like form and manner transmitted as aforesaid.

SEC. 19. *And be it further enacted*, That each of said collectors shall, within ten days after receiving his annual collection list from the assessors, respectively, as aforesaid, give notice, by advertisement published in each county in his collection district, in one newspaper printed in such county, if any such there be, and by notifications to be posted up in at least four public places in each county in his collection district, that the said duties have become due and payable, and state the time and place within said county at which he will attend to receive the same, which time shall not be less than ten days after such notification; and all persons who shall neglect to pay the duties and taxes so as aforesaid assessed upon them to the collector within the time specified, shall be liable to pay ten per centum additional upon the amount thereof, the fact of which liability shall be stated in the advertisement and notifications aforesaid. And with regard to all persons who shall neglect to pay as aforesaid, it shall be the duty of the collector, in person or by deputy, within twenty days after such neglect, to make a demand personally, or at the dwellings or usual places of business of such persons, if any they have, for payment of said duties or taxes, with the ten per centum additional aforesaid. And with respect to all such duties or taxes as are not included in the annual lists aforesaid, and all taxes and duties the collection of which is not otherwise provided for in this act, it shall be the duty of each collector, in person or by deputy, to demand payment thereof, in manner aforesaid, within ten days from and after receiving the list thereof from the assessor; and if the annual and other duties shall not be paid within ten days from and after such demand therefor, it shall be lawful for such collector or his deputies to proceed to collect the said duties or taxes, with ten per centum additional thereto, as aforesaid, by distraint and sale of the goods, chattels, or effects of the persons delinquent as aforesaid. And in case of such distraint it shall be the duty of the officer charged with the collection to make, or cause to be made, an account of the goods or chattels which may be distrained, a copy of which, signed by the officer making such distraint, shall be left with the owner or possessor of such goods, chattels, or effects, or at his or her dwelling, with some person of suitable age and discretion, with a note of the sum demanded, and the time and place of sale; and the said officer shall forthwith cause a notification to be published in some newspaper within the county wherein said distraint is made, if there is a newspaper published in said county, or to be publicly posted up at the

post-office, if there be one within five miles, nearest to the residence
of the person whose property shall be distrained, and in not less than
two other public places, which notice shall specify the articles distrained, and the time and place for the sale thereof, which time shall
not be less than ten nor more than twenty days from the date of such
notification, and the place proposed for sale not more than five miles
distant from the place of making such distraint: *Provided*, That in
any case of distraint for the payment of the duties or taxes aforesaid the goods, chattels, or effects so distrained shall and may be
restored to the owner or possessor, if prior to the sale payment of
the amount due or tender thereof shall be made to the proper officer
charged with the collection of the full amount demanded, together
with such fee for levying, and such sum for the necessary and reasonable expense of removing, advertising, and keeping the goods, chattels, or effects so distrained as may be prescribed by the Commissioner
of Internal Revenue; but in case of non-payment or tender, as aforesaid, the said officers shall proceed to sell the said goods, chattels, or
effects at public auction, and shall and may retain from the proceeds
of such sale the amount demandable for the use of the United States,
with the necessary and reasonable expenses of distraint and sale, and
a commission of five per centum thereon for his own use, rendering
the overplus, if any there be, to the person whose goods, chattels,
or effects shall have been distrained : *Provided*, That there shall be
exempt from distraint the tools or implements of a trade or profession,
one cow, arms, and provisions, and household furniture kept for use,
and apparel necessary for a family.

SEC. 20. *And be it further enacted*, That in all cases where the
property liable to distraint for duties or taxes under this act may not
be divisible, so as to enable the collector, by a sale of part thereof,
to raise the whole amount of the tax, with all costs, charges, and
commissions, the whole of such property shall be sold, and the surplus of the proceeds of the sale, after satisfying the duty or tax,
costs and charges, shall be paid to the owner of the property, or his,
her, or their legal representatives; or if he, she, or they can not be
found, or refuse to receive the same, then such surplus shall be deposited in the Treasury of the United States, to be there held for the
use of the owner, or his, her, or their legal representatives, until he,
she, or they shall make application therefor to the Secretary of the
Treasury, who, upon such application, shall, by warrant on the Treasury, cause the same to be paid to the applicant. And if the property
advertised for sale, as aforesaid, can not be sold for the amount of the
duty or tax due thereon, with the costs and charges, the collector
shall purchase the same in behalf of the United States for an amount
not exceeding the said tax or duty, with the costs and charges thereon.
And all property so purchased may be sold by said collector under
such regulations as may be prescribed by the Commissioner of Internal Revenue. And the collector shall render a distinct account
of all charges incurred in the sale of such property, and shall pay
into the Treasury the surplus, if any there be, after defraying the
charges.

SEC. 21. *And be it further enacted*, That in any case where goods, chattels, or effects, sufficient to satisfy the duties imposed by this act upon any person liable to pay the same, shall not be found by the collector or deputy collector, whose duty it may be to collect the same, he is hereby authorized to collect the same by seizure and sale of real estate; and the officer making such seizure and sale shall give notice to the person whose estate is proposed to be sold, by giving him in hand, or leaving at his last and usual place of abode, if he has any such within the collection district where said estate is situated, a notice, in writing, stating what particular estate is proposed to be sold, describing the same with reasonable certainty, and the time when, and place where, said officer proposes to sell the same; which time shall not be less than ten nor more than twenty days from the time of giving said notice; and the said officer shall also cause a notification to the same effect to be published in some newspaper within the county where such seizure is made, if any such there be, and shall also cause a like notice to be posted up at the post-office nearest to the place of residence of the person whose estate shall be so seized, and in two other public places within the county; and the place of said sale shall not be more than five miles distant from the estate seized. At the time and place appointed, the officer making such seizure shall proceed to sell the said estate at public auction, offering the same at a minimum price, including the amount of duties with the ten per centum additional thereon, and all charges for advertising, and an officer's fee of ten dollars. And if no person offers for said estate the amount of said minimum, the officer shall declare the same to be purchased by him for the United States, and shall deposit with the District Attorney of the United States a deed thereof, as hereinafter specified and provided; otherwise the same shall be declared to be sold to the highest bidder. And said sale may be adjourned by said officer for a period not exceeding five days, if he shall think it advisable so to do. If the amount bid shall not be then and there paid, the officer shall forthwith proceed to again sell said estate in the same manner. If the amount bid shall be then and there paid, the officer shall give his receipt therefor, if requested, and within five days thereafter he shall make out a deed of the estate so sold to the purchaser thereof, and execute the same in his official capacity, in the manner prescribed by the laws of the State in which said estate may [be] situated, in which said deed shall be recited the fact of said seizure and sale, with the cause thereof, the amount of duty for which said sale was made, and of all charges and fees, and the amount paid by the purchaser, and all his acts and doings in relation to said seizure and sale, and shall have the same ready for delivery to said purchaser, and shall deliver the same accordingly, upon request therefor. And said deed shall be *prima facie* evidence of the truth of the facts stated therein; and if the proceedings of the officer as set forth have been substantially in pursuance of the provisions of this act, shall be considered and operate as a conveyance to the purchaser of the title to said estate, but shall not affect the rights of third persons acquired previously to the claim of the United

States under this act. The surplus, if any, arising from such sale shall be disposed of as provided in this act for like cases arising upon sales of personal property. And any person whose estate may be seized for duties, as aforesaid, shall have the same right to pay or tender the amount due, with all proper charges thereon, prior to the sale thereof, and thereupon to relieve his said estate from sale, as aforesaid, as is provided in this act for personal property similarly situated. And any collector or deputy collector may, for the collection of duties imposed upon any person by this act, and committed to him for collection, seize and sell the lands of such person situated in any other collection district within the State in which said officer resides; and his proceedings in relation thereto shall have the same effect as if the same were had in his proper collection district; and the owners, their heirs, executors, or administrators, or any person having an interest therein, or any person on their behalf, shall have liberty to redeem the land sold as aforesaid, within one year from and after recording the said deed, upon payment to the purchaser, or in case he can not be found in the county where the lands are situate, to the collector, for the use of the purchaser, his heirs, or assigns, of the amount paid by the purchaser, with interest on the same at the rate of twenty per centum per annum. And it shall be the duty of every collector to keep a record of all sales of land made in his collection district, whether by himself or his deputies, in which shall be set forth the tax for which any such sale was made, the dates of seizure and sale, the name of the party assessed, and all proceedings in making said sale, the amount of fees and expenses, the name of the purchaser, and the date of the deed; which record shall be certified by the officer making the sale. And it shall be the duty of any deputy making sale, as aforesaid, to return a statement of all his proceedings to the collector, and to certify the record thereof. And in case of the death or removal of the collector, or the expiration of his term of office from any other cause, said record shall be deposited in the office of the clerk of the District Court of the United States for the district within which the said collector resided; and a copy of every such record, certified by the collector, or by the clerk, as the case may require, shall be evidence in any court of the truth of the facts therein stated. And when any lands sold, as aforesaid, shall be redeemed as hereinbefore provided, the collector or clerk, as the case may be, shall make an entry of the fact upon the record aforesaid, and the said entry shall be evidence of such redemption. And the claim of the government to lands sold under and by virtue of the foregoing provisions shall be held to have accrued at the time of seizure thereof.

SEC. 22. *And be it further enacted,* That if any collector shall find, upon any lists of taxes returned to him for collection, property lying within his district which is charged with any specific or ad valorem tax or duty, but which is not owned, occupied, or superintended by some person known to such collector to reside, or to have some place of business within, the United States, such collector shall forthwith take such property into his custody, and shall advertise the same, and the tax charged upon the same, in some newspaper published in his district, if any shall be published therein, otherwise in some newspaper in an adjoining district, for the space of thirty days; and if the taxes thereon, with all charges for advertising, shall not be paid within said thirty days, such collector shall proceed to sell the same, or so much as is necessary, in the manner provided for the sale of other goods distrained for the non-payment of taxes, and out of the proceeds shall satisfy all taxes charged upon such property, with the costs of advertising and selling the same. And like proceedings to those provided in the preceding section for the purchase and re-sale of property which can not be sold for the amount of duty or tax due thereon shall be had with regard to property sold under the provisions of this section. And any surplus arising from any sale herein provided for shall be paid into the treasury, for the benefit of the owner of the property. And the Secretary of the Treasury is authorized, in any case where money shall be paid into the treasury for the benefit of any owner of property sold as aforesaid, to repay the same, on proper proof being furnished that the person applying therefor is entitled to receive the same.

SEC. 23. *And be it further enacted,* That the several collectors shall, at the expiration of each and every month, after they shall, respectively, commence their collections, transmit to the Commissioner of Internal Revenue a statement of the collections made by them, respectively, within the month, and pay over monthly, or at such time or times as may be required by the Commissioner of Internal Revenue, the moneys by them respectively collected within the said term, and at such places as may be designated and required by the Commissioner of Internal Revenue; and each of the said collectors shall complete the collection of all sums annually assigned to him for collection, as aforesaid, shall pay over the same into the treasury, and shall render his final account to the Treasury Department as often as he may be required, and within six months from and after the day when he shall have received the collection lists from the said assessors or assistant assessors, as aforesaid. And the Secretary of the Treasury is authorized to designate one or more depositories in each State, for the deposit and safe keeping of the moneys collected by virtue of this act; and the receipt of the proper officer of such depository to a collector for the money deposited by him shall be a sufficient voucher for such collector in the settlement of his accounts at the Treasury Department; and the Commissioner of Internal Revenue may, under the direction of the Secretary of the Treasury, prescribe such regulations with reference to such deposits as he may deem necessary.

SEC. 24. *And be it further enacted,* That each collector shall be charged with the whole amount of taxes by him receipted, whether contained in lists delivered to him by the assessors, respectively, or delivered or transmitted to him by assistant assessors from time to time, or by other collectors; and shall be credited with the amount of duties or taxes contained in the lists transmitted in the manner above provided to other collectors, and by them receipted as aforesaid; and also for the duties or taxes of such persons as may have

absconded, or become insolvent, prior to the day when the duty or tax
ought, according to the provisions of this act, to have been collected:
Provided, That it shall be proved to the satisfaction of the First
Comptroller of the Treasury that due diligence was used by the collector, and that no property was left from which the duty or tax
could have been recovered. And each collector shall also be credited
with the amount of all property purchased by him for the use of the
United States, provided he shall faithfully account for, and pay over,
the proceeds thereof upon a re-sale of the same, as required by this
act.

Sec. 25. *And be it further enacted,* That if any collector shall
fail either to collect or to render his account, or to pay over in the
manner or within the times hereinbefore provided, it shall be the duty
of the First Comptroller of the Treasury, and he is hereby authorized
and required, immediately after such delinquency, to report the same
to the Solicitor of the Treasury, who shall issue a warrant of distress
against such delinquent collector and his sureties, directed to the
marshal of the district, therein expressing the amount of the taxes
with which the said collector is chargeable, and the sums, if any,
which have been paid. And the said marshal shall, himself, or by his
deputy, immediately proceed to levy and collect the sum which may
remain due, by distress and sale of the goods and chattels, or any
personal effects of the delinquent collector, giving at least five days'
notice of the time and place of sale, in the manner provided by law
for advertising sales of personal property on execution in the State
wherein such collector resides; and, furthermore, if such goods,
chattels, and effects can not be found sufficient to satisfy the said
warrant, the said marshal or his deputy shall and may proceed to
levy and collect the sum which remains due, by distress and sale of
the goods and chattels, or any personal effects, of the surety or sureties of the delinquent collector, giving notice as hereinbefore provided. And the bill of sale of the officer of any goods, chattels, or
other personal property, distrained and sold as aforesaid, shall be
conclusive evidence of title to the purchaser, and *prima facie* evidence of the right of the officer to make such sale, and of the correctness of his proceedings in selling the same. And for want of
goods and chattels, or other personal effects of such collector or his
sureties, sufficient to satisfy any warrant of distress, issued pursuant
to the preceding section of this act, the lands and real estate of such
collector and his sureties, or so much thereof as may be necessary
for satisfying the said warrant, after being advertised for at least
three weeks in not less than three public places in the collection district, and in one newspaper printed in the county or district, if any
there be, prior to the proposed time of sale, may and shall be sold at
public auction by the marshal or his deputy, who, upon such sale,
shall, as such marshal or deputy marshal, make and deliver to the
purchaser of the premises so sold a deed of conveyance thereof, to
be executed and acknowledged in the manner and form prescribed
by the laws of the State in which said lands are situated, which said
deed so made shall invest the purchaser with all the title and interest

of the defendant or defendants named in said warrant existing at the time of seizure thereof. And all moneys that may remain of the proceeds of such sale after satisfying the said warrant of distress, and paying the reasonable costs and charges of sale, shall be returned to the proprietor of the lands or real estate sold as aforesaid.

SEC. 26. *And be it further enacted,* That each and every collector, or his deputy, who shall exercise or be guilty of any extortion or willful oppression, under color of this act, or shall knowingly demand other or greater sums than shall be authorized by this act, shall be liable to pay a sum not exceeding double the amount of damages accruing to the party injured, to be recovered by and for the use of the party injured, with costs of suit, and shall be dismissed from office, and be disqualified from holding such office thereafter; and each and every collector, or his deputies, shall give receipts for all sums by them collected and retained in pursuance of this act.

SEC. 27. *And be it further enacted,* That a collector or deputy collector, assessor or assistant assessor, shall be authorized to enter, in the day-time, any brewery, distillery, manufactory, building, or place where any property, articles, or objects, subject to duty or taxation under the provisions of this act, are made, produced, or kept, within his district, so far as it may be necessary for the purpose of examining said property, articles, or objects, or inspecting the accounts required by this act from time to time to be made. And every owner of such brewery, distillery, manufactory, building, or place, or persons having the agency or superintendence of the same, who shall refuse to admit such officer, or to suffer him to examine said property, articles, or objects, or to inspect said accounts, shall, for every such refusal, forfeit and pay the sum of five hundred dollars.

SEC. 28. *And be it further enacted,* That if any person shall forcibly obstruct or hinder a collector or deputy collector in the execution of this act, or of any power and authority hereby vested in him, or shall forcibly rescue, or cause to be rescued, any property, articles, or objects, after the same shall have been seized by him, or shall attempt or endeavor so to do, the person so offending shall, for every such offense, forfeit and pay the sum of five hundred dollars.

SEC. 29. *And be it further enacted,* That in case of the sickness or temporary disability of a collector to discharge such of his duties as can not, under existing laws, be discharged by a deputy, they may be devolved by him upon one of his deputies: *Provided,* That information thereof be immediately communicated to the Secretary of the Treasury, and shall not be disapproved by him: *And provided, further,* That the responsibility of the collector or his sureties to the United States shall not be affected or impaired thereby.

SEC. 30. *And be it further enacted,* That in case a collector shall die, resign, or be removed, the deputies of such collector shall continue to act until their successors are appointed; and the deputy of such collector longest in service at the time immediately preceding may and shall, until a successor shall be appointed, discharge all the duties of said collector; and for the official acts and defaults of such deputy a remedy shall be had on the official bond of the collector, as in other cases; and of two or more deputy collectors, appointed on the same day, the one residing nearest the residence of the collector at the time of his death, resignation, or removal, shall in like manner discharge the said duties until the appointment of a successor; and any bond or security taken of such deputy by such collector, pursuant to the fifth section of this act, shall be available to his heirs or representatives to indemnify them for loss or damage accruing from any act of the proper deputy so continuing or so succeeding to the duties of such collector.

SEC. 31. *And be it further enacted,* That it shall be the duty of the collectors aforesaid, or their deputies, in their respective districts, and they are hereby authorized, to collect all the duties and taxes imposed by this act, however the same may be designated, and to prosecute for the recovery of the same, and for the recovery of any sum or sums which may be forfeited by virtue of this act; and all fines, penalties, and forfeitures, which may be incurred or imposed by virtue of this act, shall and may be sued for and recovered, in the name of the United States, or of the collector within whose district any such fine, penalty, or forfeiture shall have been incurred, in any proper form of action, or by any appropriate form of proceeding, before any Circuit or District Court of the United States for the district within which said fine, penalty, or forfeiture may have been incurred, or before any other court of competent jurisdiction; and where not otherwise and differently provided for, one moiety thereof shall be to the use of the United States, and the other moiety thereof to the use of the person who, if a collector or deputy collector, shall first inform of the cause, matter, or thing, whereby any such fine, penalty, or forfeiture was incurred.

SEC. 32. *And be it further enacted,* That if any person, in any case, matter, hearing, or other proceeding, in which an oath or affirmation shall be required to be taken or administered under and by virtue of this act, shall, upon the taking of such oath or affirmation, knowingly and willingly swear or affirm falsely, every person so offending shall be deemed guilty of perjury, and shall, on conviction thereof, be subject to the like punishment and penalties now provided by the laws of the United States for the crime of perjury.

SEC. 33. *And be it further enacted,* That separate accounts shall be kept at the treasury of all moneys received from internal duties or taxes in each of the respective States, Territories, and collection districts; and that separate accounts shall be kept of the amount of each species of duty or tax that shall accrue, so as to exhibit, as far as may be, the amount collected from each source of revenue, with the moneys paid to the collectors and deputy collectors, and to the other officers employed in each of the respective States, Territories, and collection districts, an abstract in tabular form of which accounts it shall be the duty of the Secretary of the Treasury, annually, in the month of December, to lay before Congress.

SEC. 34. *And be it further enacted,* That there shall be allowed to the collectors appointed under this act, in full compensation for their services and that of their deputies in carrying this act into effect, a commission of four per centum upon the first hundred thousand dollars, and two per centum upon all sums above one hundred thousand dollars; such commissions to be computed upon the amounts by them respectively paid over and accounted for under the instructions of the Treasury Department: *Provided*, That in no case shall such commissions exceed the sum of ten thousand dollars per annum, except as hereinafter provided. And there shall be further allowed to each collector his necessary and reasonable charges for stationery and blank books used in the performance of his official duties, which, after being duly examined and certified by the Commissioner of Internal Revenue, shall be paid out of the Treasury: *Provided*, That the Secretary of the Treasury be authorized to make such further allowance as may be reasonable in cases in which, from the territorial extent of the district, or from the amount of internal duties collected, it may seem just to make such allowance; but the whole compensation shall not exceed ten thousand dollars, except in collection districts embracing more than one congressional district.

Sec. 35. *And be it further enacted*, That when any duty or tax shall have been paid by levy and distraint, any person or persons, or party, who may feel aggrieved thereby may apply to the assessor of the district for relief, and exhibit such evidence as he, she, or they may have of the wrong done, or supposed to have been done, and after a full investigation the assessor shall report the case, with such parts of the evidence as he may judge material, including also such as may be regarded material by the party aggrieved, to the Commissioner of Internal Revenue, who may, if it shall be made to appear to him that such duty or tax was levied or collected, in whole or in part, wrongfully or unjustly, certify the amount wrongfully and unjustly levied or collected, and the same shall be refunded and paid to the person or persons, or party, as aforesaid, from any moneys in the treasury not otherwise appropriated, upon the presentation of such certificate to the proper officer thereof.

Sec. 36. *And be it further enacted*, That in all cases of distraint and sale of goods, or chattels, for non-payment of taxes provided for in this act, the bill of sale of such goods or chattels given by the officer making such sale to the purchaser thereof shall be conclusive evidence of the right of the officer to make such sale, and of the correctness of his proceedings in selling the same.

Sec. 37. *And be it further enacted*, That if for any cause, at any time after this act goes into operation, the laws of the United States can not be executed in a State or Territory of the United States, or any part thereof, or within the District of Columbia, it shall be the duty of the President, and he is hereby authorized, to proceed to execute the provisions of this act within the limits of such State or Territory, or part thereof, or District of Columbia, so soon as the authority of the United States therein shall be re-established, and to collect the sums which would have been due from the persons residing or holding property, goods, wares, or merchandise, object or article therein liable to any duty, license, or tax, with interest at the rate of six per centum per annum thereon from the time such duty,.

4

license, or tax ought to have been paid until paid in the manner and under the regulations prescribed in this act, so far as applicable, and where not applicable the assessment and levy shall be made, and the time and manner of collection regulated, by the instructions and directions of the Commissioner of Internal Revenue, under the direction of the Secretary of the Treasury.

SEC. 38. *And be it further enacted*, That the officers who may be appointed under this act, except within those districts within any State or Territory which have been or may be otherwise specially provided for by law, shall be, and hereby are, authorized, in all cases where the payment of such tax has not been assumed by the State, to perform all the duties relating to or regarding the assessment and collection of the direct tax imposed by an act entitled "An act to provide increased revenue from imports to pay interest on the public debt, and for other purposes," approved August fifth, eighteen hundred and sixty-one, or any direct tax which may be hereafter enacted: *Provided*, That the sum of nineteen thousand three hundred and twelve dollars, direct tax, laid upon the Territory of Nebraska by said act, shall be paid and satisfied by deducting said amount from the appropriation for legislative expenses of the Territory of Nebraska for the year ending thirtieth of June, eighteen hundred and sixty-three, and no further claim shall be made by said Territory for legislative expenses for said year: *Provided, further*, That the State of Tennessee shall have, until the first day of December next, to assume the payment of her portion of said tax.

SPIRITS, ALE, BEER, AND PORTER.

SEC. 39. *And be it further enacted*, That it shall be the duty of the collectors, within their respective districts, to grant licenses for distilling, which licenses shall contain the date thereof, the sum paid, and the time when the same will expire, and shall be granted to any person, being a resident of the United States, who shall desire the same, by application, in writing, to such collector, upon payment of the sum or duty payable by this act upon each license requested. And at the time of applying for said license, and before the same is issued, the person so applying shall give bond to the United States in such sum as shall be required by the collector, and with one or more sureties, to be approved by said collector conditioned that in case any additional still or stills, or other implements to be used as aforesaid, shall be erected by him, his agent or superintendent, he will, before using, or causing or permitting the same to be used, report in writing to the said collector the capacity thereof, and information from time to time of any change in the form, capacity, ownership, agency, or superintendence, which all or either of the said stills or other implements may undergo; and that he will, from day to day, enter, or cause to be entered, in a book to be kept for that purpose, the number of gallons of spirits that may be distilled by said still or stills, or other implements, and also of the quantities of grain or other vegetable productions, or other substances put into the mash-tub, or otherwise used by him, his agent, or superintendent, for the purpose of producing spirits, which said book shall be open at all times during the day (Sundays excepted) to the inspection of the said collector, who may make any memorandums or transcripts therefrom; and that he will render to the said collector, on the first, tenth, and twentieth days of each and every month, or within five days thereafter, during the continuance of said license, an exact account, in writing, taken from his books, of the number of gallons of spirits distilled and sold, or removed for consumption or sale, by him, his agent, or superintendent, and the proof thereof, and also of the quantities of grain or other vegetable productions, or other substances, put into the mash-tub, or otherwise used by him, his agent, or superintendent, for the purpose of producing spirits, for the period or fractional part of a month then next preceding the date of said report, which said report shall be verified by affidavit in the manner prescribed by this act; and that he will not sell or permit to be sold, or remove for consumption or sale, any spirits distilled by him under and by virtue of his said license, until the same shall have been inspected, gauged, and proved, and the quantity thereof duly entered upon his books as aforesaid; and that he will, at the time of rendering said account, pay to the said collector the duties which by this act are imposed on the spirits so distilled; and the said bond may be renewed or changed, from time to time, in regard to the amount and sureties thereof. according to the discretion of the collector.

SEC. 40. *And be it further enacted*, That the application in writing made by any person for a license for distilling, as aforesaid, shall state the place of distilling, the number and capacity of the still or stills, boiler or boilers, and the name of the person, firm, company, or corporation using the same; and any person making a false statement in either of the said particulars shall forfeit and pay the sum of one hundred dollars, to be recovered with costs of suit.

ᐧ SEC. 41. *And be it further enacted*, That, in addition to the duties payable for licenses herein provided, there shall be paid, on all spirits that may be distilled and sold, or removed for consumption or sale, of first proof, on and after the first day of August, eighteen hundred and sixty-two, the duty of twenty cents on each and every gallon, which shall be paid by the owner, agent, or superintendent of the still or other vessel in which the said spirituous liquors shall have been distilled; which duty shall be paid at the time of rendering the accounts of spirituous liquors so chargeable with duty, required to be rendered by this act: *Provided*, That the duty on spirituous liquors and all other spirituous beverages enumerated in this act shall be collected at no lower rate than the basis of first proof, and shall be increased in proportion for any greater strength than the strength of proof.

SEC. 42. *And be it further enacted*, That the term first proof used in this act and in Section six of the act of March second, eighteen hundred and sixty-one, entitled "An act to provide for the payment of outstanding treasury notes, to authorize a loan, to regulate and fix the duties on imports, and for other purposes," shall be construed, and is hereby declared to mean, that proof of a liquor which corresponds to fifty degrees of Tralles' centesimal hydrometer, adopted by regulation of the Treasury Department of August twelfth, eighteen hundred and fifty, at the temperature of sixty degrees of Fahrenheit's thermometer ; and that in reducing the temperatures to the standard of sixty, and in levying duties on liquors above and below proof, the table of commercial values, contained in the manual for inspectors of spirits, prepared by Professor McCulloh, under the superintendence of Professor Bache, and adopted by the Treasury Department, shall be used and taken as giving the proportions of absolute alcohol in the liquids gauged and proved according to which duties shall be levied.

SEC. 43. *And be it further enacted*, That there shall be designated by the collector in every assessment district where the same may be necessary, one or more inspectors, who shall take an oath faithfully to perform their duties in such form as the Commissioner of Internal Revenue shall prescribe, and who shall be entitled to receive such fees as may be fixed and prescribed by said Commissioner. And all spirits distilled as aforesaid by any person licensed as aforesaid shall, before the same is used, or removed for consumption or sale, be inspected, gauged, and proved by some person so as aforesaid designated for the performance of such duties, and who shall mark upon the cask or other package containing such spirits, in a manner to be prescribed by said Commissioner, the quantity and proof of the contents of such cask or package, with the date of inspection and the name of the inspector. And any person who shall attempt fraudulently to evade the payment of duties upon any spirits distilled as aforesaid, by changing in any manner the mark upon any such cask or package, shall forfeit the sum of five hundred dollars for each cask or package so altered or changed, to be recovered as hereinbefore provided. And the fees of such inspector shall in all cases be paid by the owner of the spirits so inspected, gauged, and proved. And any such inspector who shall knowingly put upon any such cask or package any false or fraudulent mark shall be liable to the same penalty hereinbefore provided for each cask or package so fraudulently marked. And any person who shall use any cask or package so marked, for the purpose of selling spirits of a quality different from that so inspected, shall be subject to a like penalty for each cask or package so used.

SEC. 44. *And be it further enacted*, That the owner or owners of any distillery may erect, at his or their own expense, a warehouse of iron, stone, or brick, with metal or other fire-proof roof, to be contiguous to such distillery ; and such warehouse, when approved by the collector, is hereby declared a bonded warehouse of the United States, and shall be used only for storing distilled spirits, and to be under the custody of the collector or his deputy. And the duty on the spirits stored in such warehouse shall be paid when and as it is sold or removed from such warehouse for sale.

SEC. 45. *And be it further enacted*, That every person who, on the first day of August, eighteen hundred and sixty-two, shall be the owner of any still, boiler, or other vessel, used or intended to be used for the purpose of distilling spirituous liquors, as hereinbefore provided, or who shall have such still, boiler, or other vessel under his superintendence, either as agent for the owner or on his own account, and every person who, after said day, shall use or intend to use any still, boiler, or other vessel, as aforesaid, either as owner, agent, or otherwise, shall from day to day make true and exact entry, or cause to be entered, in a book to be kept by him for that purpose, the number of gallons of spirituous liquors distilled by him, and also the number of gallons sold, or removed for consumption or sale, and the proof thereof, which book shall always be open in the daytime (Sundays excepted), for the inspection of the said collector, who may take any minutes, memorandums, or transcripts thereof, and shall render to said collector, on the first, tenth, and twentieth days of each and every month in each year, or within five days thereafter, a general account in writing, taken from his books, of the number of gallons of spirituous liquors distilled and sold, or removed for consumption or sale, and the proof thereof, for the period or fractional part of a month preceding said day, or for such portion thereof as may have elapsed from the date of said entry and report to the said day which shall next ensue ; and shall also keep a book, or books, in a form to be prescribed by the Commissioner of Internal Revenue, and to be open at all seasonable hours for inspection by the collector and assessor of the district, wherein shall be entered, from day to day, the quantities of grain, or other vegetable productions, or other substances put into the mash-tub by him, his agent, or superintendent, for the purpose of producing spirits ; and shall verify or cause to be verified the said entries, reports, books, and general accounts, by oath or affirmation, to be taken before the collector or some other officer authorized by the laws of the State to administer the same according to the form required by this act, where the same is prescribed ; and shall also pay to the collector the duties which by this act ought to be paid on the spirituous liquors so distilled and sold, or removed for consumption or sale, and in said accounts mentioned, at the time of rendering an account thereof.

SEC. 46. *And be it further enacted*, That the collector of any district may grant a permit to the owner or owners of any distillery within his district to send or ship any spirits, the product of said distillery, after the quantity and proof thereof shall have been ascertained by inspection according to the provisions of this act, to any place without said district and within the United States ; and in such case the bill of lading or receipt (which shall be in such form as the Commissioner of Internal Revenue may direct) of the same shall be taken in the name of the collector of the district in which the distillery is situate, and the spirits aforesaid shall be consigned, in such bill of lading or receipt, to the collector of the district in which the place is situate, whither the spirits is sent or shipped, and the amount of duties upon said spirits shall be stated in the receipt ; and upon the arrival of the spirits, and upon the demand of the collector aforesaid, the agent of the distillery (and the name of the agent, for the con-

venience of the collector, shall always appear in the bill of lading or
receipt) shall pay the duties upon the said spirits, with the expense
of freight, and every other expense which has accrued thereupon;
and the said collector, upon the payment of the duties aforesaid, shall
deliver the bill of lading or receipt and the spirits to the agent of the
said distillery; and if the duties are not paid as aforesaid, then the
said spirits shall be stored at the risk and cost of the owner or agent
thereof, who shall pay an addition of ten per centum thereupon; and
all the general provisions of this act, in reference to liens, penalties,
and forfeitures, as also in reference to the collection, shall apply thereto, and be enforced by the collector of the district in which the
spirits may be: *Provided,* That no permit shall be granted, under
this section, for a quantity less than fifty barrels: *And provided,*
further, That the Commissioner of Internal Revenue, under the
direction of the Secretary of the Treasury, may make such further
regulations and require such further securities as he may deem
proper, in order to protect the revenue and to carry out the spirit
and intent of this section.

SEC. 47. *And be it further enacted,* That distilled spirits may be
removed from the place of manufacture for the purpose of being exported, or for the purpose of being re-distilled for export, and refined
coal oil may be removed for the purpose of being exported, after the
quantity of spirits or oil so removed shall have been ascertained by
inspection, according to the provisions of this act, upon and with the
written permission of the collector or deputy collector of the district,
without payment of the duties thereon previous to such removal, the
owner thereof having first given bond to the United States, with
sufficient sureties, in the manner and form and under regulations
prescribed by the Commissioner of Internal Revenue, and in at least
double the amount of said duties, to export the said spirits or oil or
pay the duties thereon within such time as may be prescribed by the
Commissioner, which time shall be stated in said bond: *Provided,*
That any person desiring to give such bond shall first make oath, before the collector or deputy collector to whom he may apply for a
permit to remove any such spirits or oil, in manner and form to be
prescribed by said Commissioner, that he intends to export such
liquors or oil, and that he desires to obtain said permit for no other
purpose whatever; and any collector or deputy collector is hereby
authorized to administer such oath: *And provided, further,* That no
such removal shall be permitted where the amount of duties does not
exceed the sum of three hundred dollars, nor in any case where the
person desiring such permission has failed to perform the obligation
of any bond previously given to the United States for the removal
of any such articles, until the same shall have been fully kept and performed. And the collector of the district in which any such bond
may be given is authorized to cancel said bond on payment of said
duties, with interest thereon, at a rate to be fixed by said Commissioner, and all proper charges, if said liquors or oil shall not have
been exported, or upon satisfactory proof that the same have been
duly exported as aforesaid. And in case of the breach of the obliga-

tion of any such bond, the same shall be forthwith forwarded by the collector of the district to the Commissioner of Internal Revenue, to be by him placed in the hands of the First Comptroller of the Treasury, who shall cause the same proceedings to be taken thereon for the purpose of collecting the duties, interest, and charges aforesaid, as are provided in this act in case of a delinquent collector.

SEC. 48. *And be it further enacted*, That the entries made in the books of the distiller, required to be kept in the foregoing section, shall, on the first, tenth, and twentieth days of each and every month, or within *five* days thereafter, be verified by oath or affirmation, to be taken as aforesaid, of the person or persons by whom such entries shall have been made, which oath or affirmation shall be certified at the end of such entries by the collector or officer administering the same, and shall be, in substance, as follows : "I do swear (or affirm) that the foregoing entries were made by me on the respective days specified, and that they state, according to the best of my knowledge and belief, the whole quantity of spirituous liquors distilled and sold, or removed for consumption or sale, at the distillery owned by ———, in the county of ———, amounting to ——— gallons, according to proof prescribed by the laws of the United States."

SEC. 49. *And be it further enacted*, That the owner, agent, or superintendent aforesaid, shall, in case the original entries required to be made in his books by this act shall not have been made by himself, subjoin to the oath or affirmation of the person by whom they were made the following oath or affirmation, to be taken as aforesaid: "I do swear (or affirm) that, to the best of my knowledge and belief, the foregoing entries are just and true, and that I have taken all the means in my power to make them so."

SEC. 50. *And be it further enacted*, That on and after the first day of August, eighteen hundred and sixty-two, there shall be paid on all beer, lager beer, ale, porter, and other similar fermented liquors, by whatever name such liquors may be called, a duty of one dollar for each and every barrel containing not more than thirty-one gallons, and at a like rate for any other quantity or for fractional parts of a barrel, which shall be brewed or manufactured and sold or removed for consumption or sale within the United States or the Territories thereof, or within the District of Columbia after that day; which duty shall be paid by the owner, agent, or superintendent of the brewery or premises in which such fermented liquors shall be made, and shall be paid at the time of rendering the accounts of such fermented liquors so chargeable with duty, as required to be rendered by the following section of this act: *Provided*, That fractional parts of a barrel shall be halves, quarters, eighths, and sixteenths, and any fractional part containing less than one-sixteenth shall be accounted one-sixteenth; more than one-sixteenth, and not more than one-eighth, shall be accounted one-eighth ; more than one-eighth, and not more than one-quarter, shall be accounted one-quarter ; more than one-quarter, and not more than one-half, shall be accounted one-half; more than one-half shall be accounted one barrel.

SEC. 51. *And be it further enacted*, That every person who, on said

first day of August, eighteen hundred and sixty-two, shall be the
owner or occupant of any brewery or premises used, or intended to
be used, for the purpose of brewing or making such fermented liquors,
or who shall have such premises under his control or superintendence as agent for the owner or occupant, or shall have in his possession or custody any vessel or vessels intended to be used on said
premises in the manufacture of beer, lager beer, ale, porter, or other
similar fermented liquors, either as owner, agent, or otherwise, shall,
from day to day, enter or cause to be entered in a book to be kept by
him for that purpose, and which shall be open at all times, except
Sundays, between the rising and setting of the sun, for the inspection of said collector, who may take any minutes or memorandums
or transcripts thereof, the quantities of grain, or other vegetable productions or other substances, put into the mash-tub, or otherwise
used for the purpose of producing beer, or for any other purpose,
and the quantity or number of barrels and fractional parts of barrels
of fermented liquors made and sold, or removed for consumption or
sale, keeping separate account of the several kinds and descriptions;
and shall render to said collector, on the first day of each month in
each year, or within ten days thereafter, a general account, in writing,
taken from his books, of the quantities of grain, or other vegetable
productions or other substances, put into the mash-tub, or otherwise
used for the purpose of producing beer, or for any other purpose, and
the quantity or number of barrels and fractional parts of barrels of
each kind of fermented liquors made and sold, or removed for consumption or sale, for one month preceding said day, and shall verify,
or cause to be verified, the said entries, reports, books, and general
accounts, on oath or affirmation, to be taken before the collector or
some officer authorized by the laws of the State to administer the
same according to the form required by this act where the same is
prescribed; and shall also pay to the said collector the duties which,
by this act, ought to be paid on the liquor made and sold, or removed
for consumption or sale, and in the said accounts mentioned, at the
time of rendering the account thereof, as aforesaid. But where the
manufacturer of any beer, lager beer, or ale manufactures the same
in one collection district, and owns or hires a depot or warehouse for
the storage and sale of such beer, lager beer, or ale in another collection district, he may, instead of paying to the collector of the district
where the same was manufactured the duties chargeable thereon,
present to such collector or his deputy an invoice of the quantity or
number of barrels about to be removed for the purpose of storage and
sale, specifying in such invoice, with reasonable certainty, the depot
or warehouse in which he intends to place such beer, lager beer, or
ale; and thereupon such collector or deputy shall indorse on such invoice his permission for such removal, and shall at the same time
transmit to the collector of the district in which such depot or warehouse is situated a duplicate of such invoice; and thereafter the
manufacturer of the beer, lager beer, or ale so removed shall render
the same account, and pay the same duties, and be subject to the
same liabilities and penalties as if the beer, lager beer, or ale so re-

moved had been manufactured in the district. The Commissioner of Internal Revenue may prescribe such rules as he may deem necessary for the purpose of carrying the provisions of this section into effect.

SEC. 52. *And be it further enacted,* That the entries made in the books required to be kept by the foregoing section shall, on said first day of each and every month, or within ten days thereafter, be verified by the oath or affirmation, to be taken as aforesaid, of the person or persons by whom such entries shall have been made, which oath or affirmation shall be certified at the end of such entries by the collector or officer administering the same, and shall be, in substance, as follows:

"I do swear (or affirm) that the foregoing entries were made by me on the respective days specified, and that they state, according to the best of my knowledge and belief, the whole quantity of fermented liquors either brewed or brewed and sold at the brewery owned by ———, in the county of ———, amounting to —— barrels."

SEC. 53. *And be it further enacted,* That the owner, agent, or superintendent aforesaid, shall, in case the original entries required to be made in his books shall not have been made by himself, subjoin to the oath or affirmation the following oath or affirmation, to be taken as aforesaid:

"I do swear (or affirm) that, to the best of my knowledge and belief, the foregoing entries are just and true, and that I have taken all the means in my power to make them so."

SEC. 54. *And be it further enacted,* That the owner, agent, or superintendent of any vessel or vessels used in making fermented liquors, or of any still, boiler, or other vessel used in the distillation of spirits on which duty is payable, who shall neglect or refuse to make true and exact entry and report of the same, or to do, or cause to be done, any of the things by this act required to be done as aforesaid, shall forfeit for every such neglect or refusal all the liquors and spirits made by or for him, and all the vessels used in making the same, and the stills, boilers, and other vessels used in distillation, together with the sum of five hundred dollars, to be recovered with costs of suit; which said liquors or spirits, with the vessels containing the same, with all the vessels used in making the same, may be seized by any collector of internal duties, and held by him until a decision shall be had thereon according to law: *Provided,* That such seizure be made within thirty days after the cause for the same may have occurred, and that proceedings to enforce said forfeiture shall have been commenced by such collector within twenty days after the seizure thereof. And the proceeding to enforce said forfeiture of said property shall be in the nature of a proceeding *in rem,* in the Circuit or District Court of the United States for the district where such seizure is made, or in any other court of competent jurisdiction.

SEC. 55. *And be it further enacted,* That in all cases in which the duties aforesaid, payable on spirituous liquors distilled and sold, or removed for consumption or sale, or beer, lager beer, ale, porter, and other similar fermented liquors, shall not be paid at the time of rendering the account of the same, as herein required, the person or per-

sons chargeable therewith shall pay, in addition, ten per centum on
the amount thereof; and, until such duties with such addition shall
be paid, they shall be and remain a lien upon the distillery where such
liquors have been distilled, or the brewery where such liquors have
been brewed, and upon the stills, boilers, vats, and all other implements thereto belonging, until the same shall have been paid; and in
case of refusal or neglect to pay said duties, with the addition, within
ten days after the same shall have become payable, the amount thereof
may be recovered by distraint and sale of the goods, chattels, and
effects of the delinquent; and in case of such distraint, it shall be the
duty of the officer charged with the collection to make, or cause to
be made, an account of the goods, chattels, or effects which may be
distrained, a copy of which, signed by the officer making such distraint, shall be left with the owner or possessor of such goods, chattels, or effects, at his, her, or their dwelling, with a note of the sum
demanded, and the time and place of sale; and said officer shall forthwith cause a notification to be published in some newspaper, if any
there be, within the county, and publicly posted up at the post-office
nearest to the residence of the person whose property shall be distrained, or at the court-house of the same county, if not more than
ten miles distant, which notice shall specify the articles distrained,
and the time and place proposed for the sale thereof, which time shall
not be less than ten days from the date of such notification, and the
place proposed for sale not more than five miles distant from the place
of making such distraint: *Provided*, That in every case of distraint
for the payment of the duties aforesaid, the goods, chattels, or effects
so distrained may and shall be restored to the owner or possessor if,
prior to the sale thereof, payment or tender thereof shall be made to
the proper officer charged with the collection, of the full amount demanded, together with such fee for levying and advertising, and such
sum for the necessary and reasonable expenses of removing and keeping the goods, chattels, and effects so distrained as may be allowed
in like cases by the laws or practice of the State or Territory wherein
the distraint shall have been made; but in case of non-payment or
neglect to tender as aforesaid, the said officer shall proceed to sell the
said goods, chattels, and effects at public auction, after due notice of
the time and place of sale, and may and shall retain from the proceeds
of such sale the amount demandable for the use of the United States,
with the said necessary and reasonable expenses of said distraint and
sale, as aforesaid, and a commission of five per centum thereon for
his own use; rendering the overplus, if any there be, to the person
whose goods, chattels, and effects shall have been distrained.

SEC. 56. *And be it further enacted*, That every person licensed
as aforesaid to distill spirituous liquors, or licensed as a brewer, shall,
once in each month, upon the request of the assessor or assistant assessor for the district in which his business as a distiller or brewer
may be carried on, respectively, furnish the said assessor or assistant
assessor with an abstract of the entries upon his books, herein provided to be made, showing the amount of spirituous liquor distilled
and sold, or removed for consumption or sale, or of beer, lager beer,

ale, porter, or other fermented liquor made and sold, or removed for consumption or sale, during the preceding month, respectively; the truth and correctness of which abstract shall be verified by the oath of the party so furnishing the same. And the said assessor or assistant assessor shall have the right to examine the books of such person for the purpose of ascertaining the correctness of such abstract. And for any neglect to furnish such abstract when requested, or refusal to furnish an examination of the books as aforesaid, the person so neglecting shall forfeit the sum of five hundred dollars.

LICENSES.

SEC. 57. *And be it further enacted*, That from and after the first day of August, eighteen hundred and sixty-two, no person, association of persons, or corporation, shall be engaged in, prosecute, or carry on, either of the trades or occupations mentioned in Section sixty-four of this act, until he or they shall have obtained a license therefor in the manner hereinafter provided.

SEC. 58. *And be it further enacted*, That every person, association of persons, partnership or corporation, desiring to obtain a license to engage in any of the trades or occupations named in the sixty-fourth section of this act, shall register with the assistant assessor of the assessment district in which he shall design to carry on such trade or occupation—first, his or their name or style; and in case of an association or partnership, the names of the several persons constituting such association or partnership and their places of residence; second, the trade or occupation for which a license is desired ; third, the place where such trade or occupation is to be carried on ; fourth, if a rectifier, the number of barrels he designs to rectify ; if a peddler, whether he designs to travel on foot, or with one, two, or more horses; if an inn-keeper, the yearly rental of the house and property to be occupied for said purpose; or, if not rented, the assistant assessor shall value the same. All of which facts shall be returned duly certified by such assistant assessor, both to the assessor and collector of the district ; and thereupon, upon payment to the collector or deputy collector of the district the amount as hereinafter provided, such collector or deputy collector shall make out and deliver a license for such trade or occupation, which license shall continue in force for one year, at the place or premises described therein.

SEC. 59. *And be it further enacted*, That if any person or persons shall exercise or carry on any trade or business hereinafter mentioned for the exercising or carrying on of which trade or business a license is required by this act, without taking out such license as in that behalf required, he, she, or they shall, for every such offense, respectively, forfeit a penalty equal to three times the amount of the duty or sum of money imposed for such license, one moiety thereof to the use of the United States, the other moiety to the use of the person who, if a collector, shall first discover, and if other than a collector, shall first give information of the fact whereby said forfeiture was incurred.

SEC. 60. *And be it further enacted*, That in every license to be taken out under or by authority of this act shall be contained and set forth the purpose, trade, or business for which such license is granted, and the true name and place of abode of the person or persons taking out the same; if for a rectifier, the quantity of spirits authorized to be rectified; if by a peddler, whether authorized to travel on foot, or with one, or two, or more horses, the time for which such license is to run, and the true date or time of granting such license, and (except in the case of auctioneers and peddlers) the place at which the trade or business for which such license is granted shall be carried on: *Provided*, That a license granted under this act shall not authorize the person or persons, association or corporation mentioned therein to exercise or carry on the trade or business specified in such license in any other place than that mentioned therein, but nothing herein contained shall prohibit the storage of goods, wares, or merchandise in other places than the place of business.

SEC. 61. *And be it further enacted*, That in every case where more than one of the pursuits, employments, or occupations, hereinafter described, shall be pursued or carried on in the same place by the same person at the same time, except as therein mentioned, license must be taken out for each according to the rates severally prescribed.

SEC. 62. *And be it further enacted*, That no auctioneer shall be authorized by virtue of his license as such auctioneer to sell any goods or other property at private sale; and if any such person shall sell any such goods or commodities, as aforesaid, otherwise than by auction, without having taken out such license as aforesaid for that purpose, he or she shall be subject and liable to the penalty in that behalf imposed upon persons dealing in or retailing, trading, or selling any such goods or commodities without license, notwithstanding any license to him or her before granted, as aforesaid, for the purpose of exercising or carrying on the trade or business of an auctioneer, or selling any goods or chattels, lands, tenements, or hereditaments by auction, anything herein contained to the contrary notwithstanding: *Provided, always*, That where such goods or commodities as aforesaid are the property of any person or persons duly licensed to deal in or retail, or trade in, or sell the same, such person or persons having made lawful entry of his, her, or their house or premises for such purpose, it shall and may be lawful for any person exercising or carrying on the trade or business of an auctioneer, or selling any goods or chattels, lands, tenements, or hereditaments, by auction as aforesaid, being duly licensed for that purpose, to sell such goods or commodities as aforesaid, at auction, for and on behalf of such person or persons, and upon his, her, or their entered house or premises, without taking out a separate license for such sale. The provisions of this section shall not apply to judicial or executive officers making auction sales by virtue of any judgment or decree of any court, nor public sale made by executors and administrators.

SEC. 63. *And be it further enacted*, That upon the death of any person or persons licensed under or by virtue of this act, or upon the removal of any such person or persons from the house or premises at which he, she, or they were authorized by such license to exercise or carry on the trade or business mentioned in such license, it shall and may be lawful for the person or persons authórized to grant licenses to authorize and empower, by indorsement on such license, or otherwise, as the Commissioner of Internal Revenue shall direct, the executors or administrators, or the wife or child of such deceased person, or the assignee or assigns of such person or persons so removing as aforesaid, who shall be possessed of and occupy the house or premises before used for such purpose as aforesaid, in like manner to exercise or carry on the same trade or business mentioned in such license, in or upon the same house or premises at which such person or persons as aforesaid deceased, or removing as before mentioned, by virtue of such license to him, her, or them, in that behalf granted, before exercised or carried on such trade or business for or during the residue of the term for which such license was originally granted, without taking out any fresh license or payment of any additional duty, or any fee thereupon for the residue of such term, and until expiration thereof: *Provided, always,* That a fresh entry of the premises at which such trade or business shall continue to be so exercised or carried on as aforesaid shall thereupon be made by and in the name or names of the person or persons to whom such authority as aforesaid shall be granted.

SEC. 64. *And be it further enacted,* That on and after the first day of August, eighteen hundred and sixty-two, for each license granted the sum herewith stated shall be respectively and annually paid. Any number of persons carrying on such business in copartnership may transact such business at such place under such license, and not otherwise.

1. Bankers shall pay one hundred dollars for each license. Every person shall be deemed a banker within the meaning of this act who keeps a place of business where credits are opened in favor of any person, firm, or corporation, by the deposit or collection of money or currency, and the same, or any part thereof, shall be paid out or remitted upon the draft, check, or order of such creditor, but not to include incorporated banks or other banks legally authorized to issue notes as circulation, nor agents for the sale of merchandise for account of producers or manufacturers.

2. Auctioneers shall pay twenty dollars for each license. Every person shall be deemed an auctioneer within the meaning of this act whose occupation it is to offer property for sale to the highest or best bidder.

3. Wholesale dealers in liquors of any and every description, including distilled spirits, fermented liquors, and wines of all kinds, shall pay one hundred dollars for each license. Every person, other than the distiller, or brewer who shall sell or offer for sale any such liquors or wines in quantities of more than three gallons at one time, to the same purchaser, shall be regarded as a wholesale dealer in liquors within the meaning of this act.

4. Retail dealers in liquors, including distilled spirits, fermented

liquors, and wines of every description, shall pay twenty dollars for each license. Every person who shall sell or offer for sale such liquors in less quantities than three gallons at one time, to the same purchaser, shall be regarded as a retail dealer in liquors under this act. But this shall not authorize any spirits, liquors, wines, or malt liquors to be drank on the premises.

5. Retail dealers shall pay ten dollars for each license. Every person whose business or occupation is to sell, or offer to sell, groceries, or any goods, wares, or merchandise, of foreign or domestic production, in less quantities than a whole original piece or package at one time, to the same person (not including wines, spirituous or malt liquors, but not excluding drugs, medicines, cigars, snuff, or tobacco), shall be regarded as a retail dealer under this act.

6. Wholesale dealers shall pay fifty dollars for each license. Every person whose business or occupation is to sell, or offer to sell, groceries, or any goods, wares, or merchandise, of foreign or domestic production, by one or more original package or piece at one time, to the same purchaser, not including wines, spirituous or malt liquors, shall be deemed a wholesale dealer under this act; but having taken out a license as a wholesale dealer, such person may also sell, as aforesaid, as a retailer.

7. Pawnbrokers shall pay fifty dollars for each license. Every person whose business or occupation is to take or receive, by way of pledge, pawn, or exchange, any goods, wares, or merchandise, or any kind of personal property whatever, for the repayment or security of money lent thereon, shall be deemed a pawnbroker under this act.

8. Rectifiers shall pay twenty-five dollars for each license to rectify any quantity of spirituous liquors, not exceeding five hundred barrels or casks, containing not more than forty gallons to each barrel or cask of liquor so rectified; and twenty-five dollars additional for each additional five hundred such barrels, or any fractional part thereof. Every person who rectifies, purifies, or refines spirituous liquors or wines by any process, or mixes distilled spirits, whisky, brandy, gin, or wine, with any other materials for sale under the name of whisky, rum, brandy, gin, wine, or any other name or names, shall be regarded as a rectifier under this act.

9. Distillers shall pay fifty dollars for each license, and every person or copartnership who distills or manufactures spirituous liquors for sale shall be deemed a distiller under this act: *Provided,* That any person or copartnership distilling or manufacturing less than three hundred barrels per year shall pay twenty-five dollars for a license. *And provided, further,* That no license shall be required for any still, stills, or other apparatus used by druggists and chemists for the recovery of alcohol for pharmaceutical and chemical purposes which has been used in those processes. *And provided, further,* That distillers of apples and peaches, distilling or manufacturing less than one hundred and fifty barrels per year from the same, shall pay twelve and one-half dollars for a license for that purpose, and for a greater quantity as other distillers.

10. Brewers shall pay fifty dollars for each license. Every person

who manufactures fermented liquors of any name or description, for sale, from malt, wholly or in part, shall be deemed a brewer under this act: *Provided*, That any person who manufactures less than five hundred barrels per year shall pay the sum of twenty-five dollars for a license.

11. Hotels, inns, and taverns shall be classified and rated according to the yearly rental, or, if not rented, according to the estimated yearly rental of the house and property intended to be occupied for said purposes, as follows, to wit: All cases where the rent or the valuation of the yearly rental of said house and property shall be ten thousand dollars or more shall constitute the first class, and shall pay two hundred dollars for each license; where the rent or the valuation of the yearly rental shall be five thousand dollars and less than ten thousand dollars, the second class, and shall pay one hundred dollars for each license; where the rent or the valuation of the yearly rental shall be twenty-five hundred dollars and less than five thousand dollars, the third class, and shall pay seventy-five dollars for each license; where the rent or the valuation of the yearly rental shall be one thousand dollars and less than twenty-five hundred dollars, the fourth class, and shall pay fifty dollars for each license; where the rent or the valuation of the yearly rental shall be five hundred dollars and less than one thousand dollars, the fifth class, and shall pay twenty-five dollars for each license; where the rent or the valuation of the yearly rental shall be three hundred dollars and less than five hundred dollars, the sixth class, and shall pay fifteen dollars for each license; where the rent or the valuation of the yearly rental shall be one hundred dollars and less than three hundred dollars, the seventh class, and shall pay ten dollars for each license; where the rent or the valuation of the yearly rental shall be less than one hundred dollars, the eighth class, and shall pay five dollars for each license. Every place where food and lodging are provided for and furnished to travelers and sojourners, in view of payment therefor, shall be regarded as an hotel, inn, or tavern under this act. All steamers and vessels upon waters of the United States, on board of which passengers or travelers are provided with food or lodging, shall be required to take out a license of the fifth class, as aforesaid, under this act. The rental or estimated rental shall be fixed and established by the assessor of the proper district at its proper value, but at not less than the actual rent agreed on by the parties: *Provided*, That if there be any fraud or collusion in the return of actual rent to the assessor, there shall be a penalty equal to double the amount of licenses required by this section, to be collected as others penalties under this act are collected.

12. Eating-houses shall pay ten dollars for each license. Every place where food or refreshments of any kind are provided for casual visitors and sold for consumption therein shall be regarded as an eating-house under this act. But the keeper of any eating-house having taken out a license therefor shall not be required to take out a license as a confectioner, anything in this act to the contrary notwithstanding.

13. Brokers shall pay fifty dollars for each license. Any person

whose business is to purchase or sell stocks, coined money, bank notes, or other securities for themselves or others, or who deals in exchanges relating to money, shall be regarded a broker under this act.

14. Commercial brokers shall pay fifty dollars for each license. Any person or firm, except one holding a license as a wholesale dealer or banker, whose business it is, as the agent of others, to purchase or sell goods, or seek orders therefor, in original or unbroken packages or produce, or to manage business matters for the owners of vessels, or for the shippers and consignors of freight carried by vessels, or whose business it is to purchase, rent, or sell real estate for others, shall be regarded a commercial broker under this act.

15. Land warrant brokers shall pay twenty-five dollars for each license. Any person shall be regarded as a land warrant broker within the meaning of this act who makes a business of buying and selling land warrants, and of furnishing them to settlers or other persons under contracts to have liens upon the land procured by means of them according to the value agreed on for the warrants at the time they are furnished.

16. Tobacconists shall pay ten dollars for each license. Any person whose business it is to sell, at retail, cigars, snuff, or tobacco in any form, shall be regarded a tobacconist under this act. But wholesale and retail dealers, and keepers of hotels, inns, taverns, having taken out a license therefor, shall not be required to take out a license as tobacconist, anything in this act to the contrary notwithstanding.

17. Theaters shall pay one hundred dollars for each license. Every edifice erected for the purpose of dramatic or operatic representations, plays, or performances, and not including halls rented or used occasionally for concerts or theatrical representations, shall be regarded as a theater under this act.

18. Circuses shall pay fifty dollars for each license. Every building, tent, space, or area where feats of horsemanship or acrobatic sports are exhibited, shall be regarded as a circus under this act.

19. Jugglers shall pay for each license twenty dollars. Every person who performs by sleight of hand shall be regarded as a juggler under this act. The proprietors or agents of all other public exhibitions or shows for money, not enumerated in this section, shall pay for each license ten dollars: *Provided,* That no license procured in one State shall be held to authorize exhibitions in another State; and but one license shall be required under this act to authorize exhibitions within any one State.

20. Bowling-alleys and billiard rooms shall pay according to the number of alleys or tables belonging to or used in the building or place to be licensed. When not exceeding one alley or table, five dollars for each license ; and when exceeding one alley or table, five dollars for each additional alley or table. Every place or building where bowls are thrown or billiards played, and open to the public with or without price, shall be regarded as a bowling-alley or billiard room, respectively, under this act.

21. Confectioners shall pay ten dollars for each license. Every person who sells at retail confectionery, sweetmeats, comfits, or other confects, in any building, shall be regarded as a confectioner under this act. But wholesale and retail dealers, having taken out a license therefor, shall not be required to take out a license as confectioner, anything in this act to the contrary notwithstanding.

22. Horse-dealers shall pay for each license the sum of ten dollars. Any person whose business it is to buy and sell horses or mules shall be regarded as a horse-dealer under this act. *Provided*, That if such horse-dealer shall have taken out a license as a livery stable keeper no new license shall be required.

23. Livery stable keepers shall pay ten dollars for each license. Any person whose occupation or business is to keep horses for hire or to let shall be regarded as a livery stable keeper under this act.

24. Cattle brokers shall pay for each license the sum of ten dollars. Any person whose business it is to buy and sell and deal in cattle, hogs, or sheep shall be considered as a cattle broker.

25. Tallow-chandlers and soap-makers shall pay for each license the sum of ten dollars. Any person whose business is to make or manufacture candles or soap shall be regarded a tallow-chandler and soap-maker under this act.

26. Coal-oil distillers shall pay for each license the sum of fifty dollars. Any person who shall refine, produce, or distill crude petroleum or rock oil, or crude coal oil, or crude oil made of asphaltum, shale, peat, or other bituminous substances, shall be regarded a coal-oil distiller under this act.

27. Peddlers shall be classified and rated as follows, to wit: when traveling with more than two horses, the first class, and shall pay twenty dollars for each license; when traveling with two horses, the second class, and shall pay fifteen dollars for each license; when traveling with one horse, the third class, and shall pay ten dollars for each license; when traveling on foot, the fourth class, and shall pay five dollars for each license. Any person, except persons peddling newspapers, Bibles, or religious tracts, who sells or offers to sell, at retail, goods, wares, or other commodities, traveling from place to place, in the street, or through different parts of the country, shall be regarded a peddler under this act: *Provided*, That any peddler who sells, or offers to sell, dry goods, foreign and domestic, by one or more original packages or pieces, at one time, to the same person or persons, as aforesaid, shall pay fifty dollars for each license. And any person who peddles jewelry shall pay twenty-five dollars for each license: *Provided*, That manufacturers and producers of agricultural tools and implements, garden seeds, stoves, and hollow ware, brooms, wooden-ware, and powder, delivering and selling at wholesale any of said articles, by themselves or their authorized agents at places other than the place of manufacture, shall not be required, for any sale thus made, to take out any additional license therefor.

28. Apothecaries shall pay ten dollars for each license. Every person who keeps a shop or building where medicines are compounded or prepared according to prescriptions of physicians, and sold, shall

5

be regarded an apothecary under this act. But wholesale and retail dealers, who have taken out a license therefor, shall not be required to take out a license as apothecary, anything in this act to the contrary notwithstanding.

29. Manufacturers shall pay ten dollars for each license. Any person or persons, firms, companies, or corporations, who shall manufacture by hand or machinery, and offer for sale any goods, wares, or merchandise, exceeding annually the sum of one thousand dollars, shall be regarded a manufacturer under this act.

30. Photographers shall pay ten dollars for each license when the receipts do not exceed five hundred dollars; when over five hundred dollars and under one thousand dollars, fifteen dollars; when over one thousand dollars, twenty-five dollars. Any person or persons who make for sale photographs, ambrotypes, daguerreotypes, or pictures on glass, metal, or paper, by the action of light, shall be regarded a photographer under this act.

31. Lawyers shall pay ten dollars for each license. Every person whose business it is, for fee or reward, to prosecute or defend causes in any court of record or other judicial tribunal of the United States or of any of the States, or give advice in relation to causes or matters pending therein, shall be deemed to be a lawyer within the meaning of this act.

32. Physicians, surgeons, and dentists shall pay ten dollars for each license. Every person (except apothecaries) whose business it is, for fee and reward, to prescribe remedies or perform surgical operations for the cure of any bodily disease or ailing, shall be deemed a physician, surgeon, or dentist, as the case may be, within the meaning of this act.

33. Claim agents and agents for procuring patents shall pay ten dollars for each license. Every person whose business it is to prosecute claims in any of the executive departments of the federal government, or procure patents, shall be deemed a claim or patent agent, as the case may be, under this act.

SEC. 65. *And be it further enacted,* That where the annual gross receipts or sales of any apothecaries, confectioners, eating-houses, tobacconists, or retail dealers shall not exceed the sum of one thousand dollars, such apothecaries, confectioners, eating-houses, and retail dealers shall not be required to take out or pay for license, anything in this act to the contrary notwithstanding; the amount or estimated amount of such annual sales to be ascertained or estimated in such manner as the Commissioner of Internal Revenue shall prescribe, and so of all other annual sales or receipts, where the rate of the license is graduated by the amount of sales or receipts.

SEC. 66. *And be it further enacted,* That nothing contained in the preceding sections of this act, laying duties on licenses, shall be construed to require a license for the sale of goods, wares, and merchandise made or produced and sold by the manufacturer or producer at the manufactory or place where the same is made or produced; to vintners who sell, at the place where the same is made, wine of their own growth; nor to apothecaries, as to wines or spirituous liquors which they use exclusively in the preparation or making up of medicines for sick, lame, or diseased persons; nor shall the provisions of paragraph numbered twenty-seven extend to physicians who keep on hand medicine solely for the purpose of making up their own prescriptions for their own patients.

SEC. 67. *And be it further enacted,* That no license hereinbefore provided for, if granted, shall be construed to authorize the commencement or continuation of any trade, business, occupation, or employment therein mentioned, within any State or Territory of the United States in which it is or shall be specially prohibited by the laws thereof, or in violation of the laws of any State or Territory: *Provided,* Nothing in this act shall be held or construed so as to prevent the several States, within the limits thereof, from placing a duty, tax, or license, for State purposes, on any business matter or thing on which a duty, tax, or license is required to be paid by this act.

MANUFACTURES, ARTICLES, AND PRODUCTS.

SPECIFIC AND AD VALOREM DUTY.

SEC. 68. *And be it further enacted,* That on and after the first day of August, eighteen hundred and sixty-two, every individual, partnership, firm, association, or corporation (and any word or words in this act indicating or referring to person or persons shall be taken to mean and include partnerships, firms, associations, or corporations, when not otherwise designated or manifestly incompatible with the intent thereof), shall comply with the following requirements, that is to say:

First. Before commencing, or, if already commenced, before continuing, any such manufacture for which he, she, or they may be liable to be assessed, under the provisions of this act, and which shall not be differently provided for elsewhere, within thirty days after the date when this act shall take effect, he, she, or they shall furnish to the assistant assessor a statement, subscribed and sworn to, or affirmed, setting forth the place where the manufacture is to be carried on, name of the manufactured article, the proposed market for the same, whether foreign or domestic, and generally the kind and quality manufactured or proposed to be manufactured.

Second. He shall within ten days after the first day of each and every month, after the day on which this act takes effect, as hereinbefore mentioned, or on or before a day prescribed by the Commissioner of Internal Revenue, make return of the products and sales or delivery of such manufacture in form and detail as may be required, from time to time, by the Commissioner of Internal Revenue.

Third. All such returns, statements, descriptions, memoranda, oaths and affirmations, shall be in form, scope, and detail as may be prescribed, from time to time, by the Commissioner of Internal Revenue.

SEC. 69. *And be it further enacted,* That upon the amounts, quantities, and values of produce, goods, wares, merchandise, and articles manufactured and sold, or delivered, hereinafter enumerated, the manufacturer thereof, whether manufactured for himself or for others, shall pay to the collector of internal revenue within his district, monthly, or on or before a day to be prescribed by the Commissioner of Internal Revenue, the duties on such manufactures: *Provided*, That when thread is manufactured and sold or delivered exclusively for knitted fabrics, or for weaving or spooling, as provided for in the seventy-fifth section of this act, the duties shall be assessed on the articles finished and prepared for use or consumption to the party so finishing or preparing the same, and any party so finishing or preparing any cloth or other fabrics of cotton, wool, or other materials, whether imported or otherwise, shall be considered the manufacturer thereof for the purposes of this act; and for neglect to pay such duties within ten days after demand, either personal or written, left at his, her, or their house or place of business, or manufactory, the amount of such duties may be levied upon the real and personal property of any such manufacturer. And such duties, and whatever shall be the expenses of levy, shall be a lien from the day prescribed by the Commissioner for their payment aforesaid, in favor of the United States, upon the said real and personal property of such manufacturer, and such lien may be enforced by distraint, as provided in the general provisions of this act: *And provided, further*, That in all cases of goods manufactured, in whole or in part, upon commission, or where the material is furnished by one party and manufactured by another, if the manufacturer shall be required to pay under this act the tax hereby imposed, such person or persons so paying the same shall be entitled to collect the amount thereof of the owner or owners, and shall have a lien for the amount thus paid upon the manufactured goods: *And provided, further*, That the taxes on all articles manufactured and sold, in pursuance of contracts *bona fide* made before the passage of this act, shall be paid by the purchasers thereof, under regulations to be established by the Commissioner of Internal Revenue.

SEC. 70. *And be it further enacted*, That for neglect or refusal to pay the duties provided by this act on manufactured articles, as aforesaid, the goods, wares, and merchandise manufactured and unsold by such manufacturer shall be forfeited to the United States, and may be sold or disposed of for the benefit of the same, in manner as shall be prescribed by the Commissioner of Internal Revenue, under the direction of the Secretary of the Treasury. In such case the collector or deputy collector may take possession of said articles, and may maintain such possession in the premises and buildings where they may have been manufactured, or deposited, or may be. He shall summon, giving notice of not less than two nor more than ten days, the parties in possession of said goods, enjoining them to appear before the assessor, or assistant assessor, at a day and hour in such summons fixed, then and there to show cause, if any there be, .why, for such neglect or refusal, such articles should not be declared forfeited to the United States. Such persons or parties interested shall be deemed to be the manufacturers of the same, if the articles shall be at the time of taking such possession upon the premises where manufactured; if they shall at such time have been removed from the place of manufacture, the parties interested shall be deemed to be the person in whose custody or possession the articles shall then be. Such summons shall be served upon such parties in person, or by leaving a copy thereof at the place of abode or business of the party to whom the same may be directed. In case no such party or place can be found, which fact shall be determined by the collector's return on the summons, such notice, in the nature of a summons, shall be given by advertisement for the term of three weeks in one newspaper in the county nearest to the place of such sale. If at or before such hearing such duties shall not have been paid, and the assessor or assistant assessor shall adjudge the summons and notice, service and return of the same to be sufficient, the said articles shall be declared forfeit, and shall be sold, disposed of, or turned over to the use of any department of the government as may be directed by the Secretary of the Treasury, who may require of any officer of the government into whose possession the same may be turned over the proper voucher therefor: *Provided,* That the proceeds of the sale of said articles, if any there be after deducting the duties thereon, together with the expenses of summons, advertising, and sale, or the excess of the value of said articles, after deducting the duties and expenses accrued thereon when turned over to the use of any department of the government, shall be refunded and paid to the manufacturer, or to the person in whose custody or possession the articles were then seized. The Commissioner of Internal Revenue, with the approval of the Secretary of the Treasury, may review any such case of forfeiture and do justice in the premises. If the forfeiture shall have been wrongly declared, and sale made, the Secretary is hereby authorized, in case the specific articles can not be restored to the party aggrieved in as good order and condition as when seized, to make up to such party in money his loss and damage from the contingent fund of his department. Immediate return of seizures so forfeited shall be made to the Commissioner of Internal Revenue by the collector or deputy collector who shall make any such seizure. Articles which the collector may adjudge perishable may be sold or disposed of before declaration of forfeiture. Said sales shall be made at public auction, and notice thereof shall be given in the same manner as is provided in this section in case of forfeiture.

SEC. 71. *And be it further enacted,* That any violation of, or refusal to comply with, the provisions of the sixty-eighth section of this act, shall be good cause for seizure and forfeiture, substantially in manner as detailed in the section next preceding this, of all manufactured articles liable to be assessed under the provisions of this act, and not otherwise provided for; and such violation or refusal to comply shall further make any party so violating or refusing to comply liable to a fine of five hundred dollars, to be recovered in manner and form as provided in this act.

SEC. 72. *And be it further enacted,* That in case of the manufacture and sale or delivery of any goods, wares, merchandise, or articles as hereinafter mentioned, without compliance on the part of the party manufacturing the same with all or any of the requirements and regulations prescribed in this act in relation thereto, the assistant assessor may, upon such information as he may have, assume and estimate the amount and value of such manufactures, and upon such assumed amount assess the duties, and said duties shall be collected in like manner as in case the provisions of this act in relation thereto had been complied with, and to such articles all the foregoing provisions for liens, fines, penalties, and forfeitures shall in like manner apply.

SEC. 73. *And be it further enacted*, That all goods, wares, and merchandise, or articles manufactured or made by any person or persons not for sale, but for his, her, or their own use or consumption, and all goods, wares, and merchandise, or articles manufactured or made and sold, except spirituous and malt liquors, and manufactured tobacco, where the annual product shall not exceed the sum of six hundred dollars, shall be and are exempt from duty: *Provided*, That this shall not apply to any business or transaction where one party furnishes the materials, or any part thereof, and employs another party to manufacture, make, or finish the goods, wares, and merchandise or articles, paying or promising to pay therefor, and receiving the goods, wares, and merchandise or articles.

SEC. 74. *And be it further enacted*, That the value and quantity of the goods, wares, and merchandise required to be stated, as aforesaid, and subject to an ad valorem duty, shall be estimated by the actual sales made by the manufacturer, or by his, her, or their agent, or person or persons acting in his, her, or their behalf; and where such goods, wares, and merchandise have been removed for consumption, or for delivery to others, or placed on shipboard, or are no longer within the custody and control of the manufacturer or manufacturers, or his or their agent, not being in his, her, or their factory, store, or warehouse, the value shall be estimated by the average of the market value of the like goods, wares, and merchandise, during the time when the same would have become liable to and charged with duty.

SEC. 75. *And be it further enacted*, That from and after the said first day of August, eighteen hundred and sixty-two, upon the articles, goods, wares, and merchandise hereinafter mentioned, which shall thereafter be produced and sold, or be manufactured, or made and sold, or removed for consumption, or for delivery to others than agents of the manufacturer or producer within the United States or Territories thereof, there shall be levied, collected, and paid the following duties, to be paid by the producer or manufacturer thereof, that is to say:

On candles, of whatever material made, three per centum ad valorem;

On all mineral coals, except such as are known in the trade as pea coal and dust coal, three and a half cents per ton: *Provided*, That for all contracts of lease of coal lands made before the first day of April, eighteen hundred and sixty-two, the lessee shall pay the tax;

On lard oil, mustard-seed oil, linseed oil, and on all animal or vegetable oils not exempted nor provided for elsewhere, whether pure or adulterated, two cents per gallon: *Provided*, That red oil or oleic acid, produced in the manufacture of candles, and used as a material in the manufacture of soap, paraffine, whale and fish oil, shall be exempted from this duty;

On gas, illuminating, made of coal, wholly or in part, or any other material, when the product shall be not above five hundred thousand cubic feet per month, five cents per one thousand cubic feet; when the product shall be above five hundred thousand, and not exceeding five millions of cubic feet per month, ten cents per one thousand cubic feet; when the product shall be above five millions, fifteen cents per one thousand cubic feet; and the general average of the monthly product for the year preceding the return required by this act shall regulate the rate of duty herein imposed; and where any gas company shall not have been in operation for the year next preceding the return as aforesaid, then the rate shall be regulated upon the estimated average of the monthly product: *Provided*, That the product required to be returned by this act shall be understood to be the product charged in the bills actually rendered by any gas company during the month preceding the return, and all gas companies are hereby authorized to add the duty or tax imposed by this act to the price per thousand cubic feet on gas sold: *Provided, further*, That all gas furnished for lighting street lamps, and not measured, and all gas made for and used by any hotel, inn, tavern, and private dwelling-house, shall be subject to duty, and may be estimated; and if the returns in any case shall be understated or under-estimated, it shall be the duty of the assistant assessor of the district to increase the same as he shall deem just and proper: *And provided, further*, That coal tar produced in the manufacture of illuminating gas, and the products of re-distillation of coal tar thus produced, shall be exempt from duty: *And provided, further*, That gas companies so located as to compete with each other shall pay the rate imposed by this act upon the company having the largest production;

On coal illuminating oil, refined, produced by the distillation of coal, asphaltum, shale, peat, petroleum, or rock oil, and all other bituminous substances used for like purposes, ten cents per gallon: *Provided*, That such oil refined and produced by the distillation of coal exclusively shall be subject to pay a duty of eight cents per gallon, anything in this act to the contrary notwithstanding: *And provided, further*, That distillers of coal oil shall be subject to all the provisions of this act hereinbefore set forth and specified applicable to distillers of spirituous liquors, with regard to licenses, bonds, returns, and all other provisions designed for the purpose of ascertaining the quantity distilled, and securing the payment of duties, so far as the same may, in the judgment of the Commissioner of Internal Revenue, and under regulations prescribed by him, be necessary for that purpose;

On ground coffee, and all preparations of which coffee forms a part, or which is prepared for sale as a substitute for coffee, three mills per pound;

72 THE TAX BILL.

On ground pepper, ground mustard, ground pimento, ground cloves, ground cassia, and ground ginger, and all imitations of the same, one cent per pound;

On sugar, refined, whether loaf, lump, granulated, or pulverized, two mills per pound;

On sugar, refined or made from molasses, sirup of molasses, melado or concentrated melado, two mills per pound;

On all brown, Muscovado, or clarified sugars produced directly from the sugar-cane, and not from sorghum or imphee, other than those produced by the refiner, one cent per pound;

On sugar-candy and all confectionery, made wholly or in part of sugar, one cent per pound;

On chocolate, and cocoa prepared, one cent per pound;

On saleratus and bicarbonate of soda, five mills per pound;

On starch, made of potatoes, one mill per pound; made of corn or wheat, one and a half mills per pound; made of rice or any other material, four mills per pound;

On tobacco, cavendish, plug, twist, fine cut, and manufactured of all descriptions (not including snuff, cigars, and smoking tobacco prepared with all the stems in, or made exclusively of stems), valued at more than thirty cents per pound, fifteen cents per pound; valued at any sum not exceeding thirty cents per pound, ten cents per pound;

On smoking tobacco prepared with all the stems in, five cents per pound;

On smoking tobacco made exclusively of stems, two cents per pound;

On snuff manufactured of tobacco, ground dry or damp, of all descriptions, twenty cents per pound;

On cigars, valued at not over five dollars per thousand, one dollar and fifty cents per thousand;

On cigars, valued at over five and not over ten dollars per thousand, two dollars per thousand;

On cigars, valued at over ten and not over twenty dollars per thousand, two dollars and fifty cents per thousand;

On cigars, valued at over twenty dollars per thousand, three dollars and fifty cents per thousand;

On gunpowder, and all explosive substances used for mining, blasting, artillery, or sporting purposes, when valued at eighteen cents per pound or less, five mills per pound; when valued at above eighteen cents per pound, and not exceeding thirty cents per pound, one cent per pound; and when valued at above thirty cents per pound, six cents per pound;

On white lead, twenty-five cents per one hundred pounds;

On oxide of zinc, twenty-five cents per one hundred pounds;

On sulphate of barytes, ten cents per one hundred pounds: *Provided*, That white lead, oxide of zinc, and sulphate of barytes, or any one of them, shall not be subject to any additional duty in consequence of being mixed or ground with linseed oil, when the duties upon all the materials so mixed or ground shall have been previously actually paid;

On all paints and painters' colors, dry or ground in oil, or in paste, with water, not otherwise provided for, five per centum ad valorem :

On clock movements made to run one day, five cents each ; made to run more than one day, ten cents each ;

On pins, solid head or other, five per centum ad valorem ;

On umbrellas and parasols made of cotton, silk, or other material, five per centum ad valorem ;

On screws, commonly called wood screws, one and a half cent per pound ;

On railroad iron and all other iron advanced beyond slabs, blooms, or loops, and not advanced beyond bars or rods, and band, hoop, and sheet iron, not thinner than number eighteen wire-gauge, and plate iron not less than one-eighth of an inch in thickness, one dollar and fifty cents per ton ; on railroad iron, re-rolled, seventy-five cents per ton ; on band, hoop, and sheet iron thinner than number eighteen wire-gauge, plate iron less than one-eighth of an inch in thickness, and cut nails and spikes, two dollars per ton : *Provided*, That bars, rods, bands, hoops, sheets, plates, nails, and spikes, manufactured from iron upon which the duty of one dollar and fifty cents has been levied and paid, shall be subject only to a duty of fifty cents per ton in addition thereto, anything in this act to the contrary notwithstanding. On stoves and hollow ware, one dollar and fifty cents per ton of two thousand pounds ; cast iron used for bridges, buildings, or other permanent structures, one dollar per ton : *Provided*, That bar iron used for like purposes shall be charged no additional duty beyond the specific duty imposed by this act. On steel in ingots, bars, sheets, or wire not less than one-fourth of an inch in thickness, valued at seven cents per pound or less, four dollars per ton ; valued at above seven cents per pound, and not above eleven cents per pound, eight dollars per ton ; valued above eleven cents per pound, ten dollars per ton ;

On paper of all descriptions, including pasteboard and binders' boards, three per centum ad valorem ;

On soap, castile, palm-oil, erasive, and soap of all other descriptions, white or colored, except soft soap and soap otherwise provided for, valued not above three and a half cents per pound, one mill per pound ; valued at above three and a half cents per pound, five mills per pound ;

On soap, fancy, scented, honey, cream, transparent, and all descriptions of toilet and shaving soap, two cents per pound ;

On salt, four cents per one hundred pounds ;

On pickles and preserved fruits, and on all preserved meats, fish, and shell-fish in cans or air-tight packages, five per centum ad valorem ;

On glue and gelatine of all descriptions, in the solid state, five mills per pound ;

On glue and cement, made wholly or in part of glue, to be sold in the liquid state, twenty-five cents per gallon ;

On patent or enameled leather, five mills per square foot;

On patent Japanned split, used for dasher leather, four mills per square foot;

On patent or enameled skirting leather, one and a half cent per square foot;

On all sole and rough or harness leather, made from hides, imported east of the Cape of Good Hope, and all damaged leather, five mills per pound;

On all other sole or rough leather, hemlock tanned, and harness leather, seven mills per pound;

On all sole or rough leather, tanned in whole or in part with oak, one cent per pound;

On all finished or curried upper leather, made from leather tanned in the interest of the parties finishing or currying such leather not previously taxed in the rough, except calf skins, one cent per pound;

On bend and butt leather, one cent per pound;

On offal leather, five mills per pound;

On oil-dressed leather, and deer skins dressed or smoked, two cents per pound;

On tanned calf skins, six cents each;

On morocco, goat, kid, or sheep skins, curried, manufactured, or finished, four per centum ad valorem: *Provided*, That the price at which such skins are usually sold shall determine their value;

On horse and hog skins tanned and dressed, four per centum ad valorem;

On American patent calf skins, five per centum ad valorem;

On conducting hose of all kinds for conducting water or other fluids, a duty of three per centum ad valorem;

On wine, made of grapes, five cents per gallon;

On varnish, made wholly or in part of gum copal or other gums or substances, five per centum ad valorem;

On furs of all descriptions, when made up or manufactured, three per centum ad valorem;

On cloth and all textile or knitted or felted fabrics of cotton, wool, or other materials, before the same has been dyed, printed, bleached, or prepared in any other manner, a duty of three per centum ad valorem: *Provided*, That thread or yarn manufactured and sold or delivered exclusively for knitted fabrics, or for weaving, when the spinning and weaving for the manufacture of cloth of any kind is carried on separately, shall not be regarded as manufactures within the meaning of this act; but all fabrics of cotton, wool, or other material, whether woven, knit, or felted, shall be regarded as manufactures, and be subject to the duty, as above, of three per centum ad valorem;

On all diamonds, emeralds, and all other jewelry, a tax of three per per centum ad valorem;

On and after the first day of October, eighteen hundred and sixty-two, there shall be levied, collected, and paid, a tax of one-half of one cent per pound on all cotton held or owned by any person or persons, corporation, or association of persons; and such tax shall be a lien thereon in the possession of any person whomsoever. And further, if any person or persons, corporations, or association of persons, shall remove, carry, or transport the same from the place of its production before said tax shall have been paid, such person or persons, corporation, or association of persons, shall forfeit and pay to the United States double the amount of such tax, to be recovered in any court having jurisdiction thereof: *Provided, however*, That the Commissioner of Internal Revenue is hereby authorized to make such rules and regulations as he may deem proper for the payment of said tax at places different from that of the production of said cotton: *And provided, further*, That all cotton owned and held by any manufacturer of cotton fabrics on the first day [of] October, eighteen hundred and sixty-two, and prior thereto, shall be exempt from the tax hereby imposed;

On all manufactures of cotton, wool, silk, worsted, flax, hemp, jute, India-rubber, gutta-percha, wood, willow, glass, pottery-ware, leather, paper, iron, steel, lead, tin, copper, zinc, brass, gold, silver, horn, ivory, bone, bristles, wholly or in part, or of other materials, not in this act otherwise provided for, a duty of three per centum ad valorem : *Provided*, That on all cloths dyed, printed, bleached, manufactured into other fabrics, or otherwise prepared, on which a duty or tax shall have been paid before the same were so dyed, printed, bleached, manufactured, or prepared, the said duty or tax of three per centum shall be assessed only upon the increased value thereof: *And provided, further*, That on all oil-dressed leather, and deer skins dressed or smoked, manufactured into gloves, mittens, or other articles on which a duty or tax shall have been paid before the same were so manufactured, the said duty or tax of three per centum shall be assessed only upon the increased valuation thereof: *And provided, further*, That in estimating the duties upon articles manufactured when removed and sold at any other place than the place of manufacture, there shall be deducted from the gross amount of sales, the freight, commission, and expenses of sale actually paid, and the duty shall be assessed and paid upon the net amount after the deductions as aforesaid: *And provided, further*, That printed books, magazines, pamphlets, newspapers, reviews, and all other similar printed publications; boards, shingles, and all other lumber and timber; staves, hoops, headings, and timber only partially wrought and unfinished for chairs, tubs, pails, snathes, lasts, shovel and fork handles; umbrella stretchers; pig iron, and iron not advanced beyond slabs, blooms, or loops; maps and charts; charcoal; alcohol made or manufactured of spirits or materials upon which the duties of this act shall have been paid; plaster or gypsum; malt; burning fluid; printers' ink; flax prepared for textile or felting purposes, until actually woven or fitted into fabrics for consumption; all flour and meal made from grain; bread and breadstuffs; pearl barley and split peas; butter; cheese; concentrated milk; bullion, in the manufacture of silverware; brick; lime; Roman cement; draining tiles; marble; slate; building stone; copper, in ingots or pigs; and lead, in pigs or bars, shall not be regarded as manufactures within the meaning of this act: *Provided*, That whenever, by the provisions of this act, a duty is imposed upon any article removed for consumption or sale, it shall apply only to such articles as are manufactured on or after the first day of August, eighteen hundred and sixty-two, and to such as are manufactured and not removed from the place of manufacture prior to that date.

AUCTION SALES.

Sec. 76. *And be it further enacted*, That on and after the first day of August, eighteen hundred and sixty-two, there shall be levied, collected, and paid on all sales of real estate, goods, wares, merchandise, articles, or things at auction, including all sales of stocks, bonds, and other securities, a duty of one-tenth of one per centum on the gross amount of such sales, and every auctioneer making such sales, as aforesaid, shall at the end of each and every month, or within ten days thereafter, make a list or return to the assistant assessor of the district of the gross amount of such sales, made as aforesaid, with the amount of duty which has accrued, or should accrue thereon, which list shall have annexed thereto a declaration under oath or affirmation, in form and manner as may be prescribed by the Commissioner of Internal Revenue, that the same is true and correct, and shall at the same time, as aforesaid, pay to the collector or deputy collector the amount of duty or tax thereupon, as aforesaid, and in default thereof shall be subject to and pay a penalty of five hundred dollars. In all cases of delinquency in making said list or payment the assessment and collection shall be made in the manner prescribed in the general provisions of this act: *Provided*, That no duty shall be levied under the provisions of this section upon any sales by judicial or executive officers making auction sales by virtue of a judgment or decree of any court, nor to public sales made by executors or administrators.

CARRIAGES, YACHTS, BILLIARD-TABLES, AND PLATE.

Sec. 77. *And be it further enacted*, That from and after the first day of May, eighteen hundred and sixty-two, there shall be levied, collected, and paid, by any person or persons owning, possessing, or keeping any carriage, yacht, and billiard-table, the several duties or sums of money set down in figures against the same respectively, or otherwise specified and set forth in schedule marked A.

SCHEDULE A.

CARRIAGES, YACHTS, BILLIARD-TABLES, AND PLATE.

Carriage, gig, chaise, phæton, wagon, buggy-wagon, carryall, rockaway, or other like carriage, the body of which rests upon springs of any description, kept for use, and which shall not be exclusively employed in husbandry or for the transportation of merchandise, and valued at seventy-five dollars or over, including the harness used therewith, when drawn by one horse, one dollar......   1 00

Carriages of like description drawn by two horses, and any coach, hackney-coach, omnibus, or four-wheel carriage, the body of which rests upon springs of any description, which may be kept for use, for hire, or for passengers, and which shall not be exclusively employed in husbandry or for the transportation of merchandise, valued at seventy-five dollars, and not exceeding two hundred dollars, including the harness used therewith, drawn by two horses or more, two dollars....................   2 00

Carriages of like description, when valued above two hundred dollars, and not exceeding six hundred dollars, five dollars..   5 00

Carriages of like description, valued above six hundred dollars, ten dollars..................................   10 00

Pleasure or racing vessels, known as yachts, whether by sail or steam, under the value of six hundred dollars, five dollars...   5 00

Yachts valued above six hundred dollars, and not exceeding one thousand dollars, ten dollars....................   10 00

And for each additional one thousand dollars in value of said yachts, ten dollars...............................   10 00

Billiard-tables, kept for use, ten dollars.................   10 00

Plate of gold, kept for use, per ounce troy, fifty cents......   50

Plate of silver, kept for use, per ounce troy, three cents.....   3

Provided, That silver spoons or plate of silver, to an amount not exceeding forty ounces, as aforesaid, belonging to any one person, shall be exempt from duty.

SLAUGHTERED CATTLE, HOGS, AND SHEEP.

SEC. 78. *And be it further enacted,* That on and after the first day of August, eighteen hundred and sixty-two, there shall be levied, collected, and paid by any person or persons, firms, companies, or agents or employees thereof, the following duties or taxes, that is to say :

On all horned cattle exceeding eighteen months old, slaughtered for sale, thirty cents per head ;

On all calves and cattle under eighteen months old, slaughtered for sale, five cents per head ;

On all hogs, exceeding six months old, slaughtered for sale, when the number thus slaughtered exceeds twenty in any one year, ten cents per head ;

On all sheep, slaughtered for sale, five cents per head : *Provided,* That all cattle, hogs, and sheep, slaughtered by any person for his or her own consumption, shall be exempt from duty.

SEC. 79. *And be it further enacted,* That on and after the date on which this act shall take effect, any person or persons, firms, or companies, or agents or employees thereof, whose business or occupation it is to slaughter for sale any cattle, calves, sheep, or hogs, shall be required to make and render a list at the end of each and every month to the assistant assessor of the district where the business is transacted, stating the number of cattle, calves, if any, the number of hogs, if any, and the number of sheep, if any, slaughtered, as aforesaid, with the several rates of duty as fixed therein in this act, together with the whole amount thereof, which list shall have annexed thereto a declaration of said person or persons, agents or employees thereof, as aforesaid, under oath or affirmation, in such manner and form as may be prescribed by the Commissioner of Internal Revenue, that the same is true and correct, and shall, at the time of rendering said list, pay the full amount of duties which have accrued or should accrue, as aforesaid, to the collector or deputy collector of the district, as aforesaid ; and in case of default in making the return or payment of the duties, as aforesaid, the assessment and collection shall be made as in the general provisions of this act required, and in case of fraud or evasion the party offending shall forfeit and pay a penalty of ten dollars per head for any cattle, calves, hogs, or sheep so slaughtered upon which the duty is fraudulently withheld, evaded, or attempted to be evaded : *Provided*, That the Commissioner of Internal Revenue shall prescribe such further rules and regulations as he may deem necessary for ascertaining the correct number of cattle, calves, hogs, and sheep, liable to be taxed under the provisions of this act.

RAILROADS, STEAMBOATS, AND FERRY-BOATS.

SEC. 80. *And be it further enacted*, That on and after the first day of August, eighteen hundred and sixty-two, any person or persons, firms, companies, or corporations, owning or possessing, or having the care or management of any railroad or railroads upon which steam is used as a propelling power, or of any steamboat or other vessel propelled by steam-power, shall be subject to and pay a duty of three per centum on the gross amount of all the receipts of such railroad or railroads or steam vessel for the transportation of passengers over and upon the same ; and any person or persons, firms, companies, or corporations, owning or possessing, or having the care or management of any railroad or railroads using any other power than steam thereon, or owning, possessing, or having the care or management of any ferry-boat, or vessel used as a ferry-boat, propelled by steam or horse power, shall be subject to and pay a duty of one and a half per centum upon the gross receipts of such railroad or ferry-boat, respectively, for the transportation of passengers over and upon said railroads, steamboats, and ferry-boats, respectively ; and any person or persons, firms, companies, or corporations, owning, possessing, or having the care or management of any bridge authorized by law to receive toll for the transit of passengers, beasts, carriages, teams, and freight of any description over such bridge, shall be subject to and pay a duty of three per centum on the gross amount of all their receipts of every description. And the owner, possessor, or person or persons having the care and management of any such railroad, steamboat, ferry-boat, or other vessel, or bridge, as aforesaid, shall, within five days after the end of each and every month, commencing as hereinbefore mentioned, make a list or return to the assistant assessor of the district within which such owner, possessor, company, or corporation may have his or its place of business, or where any such railroad, steamboat, ferry-boat, or bridge is located or belongs, respectively, stating the gross amount of such receipts for the month next preceding, which return shall be verified by the oath or affirmation of such owner, possessor, manager, agent, or other proper officer, in the manner and form to be prescribed from time to time by the Commissioner of Internal Revenue, and shall also, monthly, at the time of making such return, pay to the collector or deputy collector of the district the full amount of duties which have accrued on such receipts for the month aforesaid; and in case of neglect or refusal to make said lists or return for the space of five days after such return should be made as aforesaid, the assessor or assistant assessor shall proceed to estimate the amount received and the duties payable thereon, as hereinbefore provided in other cases of delinquency to make return for purposes of assessment; and for the purpose of making such assessment, or of ascertaining the correctness of any such return, the books of any such person, company, or corporation shall be subject to the inspection of the assessor or assistant assessor on his demand or request therefor; and in case of neglect or refusal to pay the duties as aforesaid when the same have been ascertained as aforesaid for the space of five days after the same shall have become payable, the owner, possessor, or person having the management as aforesaid, shall pay, in addition, five per centum on the amount of such duties; and for any attempt knowingly to evade the payment of such duties, the said owner, possessor, or person having the care or management as aforesaid, shall be liable to pay a penalty of one thousand dollars for every such attempt, to be recovered as provided in this act for the recovery of penalties; and all provisions of this act in relation to liens and collections by distraint not incompatible herewith shall apply to this section and the objects therein embraced: *Provided,* That all such persons, companies, and corporations shall have the right to add the duty or tax imposed hereby to their rates of fare whenever their liability thereto may commence, any limitations which may exist by law or by agreement with any person or company which may have paid or be liable to pay such fare to the contrary notwithstanding.

RAILROAD BONDS.

Sec. 81. *And be it further enacted,* That on and after the first day of July, eighteen hundred and sixty-two, any person or persons owning or possessing, or having the care or management of any railroad company or railroad corporation, being indebted for any sum or sums of money for which bonds or other evidences of indebtedness have been issued, payable in one or more years after date, upon which interest is, or shall be, stipulated to be paid, or coupons representing the interest shall be or shall have been issued to be paid, and all dividends in scrip or money or sums of money thereafter declared due or payable to stockholders of any railroad company, as part of the earnings, profits, or gains of said companies, shall be subject to and pay a duty of three per centum on the amount of all such interest or coupons or dividends whenever the same shall be paid; and said railroad companies or railroad corporations, or any person or persons owning, possessing, or having the care or management of any railroad company or railroad corporation, are hereby authorized and required to deduct and withhold from all payments made to any person, persons, or party, after the first day of July, as aforesaid, on account of any interest or coupons or dividends due and payable as aforesaid, the said duty or sum of three per centum; and the duties deducted as aforesaid, and certified by the president or other proper officer of said company or corporation, shall be a receipt and discharge, according to the amount thereof, of said railroad companies or railroad corporations, and the owners, possessors, and agents thereof, on dividends and on bonds or other evidences of their indebtedness, upon which interest or coupons are payable, holden by any person or party whatsoever, and a list or return shall be made and rendered within thirty days after the time fixed when said interest or coupons or dividends become due or payable, and as often as every six months, to the Commissioner of Internal Revenue, which shall contain a true and faithful account of the duties received and chargeable, as aforesaid, during the time when such duties have accrued or should accrue, and remaining unaccounted for; and there shall be annexed to every such list or return a declaration under oath or affirmation, in manner and form as may be prescribed by the Commissioner of Internal Revenue, of the president, treasurer, or some proper officer of said railroad company or railroad corporation, that the same contains a true and faithful account of the duties so withheld and received during the time when such duties have accrued or should accrue, and not accounted for, and for any default in the making or rendering of such list or return, with the declaration annexed, as aforesaid, the person or persons owning, possessing, or having the care or management of such railroad company or railroad corporation, making such default, shall forfeit, as a penalty, the sum of five hundred dollars; and in case of any default in making or rendering said list, or of any default in the payment of the duty, or any part thereof, accruing or which should accrue, the assessment and collection shall be made according to the general provisions of this act.

BANKS, TRUST COMPANIES, SAVINGS INSTITUTIONS, AND INSURANCE COMPANIES.

SEC. 82. *And be it further enacted,* That on and after the first day of July, eighteen hundred and sixty-two, there shall be levied, collected, and paid by all banks, trust companies, and savings institutions, and by all fire, marine, life, inland, stock, and mutual insurance companies, under whatever style or name known or called, of the United States or Territories, specially incorporated or existing under general laws, or which may be hereafter incorporated or exist as aforesaid, on all dividends in scrip or money thereafter declared due or paid to stockholders, to policy holders, or to depositors, as part of the earnings, profits, or gains of said banks, trust companies, savings institutions, or insurance companies, and on all sums added to their surplus or contingent funds, a duty of three per centum : *Provided,* That the duties upon the dividends of life insurance companies shall not be deemed due, or to be collected until such dividends shall be payable by such companies. And said banks, trust companies, savings institutions, and insurance companies are hereby authorized and required to deduct and withhold from all payments made to any person, persons, or party, on account of any dividends or sums of money that may be due and payable, as aforesaid, after the first day of July, eighteen hundred and sixty-two, the said duty of three per centum. And a list or return shall be made and rendered within thirty days after the time fixed when such dividends or sums of money shall be declared due and payable, and as often as every six months, to the Commissioner of Internal Revenue, which shall contain a true and faithful account of the amount of duties accrued or which should accrue from time to time, as aforesaid, during the time when such duties remain unaccounted for, and there shall be annexed to every such list or return a declaration, under oath or affirmation, to be made in form and manner as shall be prescribed by the Commissioner of Internal Revenue, of the president, or some other proper officer of said bank, trust company, savings institution, or insurance company, respectively, that the same contains a true and faithful account of the duties which have accrued or should accrue, and not accounted for, and for any default in the delivery of such list or return, with such declaration annexed, the bank, trust company, savings institution, or insurance company making such default shall forfeit, as a penalty, the sum of five hundred dollars.

SEC. 83. *And be it further enacted,* That any person or persons owning or possessing, or having the care or management of any railroad company or railroad corporation, bank, trust company, savings institution, or insurance company, as heretofore mentioned, required under this act to make and render any list or return to the Commissioner of Internal Revenue, shall, upon rendering the same, pay to the said Commissioner of Internal Revenue the amount of the duties due on such list or return, and in default thereof shall forfeit as a penalty the sum of five hundred dollars ; and in case of neglect or refusal to make such list or return as aforesaid, or to pay the duties as aforesaid, for the space of thirty days after the time when said list should have been made and rendered, or when said duties shall have become due and payable, the assessment and collection shall be made according to the general provisions heretofore prescribed in this act.

SEC. 84. *And be it further enacted,* That on the first day of October, Anno Domini eighteen hundred and sixty-two, and on the

6

first day of each quarter of a year thereafter, there shall be paid by each insurance company, whether inland or marine, and by each individual or association engaged in the business of insurance from loss or damage by fire, or by the perils of the sea, the duty of one per centum upon the gross receipts for premiums and assessments by such individual, association, or company during the quarter then preceding; and like duty shall be paid by the agent of any foreign insurance company having an office or doing business within the United States.

SEC. 85. *And be it further enacted,* That on the first day of October next, and on the first day of each quarter thereafter, an account shall be made and rendered to the Commissioner of Internal Revenue by all insurance companies, or their agents, or associations or individuals making insurance, except life insurance, including agents of all foreign insurance companies, which shall contain a true and faithful account of the insurance made, renewed, or continued, or indorsed upon any open policy by said companies, or their agents, or associations, or individuals during the preceding quarter, setting forth the amount insured, and the gross amount received, and the duties accruing thereon under this act; and there shall be annexed to and delivered with every such quarterly account an affidavit, in the form to be prescribed by the Commissioner of Internal Revenue, made by one of the officers of said company or association, or individual, or by the agent in the case of a foreign company, that the statements in said accounts are in all respects just and true; and such quarterly accounts shall be rendered to the Commissioner of Internal Revenue within thirty days after the expiration of the quarter for which they shall be made up, and upon rendering such account, with such affidavit, as aforesaid, thereto annexed, the amount of the duties due by such quarterly accounts shall be paid to the Commissioner of Internal Revenue; and for every default in the delivery of such quarterly account, with such affidavit annexed thereto, or in the payment of the amount of the duties due by such quarterly account, the company, or agent, or association, or individual making such default shall forfeit and pay, in addition to such duty, the sum of five thousand dollars.

SALARIES AND PAY OF OFFICERS AND PERSONS IN THE SERVICE OF THE UNITED STATES, AND PASSPORTS.

SEC. 86. *And be it further enacted,* That on and after the first day of August, eighteen hundred and sixty-two, there shall be levied, collected, and paid on all salaries of officers, or payments to persons in the civil, military, naval, or other employment or service of the United States, including senators and representatives and delegates in Congress, when exceeding the rate of six hundred dollars per annum, a duty of three per centum on the excess above the said six hundred dollars; and it shall be the duty of all paymasters, and all disbursing officers, under the Government of the United States, or in the employ thereof, when making any payments to officers and persons as aforesaid, or upon settling and adjusting the accounts of such officers and persons, to deduct and withhold the aforesaid duty of three per centum, and shall, at the same time, make a certificate stating the name of the officer or person from whom such deduction was made, and the amount thereof, which shall be transmitted to the office of the Commissioner of Internal Revenue, and entered as part of the internal duties; and the pay-roll, receipts, or account of officers or persons paying such duty, as aforesaid, shall be made to exhibit the fact of such payment.

SEC. 87. *And be it further enacted,* That for every passport issued from the office of the Secretary of State, after the thirtieth day of June, eighteen hundred and sixty-two, there shall be paid the sum of three dollars; which amount may be paid to any collector appointed under this act, and his receipt therefor shall be forwarded with the application for such passport to the office of the Secretary of State, or any agent appointed by him. And the collectors shall account for all moneys received for passports in the manner hereinbefore provided, and a like amount shall be paid for every passport issued by any minister or consul of the United States, who shall account therefor to the treasury.

ADVERTISEMENTS.

SEC. 88. *And be it further enacted,* That on and after the first day of August, eighteen hundred and sixty-two, there shall be levied, collected, and paid by any person or persons, firm, or company, publishing any newspaper, magazine, review, or other literary, scientific, or news publication, issued periodically, on the gross receipts for all advertisements, or all matters for the insertion of which in said newspaper or other publication, as aforesaid, or in extras, supplements, sheets, or fly-leaves accompanying the same, pay is required or received, a duty of three per centum; and the person or persons, firm or company, owning, possessing, or having the care or management of any and every such newspaper or other publication as aforesaid, shall make a list or return quarterly, commencing as heretofore mentioned, containing the gross amount of receipts as aforesaid, and the amount of duties which have accrued thereon, and render the same to the assistant assessor of the respective districts where such newspaper, magazine, review, or other literary or news publication is or may be published, which list or return shall have annexed a declaration, under oath or affirmation, to be made according to the manner and form which may be from time to time prescribed by the Commissioner of Internal Revenue, of the owner, possessor, or person having the care or management of such newspaper, magazine, review, or other publication, as aforesaid, that the same is true and correct, and shall also, quarterly, and at the time of making said list or return, pay to the collector or deputy collector of the district, as aforesaid, the full amount of said duties; and in case of neglect or refusal to comply with any of the provisions contained in this section, or to

make and render said list or return, as aforesaid, for the space of thirty
days after the time when said list or return ought to have been made,
as aforesaid, the assistant assessor of the respective districts shall
proceed to estimate the duties, as heretofore provided in other cases
of delinquency; and in case of neglect or refusal to pay the duties,
as aforesaid, for the space of thirty days after said duties become
due and payable, said owner, possessor, or person or persons having
the care or management of said newspapers or publications, as aforesaid, shall pay, in addition thereto, a penalty of five per centum on
the amount due; and in case of fraud or evasion, whereby the revenue is attempted to be defrauded, or the duty withheld, said owners,
possessors, or person or persons having the care or management of
said newspapers or other publications, as aforesaid, shall forfeit and
pay a penalty of five hundred dollars for each offense, or for any sum
fraudulently unaccounted for; and all provisions in this act in relation to liens, assessments, and collection, not incompatible herewith,
shall apply to this section and the objects herein embraced : *Provided*,
That in all cases where the rate or price of advertising is fixed by
any law of the United States, State, or Territory, it shall be lawful
for the company, person or persons, publishing said advertisements,
to add the duty or tax imposed by this act to the price of said advertisements, any law, as aforesaid, to the contrary notwithstanding:
Provided, further, That the receipts for advertisements to the amount
of one thousand dollars, by any person or persons, firm or company,
publishing any newspaper, magazine, review, or other literary, scientific, news publication, issued periodically, shall be exempt from duty:
And provided, further, That all newspapers whose circulation does
not exceed two thousand copies shall be exempted from all taxes for
advertisements.   ·

INCOME DUTY.

Sec. 89. *And be it further enacted*, That for the purpose of modi-
fying and re-enacting, as hereinafter provided, so much of an act, entitled "An act to provide increased revenue from imports to pay
interest on the public debt, and for other purposes," approved fifth
of August, eighteen hundred and sixty-one, as relates to income tax ;
that is to say, sections forty-nine, fifty (except so much thereof as
relates to the selection and appointment of depositaries), and fifty-
one, be, and the same are hereby, repealed.

Sec. 90. *And be it further enacted*, That there shall be levied,
collected, and paid annually, upon the annual gains, profits, or income
of every person residing in the United States, whether derived from
any kind of property, rents, interest, dividends, salaries, or from any
profession, trade, employment, or vocation carried on in the United
States or elsewhere, or from any other source whatever, except as
hereinafter mentioned, if such annual gains, profits, or income exceed
the sum of six hundred dollars, and do not exceed the sum of ten
thousand dollars, a duty of three per centum on the amount of such
annual gains, profits, or income over and above the said sum of six

hundred dollars; if said income exceeds the sum of ten thousand dollars, a duty of five per centum upon the amount thereof exceeding six hundred dollars; and upon the annual gains, profits, or income, rents, and dividends accruing upon any property, securities and stocks owned in the United States by any citizen of the United States residing abroad, except as hereinafter mentioned, and not in the employment of the Government of the United States, there shall be levied, collected, and paid a duty of five per centum.

SEC. 91. *And be it further enacted,* That in estimating said annual gains, profits, or income, whether subject to a duty, as provided in this act, of three per centum, or of five per centum, all other national, State, and local taxes, lawfully assessed upon the property or other sources of income of any person as aforesaid, from which said annual gains, profits, or income of such person is or should be derived, shall be first deducted from the gains, profits, or income of the person or persons who actually pay the same, whether owner or tenant, and all gains, profits, or income derived from salaries of officers, or payments to persons in the civil, military, naval, or other service of the United States, including senators, representatives, and delegates in Congress, above six hundred dollars, or derived from interest or dividends on stock, capital, or deposits in any bank, trust company, or savings institution, insurance, gas, bridge, express, telegraph, steamboat, ferry-boat, or railroad company, or corporation or on any bonds, or other evidences of indebtedness of any railroad company or other corporation, which shall have been assessed and paid by said banks, trust companies, savings institutions, insurance, gas, bridge, telegraph, steamboat, ferry-boat, express, or railroad companies, as aforesaid, or derived from advertisements, or on any articles manufactured, upon which specific, stamp, or ad valorem duties shall have been directly assessed or paid, shall also be deducted; and the duty herein provided for shall be assessed and collected upon the income for the year ending the thirty-first day of December next preceding the time for levying and collecting said duty, that is to say, on the first of May, eighteen hundred and sixty-three, and in each year thereafter: *Provided,* That upon such portion of said gains, profits, or income, whether subject to a duty as provided in this act of three per centum or five per centum, which shall be derived from interest upon notes, bonds, or other securities of the United States, there shall be levied, collected, and paid a duty not exceeding one and one-half of one per centum, anything in this act to the contrary notwithstanding.

SEC. 92. *And be it further enacted,* That the duties on incomes herein imposed shall be due and payable on or before the thirtieth day of June, in the year eighteen hundred and sixty-three, and in each year thereafter until and including the year eighteen hundred and sixty-six, and no longer; and to any sum or sums annually due and unpaid for thirty days after the thirtieth of June, as aforesaid, and for ten days after demand thereof by the collector, there shall be levied in addition thereto, the sum of five per centum on the amount of duties unpaid, as a penalty, except from the estates of deceased and insolvent persons; and if any person or persons, or party, liable to pay such duty, shall neglect or refuse to pay the same, the amount due shall be a lien in favor of the United States from the time it was so due until paid, with the interest, penalties, and costs that may accrue in addition thereto, upon all the property, and rights to property, stocks, securities, and debts of every description from which the income upon which said duty is assessed or levied shall have accrued or may or should accrue ; and in default of the payment of said duty for the space of thirty days, after the same shall have become due, and be demanded, as aforesaid, said lien may be enforced by distraint upon such property, rights to property, stocks, securities, and evidences of debt, by whomsoever holden ; and for this purpose the Commissioner of Internal Revenue, upon the certificate of the collector or deputy collector that said duty is due and unpaid for the space of ten days after notice duly given of the levy of such duty, shall issue a warrant, in form and manner to be prescribed by said Commissioner of Internal Revenue, under the directions of the Secretary of the Treasury, and by virtue of such warrant there may be levied on such property, rights to property, stocks, securities, and evidences of debt, a further sum, to be fixed and stated in such warrant, over and above the said annual duty, interest, and penalty for non-payment, sufficient for the fees and expenses of such levy.   And in all cases of sale, as aforesaid, the certificate of such sale by the collector or deputy collector of the sale, shall give title to the purchaser, of all right, title, and interest of such delinquent in and to such property, whether the property be real or personal ; and where the subject of sale shall be stocks, the certificate of said sale shall be lawful authority and notice to the proper corporation, company, or association, to record the same on the books or records, in the same manner as if transferred or assigned by the person or party holding the same, to issue new certificates of stock therefor in lieu of any original or prior certificates, which shall be void whether canceled or not ; and said certificates of sale of the collector or deputy collector, where the subject of sale shall be securities or other evidences of debt, shall be good and valid receipts to the person or party holding the same, as against any person or persons, or other party holding, or claiming to hold, possession of such securities or other evidences of debt.

SEC. 93. *And be it further enacted,* That it shall be the duty of all persons of lawful age, and all guardians and trustees, whether such trustees are so by virtue of their office as executors, administrators, or other fiduciary capacity, to make return in the list or schedule, as provided in this act, to the proper officer of internal revenue, of the amount of his or her income, or the income of such minors or persons as may be held in trust as aforesaid, according to the requirements hereinbefore stated, and in case of neglect or refusal to make such return, the assessor or assistant assessor shall assess the amount of his or her income, and proceed thereafter to collect the duty thereon in the same manner as is provided for in other cases of neglect and refusal to furnish lists or schedules in the general provisions of this act, where not otherwise incompatible, and the assistant assessor may increase the amount of the list or return, or of any party making such return, if he shall be satisfied that the same is understated : *Provided,* That any party, in his or her own behalf, or as guardian or trustee, as aforesaid, shall be permitted to declare, under oath or affirmation, the form and manner of which shall be prescribed by the Commissioner of Internal Revenue, that he or she was not possessed of an income of six hundred dollars, liable to be assessed according to the provisions of this act, or that he or she has been assessed elsewhere and the same year for an income duty, under authority of the United States, and shall thereupon be exempt from an income duty : or, if the list or return of any party shall have been increased by the assistant assessor, in manner as aforesaid, he or she may be permitted to declare, as aforesaid, the amount of his or her annual income, or the amount held in trust, as aforesaid, liable to be assessed, as aforesaid, and the same so declared shall be received as the sum upon which duties are to be assessed and collected.

STAMP DUTIES.

SEC. 94. *And be it further enacted,* That on and after the first day of October, eighteen hundred and sixty-two, there shall be levied, collected, and paid, for and in respect of the several instruments, matters, and things mentioned, and described in the schedule (marked B) hereunto annexed, or for or in respect of the vellum, parchment, or paper upon which such instruments, matters, or things, or any of them, shall be written or printed, by any person or persons, or party who shall make, sign, or issue the same, or for whose use or benefit the same shall be made, signed, or issued, the several duties or sums of money set down in figures against the same, respectively, or otherwise specified or set forth in the said schedule.

SEC. 95. *And be it further enacted,* That if any person or persons shall make, sign, or issue, or cause to be made, signed, or issued, any instrument, document, or paper of any kind or description whatsoever, without the same being duly stamped for denoting the duty hereby imposed thereon, or without having thereupon an adhesive stamp to denote said duty, such person or persons shall incur a penalty of fifty dollars, and such instrument, document, or paper, as aforesaid, shall be deemed invalid and of no effect.

SEC. 96. *And be it further enacted,* That no stamp appropriated to denote the duty charged on any particular instrument, and bearing the name of such instrument on the face thereof, shall be used for denoting any other duty of the same amount, or if so used the same shall be of no avail.

SEC. 97. *And be it further enacted,* That no vellum, parchment, or paper, bearing a stamp appropriated by name to any particular instrument, shall be used for any other purpose, or if so used the same shall be of no avail.

SEC. 98. *And be it further enacted,* That if any person shall forge or counterfeit, or cause or procure to be forged or counterfeited, any stamp or die, or any part of any stamp or die, which shall have been provided, made, or used in pursuance of this act, or shall forge, counterfeit, or resemble, or cause or procure to be forged, counterfeited, or resembled, the impression, or any part of the impression of any such stamp or die, as aforesaid, upon any vellum, parchment, or paper, or shall stamp or mark, or cause or procure to be stamped or marked, any vellum, parchment, or paper, with any such forged or counterfeited stamp or die, or part of any stamp or die, as aforesaid, with intent to defraud the United States of any of the duties hereby imposed, or any part thereof, or if any person shall utter, or sell, or expose to sale, any vellum, parchment, or paper, article, or thing, having thereupon the impression of any such counterfeited stamp or die, or any part of any stamp or die, or any such forged, counterfeited, or resembled impression, or part of impression, as aforesaid, knowing the same respectively to be forged, counterfeited, or resembled ; or if any person shall knowingly use any stamp or die which shall have been so provided, made, or used, as aforesaid, with intent to defraud the United States ; or if any person shall fraudulently cut, tear, or get off, or procure to be cut, torn, or got off, the impression of any stamp or die which shall have been provided, made, or used in pursuance of this act, from any vellum, parchment, or paper, or any instrument or writing charged or chargeable with any of the duties hereby imposed, then, and in every such case, every person so offending, and every person knowingly and willfully aiding, abetting, or assisting in committing any such offense, as aforesaid, shall be deemed guilty of felony, and shall, on conviction thereof, forfeit the said counterfeit stamps and the articles upon which they are placed, and be punished by a fine not exceeding one thousand dollars, and by imprisonment and confinement to hard labor not exceeding five years.

SEC. 99. *And be it further enacted,* That in any and all cases where an adhesive stamp shall be used for denoting any duty imposed by this act, except as hereinafter provided, the person using or affixing the same shall write thereupon the initials of his name, and the date upon which the same shall be attached or used, so that the same may not again be used. And if any person shall fraudulently make use of an adhesive stamp to denote any duty imposed by this act without so effectually canceling and obliterating such stamp, except as before mentioned, he, she, or they shall forfeit the sum of fifty dollars : *Provided, nevertheless,* That any proprietor or proprietors of proprietary articles, or articles subject to stamp duty under schedule C of this act, shall have the privilege of furnishing, without expense to the United States, in suitable form, to be approved by the Commissioner of Internal Revenue, his or their own dies or designs for stamps to be used thereon, to be retained in the possession of the Commissioner of Internal Revenue, for his or their separate use, which shall not be duplicated to any other person. That in all cases where such stamp is used, instead of his or their writing his or their initials and the date thereon, the said stamp shall be so affixed on the box, bottle, or package, that in opening the same, or using the contents thereof, the said stamp shall be effectually destroyed ; and in default thereof shall be liable to the same penalty imposed for neglect to affix said stamp as hereinbefore prescribed in this act. Any person who shall fraudulently obtain or use any of the aforesaid stamps or designs therefor, and any person forging, or counterfeiting, or causing or procuring the forging or counterfeiting any representation, likeness, similitude, or colorable imitation of the said last-mentioned stamp, or any engraver or printer who shall sell or give away said stamps, or selling the same, or, being a merchant, broker, peddler, or person dealing, in whole or in part, in similar goods, wares, merchandise, manufactures, preparations, or articles, or those designed for similar objects or purposes, shall have knowingly or fraudulently in his, her, or their possession any such forged, counterfeited likeness, similitude, or colorable imitation of the said last-mentioned stamp, shall be deemed guilty of a misdemeanor, and, upon conviction thereof, shall be subject to all the penalties, fines, and forfeitures prescribed in section ninety-three of this act.

SEC. 100. *And be it further enacted*, That if any person or persons shall make, sign, or issue, or cause to be made, signed, or issued, or shall accept or pay, or cause to be accepted or paid, with design to evade the payment of any stamp duty, any bill of exchange, draft, or order, or promissory note for the payment of money. liable to any of the duties imposed by this act, without the same being duly stamped, or having thereupon an adhesive stamp for denoting the duty hereby charged thereon, he, she, or they shall, for every such bill, draft, order, or note, forfeit the sum of two hundred dollars.

SEC. 101. *And be it further enacted*, That the acceptor or acceptors of any bill of exchange or order for the payment of any sum of money drawn, or purporting to be drawn, in any foreign country, but payable in the United States, shall, before paying or accepting the same, place thereupon a stamp, indicating the duty upon the same, as the law requires for inland bills of exchange, or promissory notes; and no bill of exchange shall be paid or negotiated without such stamp; and if any person shall pay or negotiate, or offer in payment, or receive or take in payment, any such draft or order, the person or persons so offending shall forfeit the sum of one hundred dollars.

SEC. 102. *And be it further enacted*, That the Commissioner of Internal Revenue be, and is hereby, authorized to sell to and supply collectors, deputy collectors, postmasters, stationers, or any other persons, at his discretion, with adhesive stamps or stamped paper, vellum, or parchment, as herein provided for, upon the payment, at the time of delivery, of the amount of duties said stamps, stamped paper, vellum, or parchment, so sold or supplied, represent, and may thereupon allow and deduct from the aggregate amount of such stamps, as aforesaid, the sum of not exceeding five per centum as commission to the collectors, postmasters, stationers, or other purchasers; but the cost of any paper, vellum, or parchment shall be added to the amount, after deducting the allowance of per centum, as aforesaid: *Provided*, That no commission shall be allowed on any sum or sums so sold or supplied of less amount than fifty dollars; *And provided, further*, That any proprietor or proprietors of articles named in schedule C, who shall furnish his or their own die or design for stamps, to be used especially for his or their own proprietary articles, shall be allowed the following discount, namely: on amounts purchased at one time of not less than fifty nor more than five hundred dollars, five per centum; on amounts over five hundred dollars, ten per centum. The Commissioner of Internal Revenue may from time to time make regulations for the allowance of such of the stamps issued under the provisions of this act as may have been spoiled or rendered useless or unfit for the purpose intended, or for which the owner may have no use, or which through mistake may have been improperly or unnecessarily used, or where the rates or duties represented thereby have been paid in error, or remitted; and such allowance shall be made either by giving other stamps in lieu of the stamps so allowed for, or by repaying the amount or value, after deducting therefrom, in case of repayment, the sum of five per centum to the owner thereof.

SEC. 103. *And be it further enacted,* That it shall be lawful for any person to present to the Commissioner of Internal Revenue any instrument, and require his opinion whether or not the same is chargeable with any duty; and if the said Commissioner shall be of opinion that such instrument is not chargeable with any stamp duty, it shall be lawful for him, and he is hereby required, to impress thereon a particular stamp, to be provided for that purpose, with such word or words or device thereon as he shall judge proper, which shall signify and denote that such instrument is not chargeable with any stamp duty; and every such instrument upon which the said stamp shall be impressed shall be deemed to be not so chargeable, and shall be received in evidence in all courts of law or equity, notwithstanding any objections made to the same, as being chargeable with stamp duty, and not stamped to denote the same.

SEC. 104. *And be it further enacted,* That on and after the date on which this act shall take effect, no telegraph company or its agent or employee shall receive from any person, or transmit to any person any dispatch or message without an adhesive stamp denoting the duty imposed by this act being affixed to a copy thereof, or having the same stamped thereupon, and in default thereof shall incur a penalty of ten dollars: *Provided,* That only one stamp shall be required, whether sent through one or more companies.

SEC. 105. *And be it further enacted,* That on and after the date on which this act shall take effect, no express company or its agent or employee shall receive for transportation from any person any bale, bundle, box, article, or package of any description, without either delivering to the consignor thereof a printed receipt, having stamped or affixed thereon a stamp denoting the duty imposed by this act, or without affixing thereto an adhesive stamp or stamps denoting such duty, and in default thereof shall incur a penalty of ten dollars: *Provided,* That but one stamped receipt or stamp shall be required for each shipment from one party to another party at the same time, whether such shipment consists of one or more packages: *And provided, also,* That no stamped receipts or stamp shall be required for any bale, bundle, box, article, or package transported for the Government, nor for such bales, bundles, boxes, or packages as are transported by such companies without charge thereon.

SEC. 106. *And be it further enacted,* That all the provisions of this act relating to dies, stamps, adhesive stamps, and stamp duties shall extend to and include (except where manifestly inapplicable) all the articles or objects enumerated in schedule marked C, subject to stamp duties, and apply to the provisions in relation thereto.

SEC. 107. *And be it further enacted*, That on and after the first day of August, eighteen hundred and sixty-two, no person or persons, firms, companies, or corporations, shall make, prepare, and sell, or remove for consumption or sale, drugs, medicines, preparations, compositions, articles, or things, including perfumery, cosmetics, and playing cards, upon which a duty is imposed by this act, as enumerated and mentioned in schedule C, without affixing thereto an adhesive stamp or label denoting the duty before mentioned, and in default thereof shall incur a penalty of ten dollars: *Provided*, That nothing in this act contained shall apply to any uncompounded medicinal drug or chemical, nor to any medicine compounded according to the United States or other national pharmacopœia, nor of which the full and proper formula is published in either of the dispensatories, formularies, or text books in common use among physicians and apothecaries, including homeopathic and eclectic, or in any pharmaceutical journal now used by any incorporated college of pharmacy, and not sold or offered for sale, or advertised under any other name, form, or guise than that under which they may be severally denominated and laid down in said pharmacopœias, dispensatories, text books, or journals, as aforesaid, nor to medicines sold to or for the use of any person, which may be mixed and compounded specially for said persons, according to the written recipe or prescription of any physician or surgeon.

SEC. 108. *And be it further enacted*, That every manufacturer or maker of any of the articles for sale mentioned in schedule C, after the same shall have been so made, and the particulars hereinbefore required as to stamps have been complied with, who shall take off, remove, or detach, or cause or permit, or suffer to be taken off, or removed, or detached, any stamp, or who shall use any stamp, or any wrapper or cover to which any stamp is affixed, to cover any other article or commodity than that originally contained in such wrapper or cover, with such stamp when first used, with the intent to evade the stamp duties, shall for every such article, respectively, in respect of which any such offense shall be committed, be subject to a penalty of fifty dollars, to be recovered together with the costs thereupon accruing, and every such article or commodity as aforesaid shall also be forfeited.

SEC. 109. *And be it further enacted*, That every maker or manufacturer of any of the articles or commodities mentioned in schedule C, as aforesaid, who shall sell, send out, remove, or deliver any article or commodity, manufactured as aforesaid, before the duty thereon shall have been fully paid, by affixing thereon the proper stamp, as in this act provided, or who shall hide or conceal, or cause to be hidden or concealed, or who shall remove or convey away, or deposit, or cause to be removed or conveyed away from or deposited in any place, any such article or commodity, to evade the duty

chargeable thereon, or any part thereof, shall be subject to a penalty
of one hundred dollars, together with the forfeiture of any such
article or commodity : *Provided*, That medicines, preparations,
compositions, perfumery, and cosmetics, upon which stamp duties
are required by this act, may, when intended for exportation,
be manufactured and sold, or removed without having stamps affixed
thereto, and without being charged with duty, as aforesaid ; and
every manufacturer or maker of any article, as aforesaid, intended
for exportation, shall give such bonds and be subject to such rules
and regulations to protect the revenue against fraud as may be from
time to time prescribed by the Secretary of the Treasury.

SEC. 110. *And be it further enacted*, That every manufacturer
or maker of any of the articles or commodities, as aforesaid, or his
chief workman, agent, or superintendent, shall at the end of each
and every month make and sign a declaration in writing that no such
article or commodity, as aforesaid, has, during such preceding month,
or time when the last declaration was made, been removed, carried,
or sent, or caused, or suffered, or known to have been removed, carried, or sent from the premises of such manufacturer or maker, other
than such as have been duly taken account of and charged with the
stamp duty, on pain of such manufacturer or maker forfeiting for
every refusal or neglect to make such declaration one hundred dollars ; and if any such manufacturer or maker, or his chief workman,
agent, or superintendent, shall make any false or untrue declaration,
such manufacturer or maker, or chief workman, agent, or superintendent, making the same, shall forfeit five hundred dollars.

SCHEDULE B.

STAMP DUTIES.

	Duty. Dolls. cts.
AGREEMENT OR CONTRACT, other than those specified in this schedule ; any appraisement of value or damage, or for any other purpose ; for every sheet or piece of paper upon which either of the same shall be written, five cents	5
Bank check, draft, or order for the payment of any sum of money exceeding twenty dollars, drawn upon any bank, trust company, or any person or persons, companies, or corporations at sight or on demand, two cents	2
Bill of exchange (inland), draft, or order for the payment of any sum of money exceeding twenty and not exceeding one hundred dollars, otherwise than at sight or on de-mand, or any promissory note except bank notes issued for circulation, for a sum exceeding twenty and not ex-ceeding one hundred dollars, five cents	5
Exceeding one hundred dollars and not exceeding two hun-dred dollars, ten cents	10
Exceeding two hundred dollars and not exceeding three hundred and fifty dollars, fifteen cents	15

Duty.
Dolls. cts.

Exceeding three hundred and fifty dollars and not exceeding five hundred dollars, twenty cents............. 20

Exceeding five hundred dollars and not exceeding seven hundred and fifty dollars, thirty cents.............. · 30

Exceeding seven hundred and fifty dollars and not exceeding one thousand dollars, forty cents.............. 40

Exceeding one thousand dollars and not exceeding fifteen hundred dollars, sixty cents...................... 60

Exceeding fifteen hundred dollars and not exceeding twenty-five hundred dollars, one dollar............. 1 00

Exceeding twenty-five hundred dollars and not exceeding five thousand dollars, one dollar and fifty cents....... 1 50

And for every twenty-five hundred dollars, or part of twenty-five hundred dollars in excess of five thousand dollars, one dollar...................................... 1 00

Bill of exchange (foreign) or letter of credit, drawn in but payable out of the United States, if drawn singly, or otherwise than in a set of three or more, according to the custom of merchants and bankers, shall pay the same rates of duty as inland bills of exchange or promissory notes.

If drawn in sets of three or more : For every bill of each set, where the sum made payable shall not exceed one hundred and fifty dollars, or the equivalent thereof, in any foreign currency in which such bills may be expressed, according to the standard of value fixed by the United States, three cents............................... 3

Above one hundred and fifty dollars and not above two hundred and fifty dollars, five cents................... 5

Above two hundred and fifty dollars and not above five hundred dollars, ten cents........................ 10

Above five hundred dollars and not above a thousand dollars, fifteen cents.............................. 15

Above one thousand dollars and not above one thousand five hundred dollars, twenty cents.................... 20

Above one thousand five hundred dollars and not above two thousand two hundred and fifty dollars, thirty cents... 30

Above two thousand two hundred and fifty dollars and not above three thousand five hundred dollars, fifty cents.. 50

Above three thousand five hundred dollars and not above five thousand dollars, seventy cents.............···.. 70

Above five thousand dollars and not above seven thousand five hundred dollars, one dollar..................... 1 00

And for every two thousand five hundred dollars, or part thereof, in excess of seven thousand five hundred dollars, thirty cents...................................... 30

BILL OF LADING or receipt (other than charter-party), for any goods, merchandise, or effects, to be exported from

Duty.
Dolls. cts.

a port or place in the United States to any foreign port
or place, ten cents.. 10

EXPRESS.—For every receipt or stamp issued, or issued by
any express company, or carrier, or person whose occupation it is to act as such, for all boxes, bales, packages,
articles, or bundles, for the transportation of which such
company, carrier, or person shall receive a compensation of not over twenty-five cents, one cent.......... 1

When such compensation exceeds the sum of twenty-five
cents, and not over one dollar, two cents............. 2

When one or more packages are sent to the same address at
the same time, and the compensation therefor exceeds
one dollar, five cents..................................... 5

BOND.—For indemnifying any person who shall have become bound or engaged as surety for the payment of
any sum of money, or for the due execution or performance of the duties of any office, and to account for
money received by virtue thereof, fifty cents......... 50

BOND of any description other than such as may be required
in legal proceedings, and such as are not otherwise
charged in this schedule, twenty-five cents.......... 25

CERTIFICATE of stock in any incorporated company, twenty-
five cents... 25

CERTIFICATE of profits, or any certificate or memorandum
showing an interest in the property or accumulations
of any incorporated company, if for a sum not less than
ten dollars and not exceeding fifty dollars, ten cents... 10

For a sum exceeding fifty dollars, twenty-five cents....... 25

CERTIFICATE.—Any certificate of damage, or otherwise, and
all other certificates or documents issued by any port
warden, marine surveyor, or other person acting as such,
twenty-five cents.. 25

CERTIFICATE of deposit of any sum of money in any bank or
trust company, or with any banker or person acting as such:
If for a sum not exceeding one hundred dollars, two cents.. 2

For a sum exceeding one hundred dollars, five cents....... 5

CERTIFICATE of any other description than those specified,
ten cents.. 10

CHARTER-PARTY.—Contract or agreement for the charter of
any ship or vessel, or steamer, or any letter, memorandum, or other writing between the captain, master, or
owner, or person acting as agent of any ship or vessel,
or steamer, and any other person or persons for or relating to the charter of such ship or vessel, or steamer,
if the registered tonnage of such ship or vessel, or steamer, does not exceed three hundred tons, three dollars.. 3 00

Exceeding three hundred tons, and not exceeding six hundred tons, five dollars.................................... 5 00

Exceeding six hundred tons, ten dollars................... 10 00

Duty.

CONTRACT.—Broker's note, or memorandum of sale of any goods or merchandise, stocks, bonds, exchange, notes of hand, real estate, or property of any kind or description issued by brokers or persons acting as such, ten cents. **10**

CONVEYANCE.—Deed, instrument, or writing, whereby any lands, tenements, or other realty sold shall be granted, assigned, transferred, or otherwise conveyed to, or vested in, the purchaser or purchasers, or any other person or persons by his, her, or their direction, when the consideration or value exceeds one hundred dollars and does not exceed five hundred dollars, fifty cents. **50**

When the consideration exceeds five hundred dollars and does not exceed one thousand dollars, one dollar. **1 00**

Exceeding one thousand dollars and not exceeding two thousand five hundred dollars, two dollars. **2 00**

Exceeding two thousand five *thousand* dollars and not exceeding five thousand dollars, five dollars. **5 00**

Exceeding five thousand dollars and not exceeding ten thousand dollars, ten dollars. **10 00**

Exceeding ten thousand dollars and not exceeding twenty thousand dollars, twenty dollars. **20 00**

And for every additional ten thousand dollars, or fractional part thereof, in excess of twenty thousand dollars, twenty dollars. **20 00**

DISPATCH, TELEGRAPHIC.—Any dispatch or messsage, the charge for which for the first ten words does not exceed twenty cents, one cent. **1**

When the charge for the first ten words exceeds twenty cents, three cents. **3**

ENTRY of any goods, wares, or merchandise at any customhouse, either for consumption or warehousing, not exceeding one hundred dollars in value, twenty-five cents **25**

Exceeding one hundred dollars and not exceeding five hundred dollars in value, fifty cents. **50**

Exceeding five hundred dollars in value, one dollar. **1 00**

ENTRY for the withdrawal of any goods or merchandise from bonded warehouse, fifty cents. **50**

INSURANCE (LIFE).—Policy of insurance, or other instrument by whatever name the same shall be called, whereby any insurance shall be made upon any life or lives—

When the amount insured shall not exceed one thousand dollars, twenty-five cents. **25**

Exceeding one thousand and not exceeding five thousand dollars, fifty cents. **50**

Exceeding five thousand dollars, one dollar. **1 00**

INSURANCE (MARINE, INLAND, AND FIRE).—Each policy of insurance or other instrument, by whatever name the same shall be called, by which insurance shall be made or renewed upon property of any description, whether

Duty.
Dolla. cts

against perils by the sea or by fire, or other peril of any
kind, made by any insurance company, or its agents, or
by any other company or person, twenty-five cents....   25

LEASE, agreement, memorandum, or contract for the hire,
use, or rent of any land, tenement, or portion thereof—
If for a period of time not exceeding three years, fifty
cents   50

If for a period exceeding three years, one dollar..........   1 00.

MANIFEST for custom-house entry or clearance of the cargo
of any ship, vessel, or steamer for a foreign port—
If the registered tonnage of such ship, vessel, or steamer
does not exceed three hundred tons, one dollar.......   1 00

Exceeding three hundred tons, and not exceeding six hundred tons, three dollars............................   3 00

Exceeding six hundred tons, five dollars.................   5 00

MORTGAGE of lands, estate, or property, real or personal,
heritable or movable whatsoever, where the same shall
be made as a security for the payment of any definite
and certain sum of money lent at the time or previously
due and owing or forborne to be paid, being payable;
also any conveyance of any lands, estate, or property
whatsoever, in trust to be sold or otherwise converted
into money, which shall be intended only as security,
and shall be redeemable before the sale or other disposal thereof, either by express stipulation or otherwise;
or any personal bond given as security for the payment
of any definite or certain sum of money exceeding one
hundred dollars, and not exceeding five hundred dollars, fifty cents...................................   50

Exceeding five hundred dollars, and not exceeding one
thousand dollars, one dollar.......................   1 00

Exceeding one thousand dollars, and not exceeding two
thousand five hundred dollars, two dollars..........   2 00

Exceeding two thousand five hundred dollars, and not exceeding five thousand dollars, five dollars...........   5 00

Exceeding five thousand dollars, and not exceeding ten
thousand dollars, ten dollars......................   10 00

Exceeding ten thousand dollars, and not exceeding twenty
thousand dollars, fifteen dollars...................   15 00

And for every additional ten thousand dollars, or fractional
part thereof, in excess of twenty thousand dollars, ten
dollars..   10 00

PASSAGE TICKET, by any vessel from a port in the United
States to a foreign port, if less than thirty dollars, fifty
cents   50

Exceeding thirty dollars, one dollar.....................   1 00

POWER OF ATTORNEY for the sale or transfer of any stock,
bonds, or scrip, or for the collection of any dividends
or interest thereon, twenty-five cents..............   25

Duty.
Dolls. cts.

Power of attorney or proxy for voting at any election for officers of any incorporated company or society, except religious, charitable, or literary societies, or public cemeteries, ten cents 10

Power of attorney to receive or collect rent, twenty-five cents 25

Power of attorney to sell and convey real estate, or to rent or lease the same, or to perform any and all other acts not hereinbefore specified, one dollar............ 1 00

Probate of will, or letters of administration: Where the estate and effects for or in respect of which such probate or letters of administration applied for shall be sworn or declared not to exceed the value of two thousand five hundred dollars, fifty cents................ 50

To exceed two thousand five hundred dollars, and not exceeding five thousand dollars, one dollar............. 1 00

To exceed five thousand dollars, and not exceeding twenty thousand dollars, two dollars....................... 2 00

To exceed twenty thousand dollars, and not exceeding fifty thousand dollars, five dollars....................... 5 00

To exceed fifty thousand dollars, and not exceeding one hundred thousand dollars, ten dollars................ 10 00

Exceeding one hundred thousand dollars, and not exceeding one hundred and fifty thousand dollars, twenty dollars. 20 00

And for every additional fifty thousand dollars, or fractional part thereof, ten dollars......................... 10 00

Protest.—Upon the protest of every note, bill of exchange, acceptance, check or draft, or any marine protest, whether protested by a notary public or by any other officer who may be authorized by the law of any State or States to make such protest, twenty-five cents..... 25

Warehouse receipt for any goods, merchandise, or property of any kind held on storage in any public or private warehouse or yard, twenty-five cents.............. 25

Legal documents:

Writ, or other original process by which any suit is commenced in any court of record, either law or equity, fifty cents... 50

Provided, That no writ, summons, or other process issued by a justice of the peace, or issued in any criminal or other suits commenced by the United States or any State, shall be subject to the payment of stamp duties: *And provided, further*, That the stamp duties imposed by the foregoing schedule B on manifests, bills of lading, and passage tickets, shall not apply to steamboats or other vessels plying between ports of the United States and ports in British North America.

7

SCHEDULE C.

MEDICINES OR PREPARATIONS.—For and upon every packet, box, bottle, pot, phial, or other inclosure, containing any pills, powders, tinctures, troches or lozenges, syrups, cordials, bitters, anodynes, tonics, plasters, liniments, salves, ointments, pastes, drops, waters, essences, spirits, oils, or other preparations or compositions whatsoever, made and sold, or removed for consumption and sale, by any person or persons whatever, wherein the person making or preparing the same has, or claims to have, any private formula or occult secret or art for the making or preparing the same, or has, or claims to have, any exclusive right or title to the making or preparing the same, or which are prepared, uttered, vended, or exposed for sale under any letters patent, or held out or recommended to the public by the makers, venders, or proprietors thereof as proprietary medicines, or as remedies or specifics for any disease, diseases, or affections whatever affecting the human or animal body as follows : where such packet, box, bottle, pot, phial, or other inclosure, with its contents, shall not exceed, at the retail price or value, the sum of twenty-five cents, one cent..   **1**

Where such packet, box, bottle, pot, phial, or other inclosure, with its contents, shall exceed the retail price or value of twenty-five cents, and not exceed the retail price or value of fifty cents, two cents..............   **2**

Where such packet, box, bottle, pot, phial, or other inclosure, with its contents, shall exceed the retail price or value of fifty cents, and shall not exceed the retail price or value of seventy-five cents, three cents...........   **3**

When such packet, box, bottle, pot, phial, or other inclosure, with its contents, shall exceed the retail price or value of seventy-five cents, and shall not exceed the retail price or value of one dollar, four cents..........   **4**

When such packet, box, bottle, pot, phial, or other inclosure, with its contents, shall exceed the retail price or value of one dollar, for each and every fifty cents or fractional part thereof over and above the one dollar, as before mentioned, an additional two cents...........   **2**

PERFUMERY AND COSMETICS.—For and upon every packet, box, bottle, pot, phial, or other inclosure, containing any essence, extract, toilet, water, cosmetic, hair oil, pomade, hairdressing, hair restorative, hair dye, toothwash, dentifrice, tooth paste, aromatic cachous ; or any similar articles, by whatsoever name the same heretofore have been, now are, or may hereafter be called, known, or distinguished, used or applied, or to be used or applied as perfumes or applications to the hair,

Duty.
Dolls. cts.

Duty.
Dolls. cts.

mouth, or skin, made, prepared, and sold or removed
for consumption and sale in the United States, where
such packet, box, bottle, pot, phial, or other inclosure,
with its contents, shall not exceed at the retail price or
value the sum of twenty-five cents, one cent............ 1
Where such packet, box, bottle, pot, phial, or other inclosure, with its contents, shall exceed the retail price or
value of twenty-five cents, and shall not exceed the retail price or value of fifty cents, two cents............ 2
Where such packet, box, bottle, pot, phial, or other inclosure, with its contents, shall exceed the retail price or
value of fifty cents, and shall not exceed the retail price
or value of seventy-five cents, three cents............ 3
Where such packet, box, bottle, pot, phial, or other inclosure, with its contents, shall exceed the retail price or
value of seventy-five cents, and shall not exceed the retail price or value of one dollar, four cents............ 4
Where such packet, box, bottle, pot, phial, or other inclosure, with its contents, shall exceed the retail price or
value of one dollar, for each and every fifty cents or
fractional part thereof over and above the one dollar, as
before mentioned, an additional two cents.......... 2
PLAYING CARDS.—For and upon every pack of whatever
number, when the price per pack does not exceed
eighteen cents, one cent........................ 1
Over eighteen cents and not exceeding twenty-five cents
per pack, two cents............................ 2
Over twenty-five and not exceeding thirty cents per pack,
three cents................................. 3
Over thirty and not exceeding thirty-six cents per pack, four
cents...................................... 4
Over thirty-six cents per pack, five cents............... 5

LEGACIES AND DISTRIBUTIVE SHARES OF PERSONAL PROPERTY.

SEC. 111. *And be it further enacted,* That any person or persons
having in charge or trust, as administrators, executors, or trustees of
any legacies or distributive shares arising from personal property, of
any kind whatsoever, where the whole amount of such personal
property, as aforesaid, shall exceed the sum of one thousand dollars
in actual value, passing from any person who may die after the passage of this act possessed of such property, either by will or by the
intestate laws of any State or Territory, or any part of such property or interest therein, transferred by deed, grant, bargain, sale, or
gift, made or intended to take effect in possession or enjoyment after
the death of the grantor or bargainor, to any person or persons, or
to any body or bodies politic or corporate, in trust or otherwise, shall

be, and hereby are, made subject to a duty or tax, to be paid in the United States, as follows, that is to say :

First. Where the person or persons entitled to any beneficial interest in such property shall be the lineal issue or lineal ancestor, brother or sister, to the person who died possessed of such property as aforesaid, at and after the rate of seventy-five cents for each and every hundred dollars of the clear value of such interest in such property.

Second. Where the person or persons entitled to any beneficial interest in such property shall be a descendant of a brother or sister of the person who died possessed, as aforesaid, at and after the rate of one dollar and fifty cents for each and every hundred dollars of the clear value of such interest.

Third. Where the person or persons entitled to any beneficial interest in such property shall be a brother or sister of the father or mother, or a descendant of a brother or sister of the father or mother of the person who died possessed, as aforesaid, at and after the rate of three dollars for each and every hundred dollars of the clear value of such interest.

Fourth. Where the person or persons entitled to any beneficial interest in such property shall be a brother or sister of the grandfather or grandmother, or a descendant of the brother or sister of the grandfather or grandmother of the person who died possessed, as aforesaid, at and after the rate of four dollars for each and every hundred dollars of the clear value of such interest.

Fifth. Where the person or persons entitled to any beneficial interest in such property shall be in any other degree of collateral consanguinity than is hereinbefore stated, or shall be a stranger in blood to the person who died possessed, as aforesaid, or shall be a body politic or corporate, at and after the rate of five dollars for each and every hundred dollars of the clear value of such interest : *Provided,* That all legacies or property passing by will, or by the laws of any State or Territory, to husband or wife of the person who died possessed, as aforesaid, shall be exempt from tax or duty.

SEC. 112. *And be it further enacted,* That the tax or duty aforesaid shall be a lien and charge upon the property of every person who may die as aforesaid, until the same shall be fully paid to and discharged by the United States ; and every executor, administrator, or other person who may take the burden or trust of administration upon such property shall, after taking such burden or trust, and before paying and distributing any portion thereof to the legatees or any parties entitled to beneficial interest therein, pay to the collector or deputy collector of the district the amount of the duty or tax, as aforesaid, and shall also make and render to the assistant assessor of the district a schedule, list, or statement of the amount of such property, together with the amount of duty which has accrued or should accrue thereon, verified by his oath or affirmation, to be administered and certified thereon by some magistrate or officer having lawful power to administer such oaths, in such form and manner as may be prescribed by the Commissioner of Internal Revenue, which schedule,

list, or statement shall contain the names of each and every person
entitled to any beneficial interest therein, together with the clear
value of such interest, which schedule, list, or statement shall be by
him delivered to such collector; and upon such payment and delivery
of such schedule, list, or statement, said collector or deputy collector
shall grant to such person paying such duty or tax a receipt or receipts for the same in duplicate, which shall be prepared as is hereinafter provided; such receipt or receipts, duly signed and delivered
by such collector or deputy collector, shall be sufficient evidence to
entitle the person who paid such duty or tax as having taken the
burden or trust of administering such property or personal estate to
be allowed for such payment by the person or persons entitled to the
beneficial interest in respect to which such tax or duty was paid; and
such person administering such property or personal estate shall be
credited and allowed such payment by every tribunal which, by the
laws of any State or Territory, is or may be empowered to decide
upon and settle the accounts of executors and administrators; and in
case such person who has taken the burden or trust of administering
upon any such property or personal estate shall refuse or neglect to
pay the aforesaid duty or tax to the collector or deputy collector, as
aforesaid, within the time hereinbefore provided, or shall neglect or
refuse to deliver to said collector or deputy collector the schedule,
list, or statement of such legacies, property, or personal estate under
oath, as aforesaid, or shall deliver to said collector or deputy collector
a false schedule or statement of such legacies, property, or personal
estate, or give the names and relationship of the persons entitled to
beneficial interests therein untruly, or shall not truly and correctly set
forth and state therein the clear value of such beneficial interest, or
where no administration upon such property or personal estate shall
have been granted or allowed under existing laws, the proper officer
of the United·States shall commence such proceedings in law or
equity before any court of the United States as may be proper and
necessary to enforce and realize the lien or charge upon such property
or personal estate, or any part thereof, for which such tax or duty
has not been truly and justly paid. Under such proceedings the rate
of duty or tax enforced shall be the highest rate imposed or assessed
by this act, and shall be in the name of the United States against
such person or persons as may have the actual or constructive custody or possession of such property or personal estate, or any part
thereof, and shall subject such property or personal estate, or any
portion of the same, to be sold upon the judgment or decree of such
court, and from the proceeds of such sale, the amount of such tax or
duty, together with all costs and expenses of every description to be
allowed by such court, shall be first paid, and the balance, if any, deposited according to the order of such court, to be paid under its direction to such person or persons as shall establish their lawful title to
the same. The deed or deeds, or any proper conveyance of such
property or personal estate, or any portion thereof, so sold under such
judgment or decree, executed by the officer lawfully charged with
carrying the same into effect, shall vest in the purchaser thereof all

the title of the delinquent to the property or personal estate sold under and by virtue of such judgment or decree, and shall release every other portion of such property or personal estate from the lien or charge thereon created by this act. And every person or persons who shall have in his possession, charge, or custody, any record, file, or paper, containing or supposed to contain any information concerning such property or personal estate, as aforesaid, passing from any person who may die, as aforesaid, shall exhibit the same at the request of the collector of the revenue, his deputy, or agent, and to any law officer of the United States, in the performance of his duty under this act, his deputy or agent, who may desire to examine the same; and if any such person, having in his possession, charge, or custody any such records, files, or papers, shall refuse or neglect to exhibit the same on request, as aforesaid, he shall forfeit and pay the sum of five hundred dollars; and in case of any delinquency in making the schedule, list, or statement, or in the payment of the duty or tax accruing, or which should accrue thereon, the assessment and collection shall be made as provided for in the general provisions of this act: *Provided*, In all legal controversies where such deed or title shall be the subject of judicial investigation the recital in said deed shall be presumed to be true, and that the requirements of the law had been complied with by the officers of the Government.

SEC. 113. *And be it further enacted*, That whenever by this act any license duty, or tax of any description has been imposed on any corporate body, or property of any incorporated company, it shall be lawful for the Commissioner of Internal Revenue to prescribe and determine in what district such tax shall be assessed and collected, and to what officer thereof the official notices required in that behalf shall be given, and of whom payment of such tax shall be demanded.

SEC. 114. *And be it further enacted*, That all articles upon which duties are imposed by the provisions of this act, which shall be found in the possession of any person or persons for the purpose of being sold by such person or persons in fraud thereof and with the design to avoid payment of said duties, may be seized by any collector or deputy collector who shall have reason to believe that the same are possessed for the purpose aforesaid, and the same shall be forfeited to the United States. And the proceedings to enforce said forfeiture shall be in the nature of a proceeding *in rem* in the circuit or district court of the United States for the district where such seizure is made, or in any other court of competent jurisdiction. And any person who shall have in his possession any such articles for the purpose of selling the same, with the design of avoiding payment of the duties imposed thereon by this act, shall be liable to a penalty of one hundred dollars, to be recovered as hereinbefore provided.

APPROPRIATION.

SEC. 115. *And be it further enacted*, That the pay of the assessors, assistant assessors, collectors, and deputy collectors, shall be paid out of the accruing internal duties or taxes before the same is paid into the treasury, according to such regulations as the Commissioner of Internal Revenue, under the direction of the Secretary of the Treasury, shall prescribe ; and for the purpose of paying the Commissioner of Internal Revenue and clerks, procuring dies, stamps, adhesive stamps, paper, printing forms and regulations, advertising, and any other expenses of carrying this act into effect, the sum of five hundred thousand dollars be, and hereby is, appropriated, or so much thereof as may be necessary.

ALLOWANCE AND DRAWBACK.

SEC. 116. *And be it further enacted*, That from and after the date on which this act takes effect there shall be an allowance or drawback on all articles on which any internal duty or tax shall have been paid, except raw or unmanufactured cotton, equal in amount to the duty or tax paid thereon, and no more, when exported, the evidence that any such duty or tax has been paid to be furnished to the satisfaction of the Commissioner of Internal Revenue by such person or persons as shall claim the allowance or drawback, and the amount to be ascertained under such regulations as shall, from time to time, be prescribed by the Commissioner of Internal Revenue, under the direction of the Secretary of the Treasury, and the same shall be paid by the warrant of the Secretary of the Treasury on the Treasurer of the United States, out of any money arising from internal duties not otherwise appropriated : *Provided*, That no allowance or drawback shall be made or had for any amount claimed or due less than twenty dollars, anything in this act to the contrary notwithstanding : *And provided; further*, That any certificate of drawback for goods exported, issued in pursuance of the provisions of this act, may, under such regulations as may be prescribed by the Secretary of the Treasury, be received by the collector or his deputy in payment of duties under this act. And the Secretary of the Treasury may make such regulations with regard to the form of said certificates and the issuing thereof as, in his judgment, may be necessary : *And provided, further*, That in computing the allowance or drawback upon articles manufactured exclusively of cotton when exported, there shall be allowed, in addition to the three per centum duty which shall have been paid on such articles, a drawback of five mills per pound upon such articles, in all cases where the duty imposed by this act upon the cotton used in the manufacture thereof has been previously paid ; the amount of said allowance to be ascertained in such manner as may be prescribed by the Commissioner of Internal Revenue, under the direction of the Secretary of the Treasury.

SEC. 117. *And be it further enacted*, That if any person or persons shall fraudulently claim or seek to obtain an allowance or drawback on goods, wares, or merchandise, on which no internal duty shall have been paid, or shall fraudulently claim any greater allowance or drawback than the duty actually paid, as aforesaid, such person or persons shall forfeit triple the amount wrongfully or fraudulently claimed or sought to be obtained, or the sum of five hundred dollars, at the election of the Secretary of the Treasury, to be recovered as in other cases of forfeiture provided for in the general provisions of this act.

SEC. 118. *And be it further enacted*, That the sum of sixty thousand dollars appropriated to complete *the* capitol in New Mexico, by the second section of an act of Congress, approved June twenty-five, eighteen hundred and sixty, and the sum of fifty thousand dollars, appropriated for military roads in New Mexico, by act of Congress approved March two, eighteen hundred and sixty-one, be, and the same are hereby, credited to the Territory of New Mexico in payment of the direct annual tax of sixty-two thousand six hundred and forty-eight dollars levied upon said Territory under the eighth section of an act of Congress, approved August five, eighteen hundred and sixty-one, to be taken up on account of said direct tax under said [act] as the same may fall due to the United States from said Territory.

SEC. 119. *And be it further enacted*, That so much of an act entitled "An act to provide increased revenue from imports to pay interest on the public debt, and for other purposes," approved August fifth, eighteen hundred and sixty-one, as imposes a direct tax of twenty millions of dollars on the United States, shall be held to authorize the levy and collection of one tax to that amount; and no other tax shall be levied under and by virtue thereof, until the first day of April, eighteen hundred and sixty-five, when the same shall be in full force and effect.

GALUSHA A. GROW,
Speaker of the House of Representatives.

SOLOMON FOOT,
President of the Senate pro tempore.

Approved July 1, 1862.

ABRAHAM LINCOLN.

DEPARTMENT OF STATE,
Washington, July 8, 1862.

I certify that the foregoing is a true copy of the original act on file in this Department.

W. HUNTER, *Chief Clerk.*

AMENDMENTS.

SECTIONS 24 AND 25 OF "*An Act increasing, temporarily, the Duties on Imports, and for other purposes,*" PASSED JULY 14, 1862 (37TH CONGRESS, 1861–62, p. 560, 561), AMENDING ACT OF 1862, CH. 119, § 95.

SEC. 24. *And be it further enacted,* That *in* the fifty-ninth section of the act entitled "An act to provide internal revenue to support the Government and [to] pay interest on the public debt," approved July first, eighteen hundred and sixty-two, be so amended that no instrument, document, or paper made, signed, or issued prior to the first day of January, eighteen hundred and sixty-three, without being duly stamped, or having thereon an adhesive stamp to denote duty imposed thereon, shall for that cause be deemed invalid and of no effect : *Provided,* however, That no such instrument, document, or paper shall be admitted or used as evidence in any court until the same shall have been duly stamped, nor until the holder thereof shall have proved to the satisfaction of the court that he has paid to the Collector or Deputy Collector of the district within which such court may be held, the sum of five dollars for the use of the United States.

SEC. 25. *And be it further enacted,* That no part of the act aforesaid, in relation to stamp duties, shall be held to take effect before the first day of September, eighteen hundred and sixty-two. And so much of said act as relates to the appointment of Collectors and Assessors shall be held to take effect on the twenty-first day of July, eighteen hundred and sixty-two, instead of from and after its approval by the President.

ACT OF JULY 16, 1862.

SECOND SESSION, 37TH CONGRESS (CH. 187).

AN ACT to impose an Additional Duty on Sugars produced in the United States.

Be it enacted by the Senate and House of Representatives of the United States of America in Congress assembled, That, in addition to the duties imposed by the act entitled "An act to provide internal revenue to support the Government and to pay interest on the public debt," approved July first, eighteen hundred and sixty-two, on all brown, Muscovado, or clarified sugars, produced directly from the sugar-cane, there shall be levied, collected, and paid, under the provisions of said act, upon all such sugars produced in the United States, a duty of one cent per pound, and such additional duty and the duty specified in the act aforesaid, shall be levied, collected, and paid on all such sugars not manufactured for consumption in the family of the producer, in the hands of the producer or manufacturer thereof, on the day of the approval of this act by the President : *Provided,* That, within States or parts of States declared to be in insurrection, the said duties may be collected in such manner and by such officers as the President may direct, until the insurrection so declared shall close or have been suppressed.

SEC. 2. *And be it further enacted,* That the provisions of this act shall not apply to sugar manufactured from sorghum.

APPROVED July 16, 1862.

RESOLUTION.

SECOND SESSION, 37TH CONGRESS, 1861–62.

(No. 64.) JOINT RESOLUTION to amend Section seventy-seven of "An Act to provide Internal Revenue to support the Government and to pay Interest on the Public Debt," and for other purposes.

Resolved by the Senate and House of Representatives of the United States of America in

Congress assembled, That section seventy-seven of an act entitled " An act to provide internal revenue to support the Government and to pay interest on the public debt" be, and the same is hereby amended by striking out the word " May," and inserting " August."

SEC. 2. *And be it further resolved,* That all the sections of an act entitled " An act to provide internal revenue to support the Government and to pay interest on the public debt," which require any matter or thing to be done on or before the first day of July or August, eighteen hundred and sixty-two, shall be so amended and changed that said matters or things may be so done on or before any other day in the year eighteen hundred and sixty-two, nor later than the first day of October, eighteen hundred and sixty-two, which may be fixed and determined upon by the Secretary of the Treasury, if in his judgment a later day should be so fixed in order to put said act into practical operation ; and all parts of said act having reference to the said dates of the first days of July and August, eighteen hundred and sixty-two, shall be taken and construed as having reference to the said day, which may be so fixed and determined upon : *Provided,* That the Secretary of the Treasury shall give public notice of the day so fixed and determined upon in such manner as he may deem expedient.

APPROVED July 17, 1862.

NOTIFICATION.

[OFFICIAL.]

TREASURY DEPARTMENT, *July* 23, 1862.

By authority of a joint resolution of the Congress of the United States, approved on the seventeenth day of July instant, notice is hereby given that the first day of September next is fixed and determined upon as the day on which the " Act to provide internal revenue to support the Government and to pay interest on the public debt," shall be put into practical operation ; and any act or thing which in said Act is required to be done on or before the first day of July or August in the year eighteen hundred and sixty-two, shall be done on or before the first day of September, eighteen hundred and sixty-two ; and all parts of said Act having reference to said dates of the first days of July and August, eighteen hundred and sixty-two, shall be taken and construed as having reference to the first day of September, eighteen hundred and sixty-two.

Collectors and Assessors will be appointed, and whatever other things may be necessary to put the Act into practical operation, will be done before the date fixed by this Notice.

ACT OF JULY 2, 1862.

SECOND SESSION, 37TH CONGRESS (CH. 128).

AN ACT to prescribe an Oath of Office, and for other purposes.

Be it enacted by the Senate and House of Representatives of the United States of America in Congress assembled, That hereafter every person elected or appointed to any office of honor or profit under the Government of the United States, either in the civil, military, or naval departments of the public service, excepting the President of the United States, shall, before entering upon the duties of such office, and before being entitled to any of the salary or emoluments thereof, take and subscribe the following oath or affirmation :

I,   do solemnly   that I have never voluntarily borne arms against the United States since I have been a citizen thereof; that I have voluntarily given no aid, countenance, counsel, or encouragement to persons engaged in armed hostility thereto ; that I have neither sought nor accepted nor attempted to exercise the functions of any office whatever, under any authority, or pretended authority, in hostility to the United States; that I have not yielded a voluntary support to any pretended government, authority, power, or constitution within the United States, hostile or inimical thereto. And I do further that, to the best of my knowledge and ability, I will support and defend the Constitution of the United States against all enemies, foreign and domestic; that I will bear true faith and allegiance to the same; that I take this obligation freely, without any mental reservation or purpose of evasion ; and that I will well and faithfully discharge the duties of the office on which I am about to enter : So help me God.

and subscribed
before me, this   day
of   A.D. 186 ;

which said oath, so taken and signed, shall be preserved among the files of the court, House of Congress, or Department to which the said office may appertain. And any person who shall falsely take the said oath shall be guilty of perjury, and, on conviction, in addition to the penalties now prescribed for that offense, shall be deprived of his office and rendered incapable forever after of holding any office or place under the United States.

APPROVED July 2, 1862.

ACT OF DECEMBER 25, 1862.

THIRD SESSION, 37TH CONGRESS.

AN ACT to amend an Act entitled " An act to provide Internal Revenue to support the Government and to pay Interest on the Public Debt," approved July 1st, 1862.

Be it enacted by the Senate and House of Representatives of the United States of America in Congress assembled, That the Assessors, Assistant Assessors, and Collectors, and Deputy Collectors appointed, or who may be appointed under the provisions of an act entitled " An act to provide internal revenue to support the Government and to pay interest on the public debt," approved July first, eighteen hundred and sixty-two, and all subsequent acts in relation thereto which have been or may be enacted, are hereby authorized and empowered to administer oaths or affirmations in all cases where the same are or may be required by the acts as aforesaid : *Provided*, That no fee shall be charged or allowed therefor.

SEC. 2. *And be it further enacted*, That the Commissioner of Internal Revenue shall be authorized and empowered, and hereby is authorized and empowered, to furnish and supply the Assistant Treasurers or Collectors of the United States at San Francisco, State of California, and Portland, State of Oregon, with adhesive stamps, or stamped paper, vellum, or parchment, according to the provisions of the internal revenue laws referred to in the preceding section, under such regulations and conditions as he may from time to time prescribe, and without requiring payment in advance therefor, anything in existing laws to the contrary notwithstanding : *Provided*, That no greater commission shall be allowed than is now provided for by law.

SEC. 3. *And be it further enacted*, That no instrument, document, writing, or paper of any description required by law to be stamped, shall be deemed or held invalid and of no effect for the want of the particular kind or description of stamp designated for and denoting the duty charged on any such instrument, document, writing, or paper, provided a legal stamp or stamps denoting a duty of equal amount shall have been duly affixed and used thereon : *Provided*, That the provisions of this section shall not apply to any stamp appropriated to denote the duty charged on proprietary articles.

SEC. 4. *And be it further enacted*, That all official instruments, documents, and papers issued or used by the officers of the United States Government shall be, and hereby are, exempt from duty.

SEC. 5. *And be it further enacted*, That the ninety-fifth section of an act entitled, " An act to provide internal revenue to support the Government and to pay interest on the public debt," approved July first, eighteen hundred and sixty-two, be so amended that no instrument, document, or paper made, signed, or issued prior to the first day of March, Anno Domini eighteen hundred and sixty-three, without being duly stamped, or having thereon an adhesive stamp to denote the duty imposed thereon, shall, for that cause, be deemed invalid and of no effect : *Provided,* That no instrument, document, writing, or paper, required by law to be stamped, signed, or issued, without being duly stamped prior to the day aforesaid, or any copy thereof, shall be admitted or used as evidence in any court until a legal stamp or stamps, denoting the amount of duty charged thereon, shall have been affixed thereto, or used thereon, and the initials of the person using or affixing the same, together with the date when the same is so used or affixed, shall have been placed thereon by such person. And the person desiring to use any such instrument, document, writing, or paper as evidence, or his agent or attorney, is authorized in the presence of the court to stamp the same as hereinbefore provided.

And section twenty-four of an act entitled, "An act increasing temporarily the duties on imports, and for other purposes," approved July fourteen, Anno Domini eighteen hundred and sixty-two, is hereby repealed.

APPROVED December 25, 1862.

ACT OF MARCH 3, 1863.

THIRD SESSION, 37TH CONGRESS.

AN ACT to amend an Act entitled, "An act to provide Internal Revenue to support the Government and pay Interest on the Public Debt," approved July first, eighteen hundred and sixty-two, and for other purposes.

Be it enacted by the Senate and House of Representatives of the United States of America in Congress assembled, That "An act to provide internal revenue to support the Government and pay interest on the public debt," approved July first, eighteen hundred and sixty-two, be, and the same hereby is, amended as hereinafter set forth, namely :

That whenever any written notice, or other instrument in writing, is required, the same shall be lawful if written or partly written and printed.

That section eleven be, and hereby is, amended, so as to authorize Assistant Assessors to perform any duties therein imposed upon Assessors.

That section nineteen be so amended that the Deputy Collector, as well as the Collector, may perform all the duties required of the said Collector in the said section ; and any notice required by said section to persons who neglect to pay their taxes may be sent by mail, or left at the dwellings or usual places of business of such persons, if any they have, written or printed, and said notice shall state the amount of duty or tax for which such persons are liable, including the ten per centum additional, as provided for in said section, demanding payment of the same ; and with respect to all such duties or taxes as are not included in the annual lists as provided for in said section, and all taxes and duties the collection of which is not otherwise provided for in said act, it shall be the duty of each Collector in person, or by deputy, to demand payment therefor in the manner provided, within ten days from and after the expiration of the time within which such duty or tax should have been paid ; and any copy of distraint shall be left at the dwelling or usual place of business of the owner or possessor of the property distrained : *Provided,* That such special demand shall not be necessary in respect to taxes assessed by section seventy-seven of said act.

That section twenty-eight be, and hereby is, amended, by striking out the words "forfeit and pay the sum of five hundred dollars," and inserting in lieu thereof, "upon conviction thereof by a court of competent jurisdiction, forfeit and pay the sum of five hundred dollars, or be imprisoned for a term not exceeding two years, at the discretion of the court."

That section forty-three be amended by striking out the following words : "And any person who shall use any cask or package so marked for the purpose of selling spirits of a quality different from that so inspected, shall be subject to a like penalty for each cask or package so used," and inserting in lieu thereof, "And any person who shall fraudulently use any cask or package so marked, for the purpose of selling any other spirits than that so inspected, or for selling spirits of a quality or quantity different from that so inspected, shall be subject to a like penalty, as provided, for each cask or package so used."

That section forty-four be, and hereby is, amended, by striking out the words "to be contiguous to such distillery."

That section fifty-five be, and hereby is, amended, by inserting after the words "shall not be paid at the time of rendering the account of the same as herein required," the words, "or at the time when they shall have become payable."

LICENSES.

That section sixty-four be, and hereby is, so amended, "that no license shall be required of an attorney having taken out a license as such in consequence of being employed to purchase, rent, or sell real estate, or to collect rent thereon for others in the ordinary course of business;" in paragraph number sixteen, by inserting after the word "taverns," the words "or eating-houses;" by adding to paragraph number twenty-eight the following words: "Nor shall apothecaries who have taken out a license as such be required to take out a license as retail dealers in liquors in consequence of selling alcohol;" and in paragraph number twenty-nine, by inserting after the word "merchandise," "or who shall manufacture by hand or machinery, for any other person or persons, goods, wares, or merchandise."

That section sixty-four be, and hereby is, further amended, by adding, at the end thereof, the following paragraphs:

34. Architects and civil engineers shall pay ten dollars for each license. Every person whose business it is to plan, design, or superintend the construction of buildings, or ships, or of roads, or bridges, or canals, or railroads, shall be regarded as an architect and civil engineer under this act : *Provided*, That this shall not include a practical carpenter who labors on a building.

35. Builders and contractors shall pay twenty-five dollars for each license. Every person whose business it is to construct buildings, or ships, or bridges, or canals, or railroads by contract, shall be regarded as a builder and contractor under this act : *Provided*, That no license shall be required from any person whose building contracts do not exceed two thousand five hundred dollars in any one year.

36. Stallions and jacks, owners of, shall pay ten dollars for each license. Every person who keeps a male horse or a jackass for the use of mares, requiring or receiving pay therefor, shall be required to take out a license under this act, which shall contain a brief description of the animal, its age, and place or places where used or to be used : *Provided*, That all accounts, notes, or demands for the use of any such horse or jack without a license, as aforesaid, shall be invalid and of no force in any court of law or equity.

37. Lottery ticket dealers shall pay one thousand dollars for each license. Every person, association, firm, or corporation who shall make, sell, or offer to sell lottery tickets or fractional parts thereof, or any token, certificate, or device representing or intending to represent a lottery ticket or any fractional part thereof, or any policy of numbers in any lottery, or shall manage any lottery or prepare schemes of lotteries, or superintend the drawing of any lottery, shall be deemed a lottery ticket dealer under this act.

38. Insurance agents shall pay ten dollars for each license. Any person who shall act as agent of any fire, marine, life, mutual, or other insurance company or companies, shall be regarded as an insurance agent under this act : *Provided*, That no license shall be required of any insurance agent or broker whose receipts, as such agent, are less than the sum of six hundred dollars in any one year.

39. Butchers shall pay ten dollars for each license. Every person whose business it is to sell butchers' meat at retail shall be regarded as a butcher under this act : *Provided*, That no butcher having taken out a license, and paid ten dollars therefor, shall be required to take out a license as retail dealer on account of selling other articles at the same store, stall, or premises : *Provided further*, That butchers who retail butchers' meat exclusively from a cart or wagon, by themselves or agents, shall be required to pay five dollars only for each license, any existing law to the contrary notwithstanding, and having taken out a license therefor, shall not be required to take out a license as a peddler for retailing butchers' meat, as aforesaid : *And, provided further*, That no license shall be required of a butcher whose annual sales do not exceed one thousand dollars.

40. Retail dealers shall pay ten dollars for each license, Every person whose business or occupation it is to sell or offer for sale any goods, wares, or merchandise of foreign or domestic production, not including wines, spirituous, or malt liquors, but not excluding drugs, medicines, cigars, snuff, or tobacco, and whose annual

sales exceed one thousand dollars, and do not exceed twenty-five thousand dollars, shall be regarded as a retail dealer under this act.

41. Wholesale dealers, whose annual sales do not exceed fifty thousand dollars, shall pay twenty-five dollars for each license ; if exceeding fifty thousand, and not exceeding one hundred thousand dollars, shall pay fifty dollars for each license ; exceeding one hundred thousand, and not exceeding two hundred and fifty thousand dollars, shall pay one hundred dollars for each license ; exceeding two hundred and fifty thousand, and not exceeding five hundred thousand dollars, shall pay two hundred dollars for each license ; exceeding five hundred thousand, and not exceeding one million dollars, shall pay three hundred dollars for each license ; exceeding one million, and not exceeding two million dollars, shall pay five hundred dollars for each license ; exceeding two millions of dollars, shall pay two hundred and fifty dollars for every million of dollars in excess of two millions of dollars, in addition to the five hundred dollars. Every person shall be regarded as a wholesale dealer under this act whose business or occupation it is to sell, or offer to sell, any goods, wares, or merchandise of foreign or domestic production, not including distilled spirits, fermented liquors, or wines, but not excluding drugs, medicines, cigars, snuff, or tobacco, whose annual sales exceed twenty-five thousand dollars ; and the license required by any wholesale dealer shall not be for a less amount than his sales for the previous year, unless he has made, or proposes to make, some change in his business that will obviously reduce the amount of his annual sales ; nor shall any license as wholesale dealer allow any such person to act as a commercial broker : *Provided*, That any license understated may be again assessed.

42. Wholesale dealers in liquors shall pay for each license the amount required in this act for license to wholesale dealers. Every person other than the distiller or brewer who shall sell, or offer for sale, any distilled spirits, fermented liquors, and wines of all kinds, in quantities of more than three gallons at one time, or whose annual sales shall exceed twenty-five thousand dollars, shall take out a license as a wholesale dealer in liquors.

43. Retail dealers in liquors shall pay twenty_dollars for such license. Every person other than a distiller or brewer who shall sell, or offer for sale, any distilled spirits, fermented liquors, or wine of any description, in quantities of three gallons or less, and whose annual sales do not exceed twenty-five thousand dollars, shall be regarded as a retail dealer in liquors under this law ; but nothing herein contained shall authorize the sale of any spirits, liquors, wines, or malt liquors to be drank on the premises : *Provided*, That no person licensed to keep a hotel, inn, or tavern shall be allowed to sell any liquors to be taken off the premises, and no person licensed to keep an eating-house shall be allowed to sell spirituous or vinous liquors. And no person who has taken out a license to keep a hotel, inn, tavern, or eating-house, shall be required to take out a license as a tobacconist, because of any tobacco or cigars furnished in the usual course of business as a keeper of a hotel, inn, tavern, or eating-house.

MANUFACTURES, ARTICLES, AND PRODUCTS.

SPECIFIC AND AD VALOREM DUTY.

That section seventy-five be and hereby is amended, by inserting after the words "*Provided*, That white lead, oxide of zinc, and sulphate of barytes," the words, "and paints and painters' colors ;" by inserting before the words, "on lard oil," and attached to the next preceding sentence. as follows : "and all duties or taxes on coal mined, and delivered by coal operators at the mines on contracts made prior to July first, eighteen hundred and sixty-two, shall be paid by the purchaser thereof; by striking out the following words : "on sugar refined, whether loaf, lump, granulated, or pulverized, two mills per pound ; on sugar refined, or made from molasses, sirup of molasses, melado, or concentrated melado, two mills per pound," and inserting in lieu thereof as follows : "sugar refiners shall pay one and one half of one per cent. on the gross amount of the sales of all the products of their manufactories : *Provided*, That every person shall be regarded as a sugar refiner under this act whose business it is to advance the quality and value of sugar by melting and recrystallization, or by liquoring, claying, or other washing process, or by any other chemical or mechanical means, or who shall advance the quality or value of molasses and concentrated molasses, melado, or concentrated melado, by boiling or other process ;" and by inserting therein, in lieu of any other duties, or rates of duty, on the articles hereinafter enumerated in this section, or provisions existing in relation thereto, the following :

On marine engines, three per centum ad valorem.

On rivets, exceeding one fourth of one inch in diameter, nuts, wrought, railroad chairs, bolts, and horse-shoes, two dollars per ton : *Provided*, That where a duty upon the iron from which said articles shall have been made has been actually paid, an additional duty only shall be paid of fifty cents per ton.

On rolled brass, copper, and yellow sheathing metal, in rods or sheets, one per centum ad valorem.

On sails, tents, shades, awnings, and bags, made of cotton, flax, or hemp, or part of either, or other materials, three per centum ad valorem : *Provided*, That the sewing of sails, tents, shades, awnings, carpets, and bags, the materials whereof belonged to the employer, shall be exempt from duty, where the cloth or material from which they are made was imported, or has been subject to and paid a duty.

On tobacco, cavendish, plug, twist, fine-cut, and manufactured of all description (not including snuff, cigars, and smoking tobacco, prepared with all the stems in, or made exclusively of stems), fifteen cents per pound.

On smoking tobacco prepared with all the stems in, and on smoking tobacco made exclusively of stems, five cents per pound.

On snuff manufactured of tobacco, *on* [or] stems, or of any substitute of tobacco, ground, dry, or damp, of all descriptions, twenty cents per pound.

On mineral or medicinal waters, or waters from springs impregnated with minerals, one cent for each bottle containing not more than one quart ; when containing more than one quart, two cents for each bottle.

Tailors, boot and shoe makers, milliners, and dressmakers, making clothing or articles of dress for men's, women's, or children's wear, to order as custom work, and not for sale generally, shall, to the amount of one thousand dollars, be exempt from duty, and for any excess beyond the amount of one thousand dollars shall pay a duty of one per centum ad valorem.

On umbrellas and parasols, made of cotton, silk, or other material, three per centum ad valorem.

On all ships, barks, brigs, schooners, sloops, sail-boats, steamboats (not including the engine), canal boats, and all other vessels or water craft hereafter built, made, or constructed, two per centum ad valorem.

On sugar-candy and all confectionery made wholly or in part of sugar, valued at fourteen cents per pound or less, two cents per pound ; when valued at exceeding fourteen cents, and not exceeding forty cents per pound, three cents per pound ; when valued at exceeding forty cents per pound, or when sold otherwise than by the pound, five per centum ad valorem.

On all gold leaf fifteen cents per pack, containing not more than twenty books of twenty-five leaves each.

On castings of iron exceeding ten pounds in weight for each casting, not otherwise provided for in this act, or in the act to which this act is an amendment, one dollar and fifty cents per ton : *Provided*, That there shall be deducted from duties assessed upon railroad cars any duties which may have been assessed and paid upon car-wheels under the provisions of this act.

On clock and time-pieces, and on clock movements when sold without being cased, three per centum ad valorem.

That section seventy-seven be, and hereby is, amended, by requiring the taxes provided for in that section to be levied, collected, and paid annually, by any person or persons owning, possessing, or keeping any carriage, yacht, plate, or billiard table ; by inserting in the first paragraph of Schedule A, after the words " kept for use," the words " for hire or for passengers ;" and by exempting from duty plate belonging to religious societies.

That section seventy-eight be, and hereby is, amended, by reducing the duty so that on horned cattle slaughtered the duty shall be twenty cents per head, on sheep and lambs slaughtered the duty shall be three cents per head, and on hogs slaughtered, exceeding one hundred pounds in weight, without regard to age, six cents each, and no duty shall be charged on hogs slaughtered of less weight ; and the cattle, hogs, and sheep slaughtered by any person for his or her own consumption, not exceeding six of each, shall be exempt from duty.

That section ninety-one be amended by striking out the word "gas" wherever it occurs, and by striking out the words "or on any articles manufactured" after the word "advertisements."

That section ninety-three be amended, so that in case of neglect or refusal to make the returns referred to in said section, the proceedings thereafter for the assessment and collection of the duty shall be in the same manner as provided for in other cases of neglect.

That section ninety-nine be amended, by striking out the words "ninety-three" preceding the words "of this act," and inserting "ninety-eight."

That section one hundred and two be, and hereby is, amended, by striking out the words "thereupon allow and deduct from," and inserting in lieu thereof the words "allow upon ;" by striking out the words "added to the amount, after deducting the allowance of per centum as aforesaid," and inserting in lieu thereof the words "paid by the purchaser of such stamped paper, vellum, or parchment ;" and by striking out the word "discount," and inserting in lieu thereof the word "commission."

That section one hundred and twelve be, and hereby is, amended, by inserting after the word "district," where it first occurs, as follows : "of which the deceased person was a resident ;" and by inserting after the word "district," where it next occurs, as follows : "of which the deceased person was a resident."

STAMP DUTIES.

SEC. 2. *And be it further enacted,* That on and after the first day of May, eighteen hundred and sixty-three, no person or persons, association, firm, or corporation, shall make, sell, or offer for sale, or dispose of any lottery ticket, or fractional part thereof, or any policy of numbers in any lottery, or any token, certificate, or device representing or intended to represent the holder, or any other person or person[s], as entitled or to be entitled in any lottery, lottery scheme, or game of hazard or chance to be drawn, to any prize or share, or part of a prize, or any sum or part or share of any sum of money, or other article of value, or any fractional part thereof, without affixing thereto an adhesive stamp or stamps denoting the duty imposed by this act, and in default thereof shall incur a penalty of fifty dollars for each and every such offense ; and no prize or part of a prize drawn to or by any ticket or fractional part thereof, token, certificate, or device, as aforesaid, and no sum of money or thing of value made payable or deliverable upon any stake, or investment, or risk in or upon any policy of numbers, shall be demanded or recovered by any legal proceedings or otherwise, without the ticket or fractional part thereof, or policy of numbers, token, certificate, or device, shall have been duly stamped at the time of the making sale, or delivery, or disposal thereof : *Provided,* That in addition to all other penalties and forfeitures now imposed by law for the evasion of stamp duties, any person who shall purchase, obtain, or receive any lottery ticket, or fractional part thereof, or any token, certificate, or device representing or intended to represent a lottery ticket, or fractional part thereof, or any policy of numbers, without first having thereon the stamp imposed by this act, may recover from the person of whom the same was purchased, obtained, or received, at any time within three years thereafter, before any court of competent jurisdiction, a sum equal to twice the amount paid for such ticket, or fractional part thereof, token, certificate, or device, or staked or invested in or upon any policy of numbers as aforesaid, with just and legal costs : *Provided, further,* That the stamp duty herein provided for shall be classed in the act to which this act is an amendment under Schedule B, as follows, to wit :

"Lottery tickets, fractional parts of lottery tickets, policies of numbers in lotteries, tokens, certificates, or devices in any form, representing the holder, or any person or persons, as entitled, or to be entitled, in any lottery, scheme, or game of hazard or chance, hereafter to be drawn, to any prize or portion of a prize or sum of money, or share thereof, or other article of value, or any portion or share thereof, when such ticket, fractional part of a ticket, policy of numbers, token, certificate, or device shall not exceed one dollar in the amount risked, or in the retail price thereof, fifty cents (50) ; when such ticket, fractional part of a ticket, policy, token, certificate, or device shall exceed one dollar in the amount risked or in the retail price thereof, then for each and every dollar, or fractional part thereof over and above one dollar, as before mentioned, an additional fifty cents (50) : *Provided, however*, That no stamp duty herein provided for shall be construed to authorize any lottery, or the sale of any lottery, tickets, tokens, or certificates, representing shares, or fractional parts of shares therein, within any State or Territory of the United States in which lotteries or the sale of lottery tickets is or shall be specially prohibited by the laws thereof, or in violation of the laws of any State or Territory ; and nothing in this act shall be held or construed so as to prevent the several States, within the limits thereof, from placing a duty, tax, or license, for State purposes, on any sale of lottery tickets on which a duty is required to be paid by this act."

Sec. 3. *And be it further enacted*, That any person or persons, firm, company, or corporation, who shall issue tickets or contracts of insurance against fatal or non-fatal injury to persons while traveling by land or water, shall pay a duty of one per centum on the gross amount of all the receipts for such insurance, and shall be subject to all the provisions and regulations of existing law applicable thereto, in relation to insurance companies : *Provided*, That no stamp duty shall be required upon tickets or contracts of insurance, as aforesaid, when limited to fatal or non-fatal injury to persons while traveling.

Sec. 4. *And be it further enacted*, That all contracts for the purchase or sale of gold or silver coin or bullion, and all contracts for the loan of money or currency secured by pledge or deposit, or other disposition of gold or silver coin of the United States, if to be performed after a period exceeding three days, shall be in writing or printed, and signed by the parties or their agents or attorneys ; and shall have one or more adhesive stamps, as provided in the act to which this is an amendment, equal in amount to one-half of one per centum, and interest at the rate of six per centum per annum on the amount so loaned, pledged, or deposited. And if any such loan, pledge, or deposit, made for a period not exceeding three days, shall be renewed or in any way extended for any time whatever, said loan, pledge, or deposit shall be subject to the duty imposed on loans exceeding three days. And no loan of currency or money on the security of gold or silver coin of the United States, as aforesaid, or of any certificate or other evidence of deposit payable in gold or silver coin, shall be made exceeding in amount the par value of the coin pledged or deposited as security ; and any such loan so made or attempted to be made shall be utterly void : *Provided*, That if gold or silver coin be loaned at its par value, it shall be subject only to the duty imposed on other loans : *Provided, however*, That nothing herein contained shall apply to any transaction by or with the Government of the United States.

Sec. 5. *And be it further enacted*, That all contracts, loans, or sales of gold and silver coin and bullion, not made in accordance with this act, shall be wholly and absolutely void ; and in addition to the penalties provided in the act to which this is an amendment, any party to said contract may, at any time within one year from the date of the contract, bring suit before any court of competent jurisdiction to recover back, for his own use and benefit, the money paid on any contract not made in accordance with this act.

Sec. 6. *And be it further enacted*, That section one hundred and ten be, and hereby is, amended as follows : "Any memorandum, check, receipt, or other written or printed evidence of an amount of money to be paid on demand, or at a time designated, shall be considered as a promissory note within the meaning of that section, and shall be stamped accordingly ; and that Schedule B, following said section, be and is hereby amended, so that any inland bill of exchange, draft, or order for the payment of any sum of money exceeding twenty dollars, otherwise than at sight or on demand, and any promissory note, shall (in lieu of the duties prescribed in Schedule B) have a stamp or stamps affixed thereon denoting a duty, upon every sum of two hundred dollars or any fractional part thereof, if payable on demand or at any time not exceeding thirty-three days, including the grace, from the date or sight, of one cent (01).

If payable at any time not less than thirty-three days, as aforesaid, and not exceeding sixty-three days, including the grace, from date or sight, of two cents (02).

If payable at any time not less than sixty-three days, as aforesaid, and not exceeding ninety-three days, including the grace, from date or sight, of three cents (03).

If payable at any time not less than ninety-three days, as aforesaid, and not exceeding four months from date or sight and grace, of four cents (04).

If payable at any time not less than four months, as aforesaid, and not exceeding six months from date or sight, or grace, of six cents (06).

8

If payable at any time exceeding six months from date or sight and grace, of ten cents (10).

And that Schedule B, following section one hundred and ten, be, and is hereby, further amended, so that the stamp duty on certificates of any other description than those specified in said schedule, in lieu of ten cents as therein prescribed, shall be five cents (05).

On passage tickets by any vessel from a port of the United States to a foreign port, costing thirty dollars or less, fifty cents (50).

On any power of attorney for the sale or transfer of any scrip or certificate of profits or memorandum, showing an interest in the profits or accumulations of any corporation or association, if for a sum not exceeding fifty dollars, ten cents (10).

On any policy of insurance or other instrument, by whatever name the same shall be called, by which insurance shall be made or renewed upon property of any description, whether against perils by sea, or by fire, or other peril of any kind, made by any insurance company or its agents, or by any other company or person, in which the premium or assessment shall not exceed ten dollars, ten cents (10).

On any bill of sale by which any ship or vessel, or any part thereof, shall be conveyed to or vested in any other person or persons, when the consideration shall not exceed five hundred dollars, there shall be affixed a stamp or stamps denoting a duty of twenty-five cents (25).

If the consideration exceeds five hundred, and does not exceed one thousand dollars, the duty shall be fifty cents (50).

If the consideration exceeds one thousand dollars, for each and every additional amount of one thousand dollars, or any fractional part thereof, in excess of one thousand dollars, the duty in addition shall be fifty cents (50).

On each and every assignment or transfer of a mortgage, lease, or policy of insurance, a stamp duty shall be paid equal to that imposed on the original instrument.

Any power of attorney, conveyance, or document of any kind, made, or purporting to be made, in any foreign country, to be used in the United States, shall pay the same duty as is required by law on similar instruments or documents when made or issued in the United States ; and the party to whom the same is issued or by whom it is to be used, shall, before using the same, affix thereon the stamp or stamps indicating the duty required.

Any mortgage or personal bond for the payment of money, or as security for the payment of any definite or certain sum of money, in lieu of the duties imposed as prescribed in Schedule B, following the one hundred and tenth section, shall have a stamp or stamps affixed thereon denoting a duty upon every sum of two hundred dollars, or any fractional part thereof, of ten cents (10).

No conveyance, deed, mortgage, or writing, whereby any lands, tenements, realty, or other property shall be sold, granted, assigned, or otherwise conveyed, or shall be made as security for the payment of any sum of money, shall be required to pay a stamp duty of more than the sum of one thousand dollars, anything to the contrary notwithstanding.

No stamp duty shall be required on powers of attorney or any other paper relating to applications for bounties, arrearages of pay, or pensions, or to the receipt thereof from time to time, or indemnity awarded for depredations and injuries by certain bands of Sioux Indians ; nor on any warrant of attorney accompanying a bond or note, when such bond or note shall have affixed thereto the stamp or stamps denoting the duty required ; and whenever any bond or note shall be secured by a mortgage, but one stamp duty shall be required to be placed on such papers : *Provided*, That the stamp duty placed thereon is the highest rate required for said instruments, or either of them ; nor on certificates of the measurement or weight of animals, wood, coal, or other articles ; nor on deposit notes to mutual insurance companies for insurance upon which policies subject to stamp duties have been, or are to be, issued ; nor any certificate of the record of a deed or other instrument in writing, or of the acknowledgment or proof thereof by attesting witnesses.

The duty or stamp required for transportation by express companies and others is hereby repealed, and such transportation shall be exempt from stamp duty.

That the stamp duty on a contract or agreement for the charter of any ship, or vessel, or steamer, as now provided for in Schedule B, or any letter, memorandum, or other writing between the captain, master, or owner, or person acting as agent of any ship, or vessel, or steamer, and any other person or persons for or relating to the charter of such ship, or vessel, or steamer, if the registered tonnage of such ship, or vessel, or steamer does not exceed one hundred and fifty tons, shall be one dollar ($1).

Exceeding one hundred and fifty tons, and not exceeding three hundred tons, three dollars ($3).

Exceeding three hundred tons, and not exceeding six hundred tons, five dollars ($5).

Exceeding six hundred tons, ten dollars ($10).

SEC. 7. *And be it further enacted*, That the Commissioner of Internal Revenue be, and he is hereby authorized to prescribe such method for the cancellation of stamps as a substitute for, or in addition to, the method now prescribed by law, as he may deem expedient and effectual. And he is further authorized in his discretion to make the application of such method imperative upon the manufacturers of proprietary articles, and upon stamps of a nominal value exceeding twenty-five cents each.

CANAL AND TURNPIKE COMPANIES.

SEC. 8. *And be it further enacted*, That on and after the passage of this act, any person or persons owning or possessing, or having the care or management of any canal company, or canal navigation or slack-water corporation, or turnpike companies, being indebted for any sum or sums of money for which bonds or other evidences of indebtedness have been issued, payable in one or more years after date, upon which interest is, or shall be, stipulated to be paid, or coupons representing the interest shall be or shall have been issued to be paid ; and all dividends in scrip or money, or sums of money thereafter declared due or payable to stockholders of any canal navigation, or slack-water or turnpike company, as part of the earnings, profits, or gains of said companies, shall be subject to and pay a duty of three per centum on the amount of all such interest, or coupons, or dividends, whenever the same shall be paid ; and said canal companies or canal navigation, or slack-water corporations, or turnpike companies, or any person or persons owning, possessing, or having the care or management of any canal company, or canal navigation or slack-water corporation, or turnpike company, are hereby authorized and required to deduct and withhold from all payments made to any person, persons, or party, after the first day of July, as aforesaid, on account of any interest, or coupons, or dividends due and payable, as aforesaid, the said duty or sum of three per centum ; and the duties deducted, as aforesaid, and certified by the president or other proper officer of said company or corporation, shall be a receipt and discharge, according to the amount thereof, of said canal companies, or canal navigation, or slack-water corporations, or turnpike companies, and the owners, possessors, and agents thereof, on dividends and on bonds or other evidences of their indebtedness upon which interest or coupons are payable, holden by any person or party whatsoever, and a list or return shall be made and rendered within thirty days after the time fixed when said interest, or coupons, or dividends become due or payable, and as often as every six months, to the Commissioner of Internal Revenue, which shall contain a true and faithful account of the duties received and chargeable as aforesaid, during the time when such duties have accrued, or should accrue, and remaining unaccounted for ; and there shall be annexed to every such list or return a declaration, under oath or affirmation, in manner and form as may be prescribed by the Commissioner of Internal Revenue, of the president, treasurer, or some proper officer of said canal company, or canal or navigation and slack-water corporation or turnpike companies, that the same contains a true and faithful account of the duties so withheld and received during the time when such duties have accrued, or should accrue, and not accounted for ; and for any default in the making or rendering of such list or return, with the declaration annexed, as aforesaid, the person or persons owning, possessing, or having the care or management of such canal company or canal, navigation, or slack-water corporation, or turnpike companies, making such default, shall forfeit, as a penalty, the sum of five hundred dollars ; and in case of any default in making or rendering said list, or of any default in the payment of the duty, or any part thereof, accruing or which should accrue, the assessment and collection shall be made according to the general provisions of the act to which this act is an amendment.

FERRY-BOATS.

SEC. 9. *And be it further enacted*, That any person or persons, firms, companies, or corporations, owning or possessing, or having the care or management of any ferry-boat, or vessel used as a ferry-boat, propelled by steam or horse power, in lieu of the duties now imposed by law, shall be subject to pay a duty of one and one half of one per centum upon the gross receipts of such ferry-boat; and the return and payment thereof shall be made in the manner prescribed in the act to which this act is an amendment.

EXPRESS COMPANIES.

SEC. 10. *And be it further enacted*, That on and after the first day of April, eighteen hundred and sixty-three, any person or persons, firms, companies, or corporations carrying on or doing an express business, shall, in lieu of the tax and stamp duties imposed by existing laws, be subject to and pay a duty of two per centum on the gross amount of all the receipts of such express business, and shall be subject to the same provisions, rules, and penalties as are prescribed in section eighty of the act to which this is an amendment, for the persons, firms, companies, or corporations owning or possessing or having the management of railroads, steamboats, and ferry-boats; and all acts, or part of acts, inconsistent herewith, are hereby repealed.

INCOME.

SEC. 11. *And be it further enacted*, That in estimating the annual gains, profit, or income of any person under the act to which this act is an amendment, the amount actually paid by such person for the rent of the dwelling-house or estate on which he resides shall be first deducted from the gains, profit, or income of such person.

ALE, BEER, ETC., COAL OIL, DISTILLED SPIRITS, COTTON OR WOOLEN FABRICS MANUFACTURED PRIOR TO SEPTEMBER 1st, 1862.

SEC. 12. *And be it further enacted*, That no duty shall be required to be assessed or collected on beer, lager beer, ale, or porter, brewed or manufactured, or on coal illuminating oil, refined, produced by the distillation of coal, asphaltum, shale, peat, petroleum, or rock oil, distilled spirits, cotton or woolen fabrics, when brewed, manufactured, or distilled prior to the first day of September, eighteen hundred and sixty-two, whether the same was removed for consumption or sale, or not, when the owner, agent, or superintendent of the brewery or premises in which such articles as aforesaid were made, manufactured, produced, or distilled, shall furnish to the assessor of the district, without costs or expense to the United States, satisfactory proof that such beer, lager beer, ale, or porter, or such coal illuminating oil, refined, produced by the distillation of coal, asphaltum, shale, peat, petroleum, or rock oil, distilled spirits, cotton or woolen fabrics, was actually brewed, manufactured, produced, or distilled prior to the first day of September, eighteen hundred and sixty-two, as aforesaid : *Provided*, That, in addition to the fractional parts of a barrel allowed in section fifty of the act to which this act is an amendment, fractional parts of a barrel may be thirds and sixths when the quantity therein contained is not greater than such fractional part represents : *Provided, further*, That from and after the passage of this act, and until the first day of April, eighteen hundred and sixty-four, there shall be paid on all beer, lager beer, ale, porter, and other similar fermented liquors, by whatever name such liquors may be called, a duty only of sixty cents for each and every barrel containing not more than thirty-one gallons, and at a like rate for any other quantity or for fractional parts of a barrel : *And provided, further*, That the Commissioner of Internal Revenue is authorized to make rules providing for deductions on account of leakage, from the quantity of spirituous liquors subject to taxation, under the act to which this act is an amendment, not exceeding five per centum of the amount removed for sale ; and said deduction shall be so adjusted in the different parts of the United States as to be proportioned, as nearly as practicable, to the distances over which the manufacturer usually transports said liquors for the wholesale thereof ; and the owner of the aforesaid liquors shall be charged with and pay the expense of ascertaining the leakage.

SEC. 13. *And be it further enacted*, That any brewer of ale, beer, lager beer, porter, or other malt liquors, shall be required to render accounts and make returns on the first day of each and every month, and no oftener. And no brewer of ale, beer, lager beer, porter, or other malt liquors, shall hereafter be required to keep a record or an account, or to report or return the quantities of grain or other vegetable productions, or other substances put into the mash-tub by him or his agent or superintendent, for the purpose of producing malt liquors, any law to the contrary notwithstanding.

BANKS.

SEC. 14. *And be it further enacted*, That every incorporated bank, or other bank legally authorized to issue notes as circulation, which shall neglect or omit to make dividends or additions to its surplus or contingent fund as often as once in six months, shall, in lieu thereof, make returns, under oath, to the Commissioner of Internal Revenue, on the first days of January and July in each year, or within thirty days thereafter, of the amount of profits which have accrued or been earned and received by said bank during the six months next preceding said first days of January and July; and, at the time of making such returns, shall pay to the Commissioner of Internal Revenue a duty of three per cent. on such profits, and shall be subject to the provisions of the eighty-second section of the act to which this is an addition : *Provided*, That the return for the first day of January, eighteen hundred and sixty-three, shall be made within thirty days after the passage of this act.

ASSESSMENT OF LICENSES.

SEC. 15. *And be it further enacted*, That the several Assessors shall, on the first Monday of May next, and on the first Monday of May in each succeeding year, direct and cause the several Assistant Assessors to proceed through every part of their respective districts, and inquire after and concerning all persons being within the assessment districts where they respectively reside, and liable to license duty under the provisions of this act, or of the act to which this is an addition, and assess such persons as in said acts is required. And all licenses so assessed shall continue in force until the first day of May next succeeding. And all licenses granted after the first day of May in any year shall expire on the first day of May following, and shall be issued upon the payment of a ratable proportion of the whole amount of duty imposed for such license ; and each license so granted shall be dated on the first day of the month in which it is issued : *Provided*, That any person, firm, or corporation that on the first day of May next shall hold an unexpired license, shall be assessed a ratable proportion for the time between the expiration of the license and the first day of May, eighteen hundred and sixty-four.

ADHESIVE STAMPS AND STAMPED PAPER.

SEC. 16. *And be it further enacted*, That in any Collection District where, in the judgment of the Commissioner of Internal Revenue, the facilities for the procurement and distribution of stamped vellum, parchment, or paper, and adhesive stamps are or shall be insufficient, the Commissioner, as aforesaid, is authorized to furnish, supply, and deliver, to the Collector of any such district a suitable quantity or amount of stamped vellum, parchment, or paper, and adhesive stamps, without prepayment therefor, and shall allow the highest rate of commissions to the collector allowed by law to any other parties purchasing the same, and may, in advance, require of any such collector a bond, with sufficient sureties to an amount equal to the value of any stamped vellum, parchment, or paper, and adhesive stamps which may be placed in his hands and remain unaccounted for, conditioned for the faithful return, whenever so required, of all quantities or amounts undisposed of, and for the payment, monthly, of all quantities or amounts sold or not, remaining on hand. And it shall be the duty of such collector to supply his deputies with, or sell to other parties within his district who may make applications therefor, stamped vellum, parchment, or paper, and adhesive stamps upon the same terms allowed by law, or under the regulations of the Commissioner of Internal Revenue, who is hereby authorized to make such other regulations, not inconsistent herewith, for the security of the United States and the better accommodation of the public in relation to the matters hereinbefore mentioned, as he may judge necessary and expedient : *Provided*, That no instrument, document, or

paper made, signed, or issued prior to the first day of June, Anno Domini eighteen
hundred and sixty-three, without being duly stamped, or having thereon an adhesive stamp to denote the duty imposed thereon, shall, for that cause, be deemed invalid and of no effect: *And provided*, That no instrument, document, writing, or
paper, required by law to be stamped, signed, or issued, without being duly stamped
prior to the day aforesaid, or any copy thereof, shall be admitted or used as evidence
in any court until a legal stamp, or stamps, denoting the amount of duty charged
thereon, shall have been affixed thereto or used thereon, and the initials of the
persons using or affixing the same, together with the date when the same is so used
or affixed, shall have been placed thereon by such person. And the person desiring
to use any such instrument, document, writing, or paper as evidence, or his agent
or attorney, is authorized in the presence of the court to stamp the same as heretofore provided by law.

OFFICERS OF INTERNAL REVENUE.

SEC. 17. *And be it further enacted*, That, in addition to the compensation now allowed to Collectors for their services, and that of their deputies, there shall be
allowed their necessary and reasonable charges for postage actually paid on letters
and documents received or sent and exclusively relating to official business ; and in
calculating the commission of Collectors of Internal Revenue in districts where
distilled spirits are shipped to be sold in other districts in pursuance of the provisions of the act to which this act is an amendment, the amount of duties due on
the quantity of spirits so shipped shall be added to the principal on which the commissions of such Collectors are calculated, and a corresponding amount shall be deducted from the principal sum on which the commissions of the Collectors in the
districts to which such spirits are shipped are calculated : *Provided, however*, That the
salary of no Collector shall exceed ten thousand dollars in the aggregate, or more
than five thousand dollars exclusive of the expenses of administering the office.

SEC. 18. *And be it further enacted*, That it shall be the duty of the Commissioner of
Internal Revenue to pay over to the Treasurer of the United States monthly, or
oftener, if required by the Secretary of the Treasury, all public moneys which may
come into his hands or possession, for which the Treasurer shall give proper receipts,
and keep a faithful account, and at the end of each month the Commissioner, as
aforesaid, shall render true and faithful accounts of all public moneys received or
paid out, or paid to the Treasurer of the United States, exhibiting proper vouchers
therefor, and the same shall be received and examined by the Fifth Auditor of the
Treasury, who shall thereafter certify the balance, if any, and transmit the accounts,
with the vouchers and certificate, to the First Comptroller for his decision thereon ;
and the Commissioner, as aforesaid, when such accounts are settled as herein provided for, shall transmit a copy thereof to the Secretary of the Treasury. He shall
at all times submit to the Secretary of the Treasury and the Comptroller, or either
of them, the inspection of moneys in his hands, and shall, prior to the entering
upon the duties of his office, execute a bond, with sufficient sureties, to be approved
by the Secretary of the Treasury and by the First Comptroller, in a sum of not less
than one hundred thousand dollars, payable to the United States, conditioned that
said Commissioner shall faithfully perform the duties of his office according to law,
and shall justly and faithfully account for and pay over to the United States, in
obedience to law and in compliance with the order or regulations of the Secretary
of the Treasury, all public moneys which may come into his hands or possession,
and for the safe-keeping and faithful account of all stamps, adhesive stamps, or
vellum, parchment, or paper, bearing a stamp denoting any duty thereon ; which
bond shall be filed in the office of the First Comptroller of the Treasury, and such
Commissioner shall, from time to time, renew, strengthen, and increase his official
bond as the Secretary of the Treasury may direct.

SEC. 19. *And be it further enacted*, That the President shall appoint in the Department of the Treasury, by and with the advice and consent of the Senate, a competent person, who shall be called the Deputy Commissioner of Internal Revenue,
with an annual salary of twenty-five hundred dollars, who shall be charged with
such duties in the Bureau of Internal Revenue as may be prescribed by the Secretary
of the Treasury, or as may be required by law, and who shall act as Commissioner
of Internal Revenue in the absence of that officer, and exercise the privilege of franking all letters and documents pertaining to the Office of Internal Revenue.

Sec. 20. *And be it further enacted*, That the Secretary of the Treasury may appoint, not exceeding three revenue agents, whose duties shall be, under the direction of the Secretary of the Treasury, to aid in the prevention, detection, and punishment of frauds upon the revenue, who shall be paid such compensation as the Secretary of the Treasury may deem just and reasonable, not exceeding two thousand dollars per annum. The above salaries to be paid in the same manner as are other expenses for collecting the revenue.

Sec. 21. *And be it further enacted*, That the President of the United States be, and he is hereby, authorized to appoint, by and with the advice and consent of the Senate, a competent person, who shall be called the Cashier of Internal Duties, with a salary of twenty-five hundred dollars, who shall have charge of the moneys received in the office of the Commissioner of Internal Revenue, and shall perform such duties as may be assigned to his office by said Commissioner, under the regulations of the Secretary of the Treasury; and before entering upon his duties as cashier he shall give a bond with sufficient sureties, to be approved by the Secretary of the Treasury and by the Solicitor, that he will faithfully account for all the moneys, or other articles of value, belonging to the United States, which may come into his hands, and perform all the duties enjoined upon his office, according to law and regulations, as aforesaid; which bond shall be deposited with the First Comptroller of the Treasury.

Sec. 22. *And be it further enacted*, That in lieu of the pay allowed by law, the several Assessors, from the date of their appointment, shall be allowed and paid a salary of fifteen hundred dollars per annum, payable quarterly, and in addition thereto, where the receipts of the collection district shall exceed the sum of two hundred thousand dollars, and shall not exceed the sum of four hundred thousand dollars annually, one half of one per centum upon the excess of receipts over two hundred thousand dollars; where the receipts of a collection district shall exceed four hundred thousand dollars, and shall not exceed eight hundred thousand dollars, one fourth of one per centum upon the excess of receipts over four hundred thousand dollars; where the receipts shall exceed eight hundred thousand dollars, one tenth of one per centum upon such excess; but the salary of no Assessor shall in any case exceed the sum of three thousand dollars. And the several Assessors shall be allowed and paid the sums actually expended for office rent, not exceeding the rate of five hundred dollars per annum. The Commissioner of Internal Revenue, under the direction of the Secretary of the Treasury, is authorized to allow each Assessor such clerks as he may deem necessary for the proper transaction of business, and to fix their compensation. Such Assessors shall also be allowed their necessary and reasonable charges for postage actually paid on letters and documents received or sent, and exclusively relating to official business, and for stationery and blank books used in the execution of their duties; and the compensation herein specified shall be in full for all expenses not otherwise particularly authorized. And Assistant Assessors shall, in addition to pay and charges allowed by law, also be allowed their necessary and reasonable charges for postage actually paid on letters and documents received or sent, and exclusively relating to official business : *Provided*, That the Secretary of the Treasury shall be, and he is hereby, authorized to fix such additional rates of compensation to be made to Assessors and Assistant Assessors in the States of California and Oregon, and the Territories, as may appear to him to be just and equitable in consequence of the greater cost of living and traveling in those States and Territories, and as may, in his judgment, be necessary to secure the services of competent and efficient men : *Provided further*, That the rates of compensation thus allowed shall not exceed the rates paid to similar officers in such States and Territories, respectively.

Sec. 23. *And be it further enacted*, That Assistant Assessors shall make out their accounts for pay and charges allowed by law monthly, specifying each item and including the date of each day of service, and shall transmit the same to the Assessor of the District, who shall thereupon examine the same, and if it appear just and in accordance with law, he shall indorse his approval thereon, but otherwise shall return the same with objections. Any such account so approved may be presented by the Assistant Assessor to the Collector of the district for payment, who shall thereupon pay the same, and, when receipted by the Assistant Assessor, be allowed therefor upon presentation to the Commissioner of Internal Revenue. Where any account, so transmitted to the Assessor, shall be objected to, in whole or in part, the Assistant Assessor may appeal to the Commissioner of Internal Revenue, whose decision on the case shall be final ; and should it appear at any time that any Assessor has willfully and corruptly approved any account, as aforesaid, allowing any Assistant Assessor a sum larger than was due according to law, it shall be the duty of the Commissioner of Internal Revenue, upon proper proof thereof, to deduct the sum so allowed from any pay which may be due to such Assessor ; or the Commissioner, as aforesaid, may direct a suit to be brought in any court of competent jurisdiction against the Assessor or Assistant Assessor in default for the recovery of the amount willfully and corruptly allowed, as hereinbefore mentioned.

GENERAL PROVISIONS.

SEC. 24. *And be it further enacted,* That if any person or persons shall knowingly exercise or carry on any trade or business, for the exercising or carrying on of which trade or business a license is required, without taking out such license as is in that behalf required, he, she, or they shall, for every such offense, upon conviction thereof, in lieu of or in addition to other penalties now imposed by law, at the discretion of the court, be subject to imprisonment for a term not exceeding two years.

SEC. 25. *And be it further enacted,* That no auctioneer shall be authorized, by virtue of his license as such auctioneer, to sell any goods or other property in any other district than that in which the license shall have been granted ; but lawyers, physicians, surgeons, or dentists, having taken out a license as such, shall not be required to take out any additional license in consequence of practicing their profession within or beyond the limits of the district where licensed.

SEC. 26. *And be it further enacted,* That, upon the removal of any person or persons from the house or premises at which he, she, or they were authorized by license to exercise or carry on any trade or business mentioned in such license, and authorized by the act to which this act is an amendment, it shall and may be lawful for the person or persons authorized to grant licenses to authorize and empower, by indorsement on such license or otherwise, as the Commissioner of Internal Revenue shall direct, the person or persons so removing, as aforesaid, to any other place, to carry on the trade or business specified in such license at the place to which such person or persons may have removed, for or during the residue of the term for which such license was originally granted, without taking out any fresh license or payment of any additional duty, or any fee thereupon, for the residue of such term, and until the expiration thereof: *Provided, always,* that a fresh entry of the premises at which such trade or business shall continue to be so exercised or carried on, as aforesaid, shall thereupon be made by and in the name or names of the person or persons to whom such authority, as aforesaid, shall be granted.

SEC. 27. *And be it further enacted,* That any person who shall offer for sale, after the thirtieth of September, eighteen hundred and sixty-three, any of the articles named in Schedule C of the act to which this act is an amendment, whether the articles so offered are imported or are of foreign or domestic manufacture, shall be deemed the manufacturer thereof, and subject to all the duties, liabilities, and penalties in said act imposed in regard to the sale of such articles without the use of the proper stamp or stamps as in said act is required.

SEC. 28. *And be it further enacted,* That all medicines, preparations, compositions, perfumery, and cosmetics, intended for exportation, as provided for in section one hundred and nine of the act to which this act is an amendment, in order to be manufactured and sold or removed, without being charged with duty, and without having a stamp affixed thereto, may, under such rules and regulations as the Secretary of the Treasury may prescribe, be made and manufactured in warehouses known and designated in treasury regulations as bonded warehouses, class two : *Provided,* Such manufacturer shall first give satisfactory bonds to the Collector of Internal Revenue for the faithful observance of the rules and regulations herein provided for. in amount not less than half required by the regulations of the Secretary of the Treasury from persons allowed bonded warehouses, class two. Such goods, when manufactured in such warehouses, may be removed for exportation, under the direction of the revenue officer having charge thereof, without being charged with duty, and without having a stamp affixed thereto. Any manufacturer of the articles aforesaid, or of any of them, having such bonded warehouse as aforesaid, shall be at liberty, under such rules and regulations as the Secretary of the Treasury may prescribe, to convey therein any materials to be used in such manufacture which are allowed by the provisions of the said act to be exported free from tax or duty, as well as the necessary materials, implements, packages, vessels, brands, and labels for the preparation, putting up, and export of the said manufactured articles; and every article so used shall be exempt from stamp and excise duty. Articles and materials so to be used may be transferred from any bonded warehouse in which the same may be, under such regulations as the Secretary of the Treasury may prescribe, into any bonded warehouse, class two, in which such manufacture may be conducted, and may be used in such manufacture, and when so used shall be exempt from stamp and excise duty, and the receipt of the officer of the revenue in charge shall be received as a voucher for the manufacture of such articles. Any materials imported into the United States may, under such rules as the Secretary of the Treasury may prescribe, and under the direction of the proper officer of the customs, be removed in original packages from on ship-board, or from the bonded warehouses in which the same may be, into the bonded warehouse, class two, in which such manufacture may be carried on, for the purpose of being used in such manufacture, without payment of duties thereon, and may there be used in such manufacture. No article so removed, nor any article manufactured in said bonded warehouse, class two, shall be taken therefrom except for exportation, under the direction of the proper officer of the customs having charge thereof, whose certificate, describing the articles by their marks, or otherwise, the quantity, the date of importation, and name of vessel, with such additional particulars as may from time to time be required, shall be received by the Collector of Customs in cancellation of the bonds, or return of the amount of foreign import duties. All labor performed and services rendered under these regulations shall be under the supervision of an officer of the customs, and at the expense of the manufacturer.

Sec. 29. *And be it further enacted*, That spokes, hubs, felloes, grindstones, coke, silver bullion, rolled or prepared for platers' use exclusively; materials for the manufacture of hoop skirts exclusively, and unfitted for other use (such as steel wire, rolled, tempered, or covered, cut tapes, and small wares for joining hoops together); spindles, and castings of all descriptions, where made exclusively for instruments, articles, or machinery upon which duties are assessed and paid, shall be exempt from duty; and all goods, wares, and merchandise, and articles made or manufactured from materials which have been subject to and upon which internal duties have been actually paid, or materials imported upon which duties have been paid, or upon which no duties are imposed by law, where the increased value of such goods, wares, and merchandise, and articles so made and manufactured shall not exceed the amount of five per centum ad valorem, shall be, and hereby are, exempt from duty.

Sec. 30. *And be it further enacted*, That on oil cloths of silk, cotton, or other materials, dyed, printed, bleached, manufactured, or prepared into other fabrics, which were removed from the place of manufacture prior to the first of September, eighteen hundred and sixty-two, or which have been or shall be imported, the duty or tax of three per centum shall be assessed only upon the increased value thereof: *Provided further*, That whenever the duty has been assessed, or assessed and collected at the full value thereof upon cloths of silk, cotton, or other material manufactured and removed from the place of manufacture prior to the first of September, eighteen hundred and sixty-two, or which were imported prior to the passage of this act, and which have been dyed, printed, bleached, manufactured, or otherwise prepared into other fabrics since the said first of September, eighteen hundred and sixty-two, the Commissioner of Internal Revenue, subject to the regulation of the Secretary of the Treasury, shall be, and he hereby is, authorized and directed to remit, refund, and pay back such proportion of said duties as were assessed upon the value of such cloths before the same were so dyed, printed, bleached, manufactured, or otherwise prepared.

Sec. 31. *And be it further enacted*, That the Commissioner of Internal Revenue, subject to the regulations of the Secretary of the Treasury, shall be, and hereby is, authorized to remit, refund, and pay back all duties erroneously or illegally assessed or collected, and all judgments or sums of money recovered in any court against any Collector or Deputy Collector for any duties or licenses paid under protest.

Sec 32. *And be it further enacted*, That manufacturers of lard oil, lubricating oil, and linseed oil shall be subject to the provisions of the act to which this is an amendment, relating to distillers of spirituous liquors, and designed for the purpose of ascertaining the quantity produced, so far as the same may, in the judgment of the Commissioner of Internal Revenue, and under regulations to be prescribed by him, be deemed necessary.

SEC. 33. *And be it further enacted,* That the provisions of the act to which this act is an amendment, in relation to returns by manufacturers, and the payment and collection of duties upon manufactured articles, enumerated in section seventy-five of said act, shall be, and hereby are, made applicable to the producers of articles which are also mentioned in said section, and on which taxes are levied.

INSPECTORS OF MANUFACTURED TOBACCO.

SEC. 34. *And be it further enacted,* That there shall be designated by the Collector in every district where the same may be necessary one or more inspectors of manufactured tobacco, who shall take an oath faithfully to perform their duties in such form as the Commissioner of Internal·Revenue shall prescribe, and who shall be entitled to receive such fees as may be fixed and prescribed by said Commissioner. And all manufactured tobacco shall, before the same is used or removed for consumption or sale, be inspected and weighed by an inspector, designated as aforesaid, who shall mark upon the box or other package containing such tobacco, in a manner to be prescribed by said Commissioner, the quality and weight of the contents of such package, with the date of inspection and the name of the inspector. The fees of such inspector shall in all cases be paid by the owner of the tobacco so inspected and weighed. The penalties for the fraudulent marking of any package of tobacco, and for any fraudulent attempt to evade, the duties on tobacco, so inspected, by changing in any manner the package or the marks thereon, shall be the same as are provided in relation to distilled spirits by existing laws. That manufactured tobacco may be removed from the place of manufacture for the purpose of being exported, after the quantity and quality to be so removed shall have been ascertained by inspection, according to the provisions of this act, upon and with the written permission of the Collector or Deputy Collector of the district, without payment of the duties thereon previous to such removal, the owner thereof having given bond to the United States, with sufficient sureties in the manner and form and under regulations to be prescribed by the Commissioner of Internal Revenue, and in at least double the amount of said duties, to export the said manufactured tobacco or pay the duties thereon within such time as may be stated in the bond ; and all the provisions relative to the exportation of distilled spirits in bond, contained in the act to which this is an amendment, as far as the same may be applicable, shall be applied to the exportation of tobacco in bond : *Provided, however,* that nothing herein contained shall be considered to apply to snuff, fine-cut tobacco, or cigars.

DRAWBACK.

SEC. 35. *And be it further enacted,* That the evidence of exportation to entitle to benefit of drawback under the act to provide internal revenue to which this act is an amenduent, and the rules and regulations pertaining thereto, shall be the same as those which are now or may be required to entitle the exporter to benefit of drawback under the acts relating to drawbacks of duties on imports, with such other rules and regulations as the Secretary of the Treasury may prescribe ; that the bureau in charge of exports for the benefit of drawback under the acts as aforesaid at the port of New York (and at such other ports as the Secretary of the Treasury may designate), shall have charge of the same under the act to which this act is an amendment ; that the head of such bureau shall be invested with the authority and receive the emoluments of a deputy of the Collector of Customs; and that the said bureau shall, under the direction of the Collector of the Customs, embrace the supervision of all exports entitled to remission of duties, or to drawback of duties paid, under the acts above mentioned ; the ascertaining and certifying such duties ; the taking and cancellation of required bonds ; the charge of all export entry papers for benefit of drawback and officers' returns thereon, and of certificates in proof of the landing of such exports abroad : *Provided,* That nothing herein contained shall be construed to change or modify the existing mode of paying the drawbacks and debentures allowed by the laws before referred to.

SEC. 36. *And be it further enacted,* That the Assistant Treasurer of the United States at San Francisco is required, under such instructions as the Commissioner of Internal Revenue shall prescribe, to audit, allow, and pay the accounts for services of the Collectors and Assessors of California, Oregon, and Nevada Territory, subject to the revision of the said Commissioner.

SEC. 37. *And be it further enacted,* That this act, except where otherwise indicated, shall take effect from and after its passage, and all acts and parts of acts repugnant to the provisions of this act be, and the same are hereby, repealed : *Provided,* That the existing laws shall extend to and be in force, as modified, for the collection of the duties imposed by this act, for the prosecution and punishment of all offenses, and for the recovery, collection, distribution, and remission of all fines, penalties, and forfeitures, as fully and effectually as if every regulation, penalty, forfeiture, provision, clause, matter, and thing to that effect, in the existing laws contained, had been inserted in, and re-enacted by, this act.

SEC. 38. *And be it further enacted,* That from and after the date when this act takes effect, there shall be an allowance or drawback on cordials and other liquors manufactured wholly or in part of domestic spirits, on which a duty shall have been paid equal in amount to the duty paid on such spirits when exported, with such deduction as the Secretary of the Treasury may think reasonable, not exceeding five per centum of the amount of duty so paid, the amount to be ascertained in the manner and under the regulations prescribed in section one hundred and sixteen of the act to which this is additional, and the same to be subject to all the provisions of said section applicable thereto : *Provided,* That no such allowance shall be made unless the value of the spirits used in such manufacture shall exceed one half of the whole value of the article manufactured, as aforesaid.

GALUSHA A. GROW,
Speaker of the House of Representatives.
SOLOMON FOOT,
President of the Senate pro tempore.

APPROVED March 3, 1863.

ABRAHAM LINCOLN.

THE FINANCE ACT.

AN act to provide ways and means for the support of the Government:

Be it enacted by the Senate and House of Representatives of the United States of America in Congress assembled, That the Secretary of the Treasury be and he is hereby authorized to borrow, from time to time, on the credit of the United States, a sum not exceeding three hundred millions of dollars for the current fiscal year, and six hundred millions for the next fiscal year, and to issue therefor coupon or registered bonds, payable at the pleasure of the Government after such periods as may be fixed by the Secretary, not less than ten nor more than forty years from date, in coin, and of such denominations not less than fifty dollars as he may deem expedient, bearing interest at a rate not exceeding six per centum per annum, payable on bonds not exceeding one hundred dollars, annually, and on all other bonds semi-annually, in coin; and he may in his discretion dispose of such bonds at any time, upon such terms as he may deem most advisable, for lawful money of the United States, or for any of the certificates of indebtedness or deposit that may at any time be unpaid, or for any of the treasury notes heretofore issued or which may be issued under the provisions of this act. And all the bonds and treasury notes or United States notes issued under the provisions of this act shall be exempt from taxation by or under State or municipal authority: *Provided,* That there shall be outstanding of bonds, treasury notes, and United States notes, at any time, issued under the provisions of this act, no greater amount altogether than the sum of nine hundred millions of dollars. ◆

SEC. 2. *And be it further enacted,* That the Secretary of the Treasury be and he is hereby authorized to issue, on the credit of the United States, four hundred millions of dollars in treasury notes, payable at the pleasure of the United States, or at such time or times not exceeding three years from date as may be found most beneficial to the public interest, and bearing interest at a rate not exceeding six per centum per annum, payable at periods expressed on the face of said treasury notes; and the interest on the said treasury notes and on certificates of indebtedness and deposit hereafter issued shall be paid in lawful money. The treasury notes thus issued shall be of such denomination as the Secretary may direct, not less than ten dollars, and may be disposed of on the best terms that can be obtained, or may be paid to any creditor of the United States willing to receive the same at par. And said treasury notes may be made a legal tender to the same extent as United States notes, for their face value excluding interest; or they may be made exchangeable under regulations prescribed by the Secretary of the Treasury, by the holder thereof at the Treasury in the city of Washington, or at the office of any assistant treasurer or depositary designated for that purpose, for United States notes equal in amount to the treasury notes offered for exchange, together with the interest accrued and due thereon at the date of interest payment next preceding such exchange. And in lieu of any amount of said treasury notes thus exchanged, or redeemed, or paid at maturity, the Secretary may issue an equal amount of other treasury notes; and the treasury notes so exchanged, redeemed, or paid, shall be canceled and destroyed as the Secretary may direct. In order to secure certain and prompt exchanges of United *of* States notes for treasury notes when required as above provided, the Secretary shall have power to issue United States notes to the amount of one hundred and fifty millions of dollars, which may be used if necessary for such exchanges; but no part of the United States notes authorized by this section shall be issued for or applied to any other purposes than said exchanges; and whenever any amount shall have been so issued and applied, the same shall be replaced as soon as practicable from the sales of treasury notes for United States notes.

SEC. 3. *And be it further enacted,* That the Secretary of the Treasury be and he is hereby authorized, if required by the exigencies of the public service, for the payment of the army and navy, and other creditors of the Government, to issue on the credit of the United States the sum of one hundred and fifty millions of dollars of United States notes, including the amount of such notes heretofore authorized by the joint resolution approved January seventeen, eighteen hundred and sixty-three, in such form as he may deem expedient, not bearing interest, payable to bearer, and of such denominations, not less than one dollar, as he may prescribe, which notes so issued shall be lawful money and a legal tender in payment of all debts, public and private, within the United States, except for duties on imports and interest on the public debt; and any of the said notes, when returned to the Treasurer, may be reissued from time to time as the exigencies of the public service may require. And in lieu of any of said notes, or any other United States notes, returned to the Treasury, and canceled or destroyed, there may be issued equal amounts of the United States notes, such as are authorized by this act. And so much of the act to authorize the issue of the United States notes, and for other purposes, approved February twenty-five, eighteen hundred and sixty-two, and of the act to authorize an additional issue of United States notes, and for other purposes, approved July eleven, eighteen hundred and sixty-two, as restricts the negotiation of bonds to market value, is hereby repealed. And the holders of United States notes, issued under and by virtue of said acts, shall present the same for the purpose of exchanging the same for bonds, as therein provided, on or before the first day of July, eighteen hundred and sixty-three, and thereafter the right so to exchange the same shall cease and determine.

SEC. 4. *And be it further enacted,* That in lieu of postage and revenue stamps for fractional currency, and of fractional notes, commonly called postage currency, issued or to be issued, the Secretary of the Treasury may issue fractional notes of like amounts in such form as he may deem expedient, and may provide for the engraving, preparation, and issue thereof in the Treasury Department building. And all such notes issued shall be exchangeable by the Assistant Treasurers and designated depositors for United States notes, in sums not less than three dollars, and shall be receivable for postage and revenue stamps, and also in payment of any dues to the United States less than five dollars, excepts duties on imports, and shall be redeemed on presentation at the Treasury of the United States in such sums and under such regulations as the Secretary of the Treasury shall prescribe : *Provided*, That the whole amount of fractional currency issued, including postage and revenue stamps issued as currency, shall not exceed fifty millions of dollars.

SEC. 5. *And be it further enacted*, That the Secretary of the Treasury is hereby authorized to receive deposits of gold coin and bullion with the Treasurer or any Assistant Treasurer of the United States, in sums not less than twenty dollars, and to issue certificates therefor in denominations of not less than twenty dollars each, corresponding with the denominations of the United States notes. The coin and bullion deposited for or representing the certificates of deposit shall be retained in the Treasury for the payment of the same on demand. And certificates representing coin in the Treasury may be issued in payment of interest on the public debt, which certificates, together with those issued for coin and bullion deposited, shall not at any time exceed twenty per centum beyond the amount of coin and bullion in the Treasury ; and the certificates for coin or bullion in the Treasury shall be received at par in payment for duties on imports.

SEC. 6. *And be it further enacted*, That the coupon or registered bonds, treasury notes, and United States notes authorized by this act, shall be in such form as the Secretary of the Treasury may direct, and shall have printed upon them such statements, showing the amount of accrued or accruing interest, the character of the notes, and the penalties or punishment for altering or counterfeiting them, as the Secretary of the Treasury may prescribe, and shall bear the written or engraved signatures of the Treasurer of the United States and the Register of the Treasury, and also, as evidence of lawful issue, the imprint of the copy of the seal of the Treasury Department, which imprint shall be made, under the direction of the Secretary, after the said notes or bonds shall be received from the engravers and before they are issued ; or the said notes and bonds shall be signed by the Treasurer of the United States, or for the Treasurer by such persons as may be specially appointed by the Secretary of the Treasury for that purpose, and shall be countersigned by the Register of the Treasury, or for the Register by such persons as the Secretary of the Treasury may specially appoint for that purpose. And all the provisions of the act entitled " An act to authorize the issue of treasury notes," approved the twenty-third day of December, eighteen hundred and fifty-seven, so far as they can be applied to this act, and not inconsistent therewith, are hereby revived and re-enacted.

SEC. 7. *And be it further enacted,* That all banks, associations, corporations, or individuals, issuing notes or bills for circulation as currency, shall be subject to and pay a duty of one per centum each half year from and after April first, eighteen hundred and sixty-three, upon the average amount of circulation of notes or bills as currency issued beyond the amount hereinafter named—that is to say, banks, associations, corporations, or individuals having a capital of not over one hundred thousand dollars, ninety per centum thereof; over one hundred thousand and not over two hundred thousand dollars, eighty per centum thereof; over two hundred thousand and not over three hundred thousand dollars, seventy per centum thereof; over three hundred thousand and not over five hundred thousand dollars, sixty per centum thereof; over five hundred thousand and not over one million of dollars, fifty per centum thereof; over one million and not over one million and a half of dollars, forty per centum thereof; over one million and a half, and not over two millions of dollars, thirty per centum thereof; over two millions of dollars, twenty-five per centum thereof. In the case of banks with branches, the duty herein provided for shall be imposed upon the circulation of the notes or bills of such branches severally, and not upon the aggregate circulation of all; and the amount of capital of each branch shall be considered to be the amount allotted to or used by such branch; and all such banks, associations, corporations, and individuals shall also be subject to and pay a duty of one-half of one per centum each half year from and after April first, eighteen hundred and sixty-three, upon the average amount of notes or bills not otherwise herein taxed and outstanding as currency during the six months next preceding the return hereinafter provided for ; and the rate of tax or duty imposed on the circulation of associations which may be organized under the act " to provide a national currency, secured by a pledge of United States stocks, and to provide for the circulation and redemption thereof," approved February twenty-fifth, eighteen hundred and sixty-three, shall be the same as that hereby imposed on the circulation and deposits of all banks, associations, corporations, or individuals, but shall be assessed and collected as required by said act ; all banks, associations, or corporations, and individuals issuing or reissuing notes or bills for circulation as currency after April first, eighteen hundred and sixty-three, in sums representing any fractional part of a dollar, shall be subject to and pay a duty of five per centum each half year thereafter upon the amount of such fractional notes or bills so issued. And all banks, associations, corporations, and individuals receiving deposits or money subject to payment on check or draft, except savings institutions, shall be subject to a duty of one-eighth of one per centum each half year from and after April first, eighteen hundred and sixty-three, upon the average amount of such deposits beyond the average amount of their circulating notes or bills lawfully issued and outstanding as currency. And a list or return shall be made and rendered within thirty days after the first day of October, eighteen hundred and sixty-three, and each six months thereafter, to the Commissioner of Internal Revenue, which shall contain a true and faithful account of the amount duties accrued, or which should accrue, on the full amount of the fractional note circulation and on the average amount of all other circulation and of all such deposits for the six months next preceding. And there shall be annexed to every such list or return a declaration, under oath or affirmation, to be made in form and manner as shall be prescribed by the Commissioner of Internal Revenue, of the president, or some other proper officer of said bank, association, corporation, or individual, respectively, that the same contains a true and faithful account of the duties which have accrued, or which should accrue, and not accounted for; and for any default in the delivery of such list or return, with such declaration annexed, the bank, association, corporation, or individual making such default, shall forfeit, as a penalty, the sum of five hundred dollars. And such bank, association, corporation, or individual shall, upon rendering the list or return as aforesaid, pay to the Commissioner of Internal Revenue the amount of the duties due on such list or return, and in default thereof shall forfeit, as a penalty, the sum of five hundred dollars ; and in case of neglect or refusal to make such list or return as aforesaid, or to pay the duties as aforesaid, for the space of thirty days after the time when said list should have been made or rendered, or when said duties shall have become due and payable, the assessment and collection shall be made according to the general provisions prescribed in an act entitled " An act to provide internal revenue to support the government and to pay interest on the public debt," approved July one, eighteen hundred and sixty-two.

Sec. 8. *And be it further enacted,* That, in order to prevent and punish counterfeiting and fraudulent alterations of the bonds, notes, and fractional currency authorized to be issued by this act, all the provisions of the sixth and seventh sections of the act entitled " An act to authorize the issue of United States notes, and for the redemption or funding thereof, and for funding the floating debt of the United States," approved February twenty-fifth, eighteen hundred and sixty-two, shall, so far as applicable, apply to the bonds, notes, and fractional currency hereby authorized to be issued, in like manner as if the said sixth and seventh sections were hereby adopted as additional sections of this act. And the provisions and penalties of said sixth and seventh sections shall extend and apply to all persons who shall imitate, counterfeit, make, or sell any paper such as that used, or provided to be used, for the fractional notes prepared, or to be prepared, in the Treasury Department building, and to all officials of the Treasury Department engaged in engraving and preparing the bonds, notes, and fractional currency hereby authorized to be issued, and to all official and unofficial persons in any manner employed under the provisions of this act. And the sum of six hundred thousand dollars is hereby appropriated, out of any money in the treasury not otherwise appropriated, to enable the Secretary of the Treasury to carry this act into effect.

Approved March 3, 1863.

THE CONSCRIPTION ACT.

AN act for enrolling and calling out the national forces, and for other purposes:

Whereas, There now exist in the United States an insurrection and rebellion against the authority thereof, and it is, under the Constitution of the United States, the duty of the Government to suppress insurrection and rebellion, to guarantee to each State a republican form of government, and to preserve the public tranquillity; and *whereas*, for these high purposes, a military force is indispensable, to raise and support which all persons ought willingly to contribute; and *whereas*, no service can be more praiseworthy and honorable than that which is rendered for the maintenance of the Constitution and Union, and the consequent preservation of free government, therefore

Be it enacted by the Senate and House of Representatives of the United States of America, in Congress assembled, That all able-bodied male citizens of the United States, and persons of foreign birth who shall have declared on oath their intention to become citizens under and in pursuance of the laws thereof, between the ages of twenty and forty-five years, except as hereinafter excepted, are hereby declared to constitute the national forces, and shall be liable to perform military duty in the service of the United States when called out by the President for that purpose.

SEC. 2. *And be it further enacted,* That the following persons be, and they are hereby, excepted and exempt from the provisions of this act, and shall not be liable to military duty under the same, to wit: Such as are rejected as physically or mentally unfit for the service; also, first, the Vice-President of the United States, the judges of the various courts of the United States, the heads of the various executive departments of the Government, and the governors of the several States. Second, the only son liable to military duty of a widow dependent upon his labor for support. Third, the only son of aged or infirm parent or parents dependent upon his labor for support. Fourth, where there are two or more sons of aged or infirm parents subject to draft, the father, or if he be dead, the mother, may elect which son shall be exempt. Fifth, the only brother of children not twelve years old, having neither father nor mother, dependent upon his labor for support. Sixth, the father of motherless children under twelve years of age dependent upon his labor for support. Seventh, where there are a father and sons in the same family and household, and two of them are in the military service of the United States as non-commissioned officers, musicians, or privates, the residue of such family and household, not exceeding two, shall be exempt. And no person but such as are herein excepted shall be exempt: *Provided,*

9

however, That no person who has been convicted of any felony shall be enrolled or permitted to serve in said forces.

SEC. 3. *And be it further enacted*, That the national forces of the United States not now in the military service, enrolled under this act, shall be divided into two classes, the first of which shall comprise all persons subject to do military duty between the ages of twenty and thirty-five years, and all unmarried persons subject to do military duty above the age of thirty-five and under the age of forty-five; the second class shall comprise all other persons subject to do military duty; and they shall not, in any district, be called into the service of the United States until those of the first class shall have been called.

SEC. 4. *And be it further enacted*, That for greater convenience in enrolling, calling out, and organizing the national forces, and for the arrest of deserters and spies of the enemy, the United States shall be divided into districts, of which the District of Columbia shall constitute one, each Territory of the United States shall constitute one or more, as the President shall direct, and each Congressional district of the respective States as fixed by a law of the State next preceding the enrollment, shall constitute one: *Provided*, That in States which have not by their laws been divided into two or more Congressional districts, the President of the United States shall divide the same into so many enrollment districts as he may deem fit and convenient.

SEC. 5. *And be it further enacted*, That for each of said districts there shall be appointed by the President a provost marshal, with the rank, pay, and emoluments of a captain of cavalry, or an officer of said rank shall be detailed by the President, who shall be under the direction and subject to the orders of a provost marshal general, appointed or detailed by the President of the United States, whose office shall be at the seat of government, forming a separate bureau of the War Department, whose rank, pay, and emoluments shall be those of a colonel of cavalry.

SEC. 6. *And be it further enacted*, That it shall be the duty of the provost marshal general, with the approval of the Secretary of War, to make rules and regulations for the government of his subordinates; to furnish them with the names and residences of all deserters from the army, or any of the land forces in the service of the United States, including the militia, when reported to him by the commanding officers; to communicate to them all orders of the President in reference to calling out the national forces; to furnish proper blanks and instructions for enrolling and drafting; to file and preserve copies of all enrollment lists; to require stated reports of all proceedings on the part of his subordinates; to audit all accounts connected with the service under his direction; and to perform such other duties as the President may prescribe in carrying out the provisions of this act.

SEC. 7. *And be it further enacted*, That it shall be the duty of the provost marshals to arrest all deserters, whether regulars, volunteers, militiamen, or persons called into the service under this or any other act of Congress, wherever they may be found, and to send them to the nearest military commander or military post; to detect, seize, and confine spies of the enemy who shall, without unreasonable delay, be delivered to the custody of the general commanding the department in which they may be arrested, to be tried as soon as the exigencies of the service permit; to obey all lawful orders and regulations of the provost marshal general, and such as may be prescribed by law concerning the enrollment and calling into service of the national forces.

SEC. 8. *And be it further enacted,* That in each of said districts there shall be a board of enrollment, to be composed of the provost marshal, as president, and two other persons, to be appointed by the President of the United States, one of whom shall be a licensed and practicing physician and surgeon.

SEC. 9. *And be it further enacted,* That it shall be the duty of the said board to divide the district into sub-districts of convenient size, if they shall deem it necessary, not exceeding two, without the direction of the Secretary of War, and to appoint, on or before the tenth day of March next, and in each alternate year thereafter, an enrolling officer for each sub-district, and to furnish him with proper blanks and instructions; and he shall immediately proceed to enroll all persons subject to military duty, noting their respective places of residence, ages, on the first day of July following, and their occupation, and shall, on or before the first day of April, report the same to the board of enrollment, to be consolidated into one list, a copy of which shall be transmitted to the provost marshal general on or before the first day of May succeeding the enrollment. *Provided,* nevertheless, That if, from any cause, the duties prescribed by this section can not be performed within the time specified, then the same shall be performed as soon thereafter as practicable.

SEC. 10. *And be it further enacted,* That the enrollment of each class shall be made separately, and they shall only embrace those whose ages shall be on the first day of July thereafter between twenty and forty-five years.

SEC. 11. *And be it further enacted,* That all persons thus enrolled shall be subject for two years after the first day of July succeeding the enrollment, to be called into the military service of the United States, and to continue in service for three years, or during the war; and when called into service shall be placed on the same footing, in all respects, as volunteers during the present rebellion; not, however, exceeding the term of three years, including advance pay and bounty as now provided by law.

SEC. 12. *And be it further enacted,* That whenever it may be necessary to call out the national forces for military service, the President is hereby authorized to assign to each district the number of men to be furnished by said district; and thereupon the enrolling board shall, under the direction of the President, make a draft of the required number, and fifty per centum in addition, and shall make an exact and complete roll of the names of the persons so drawn, and of the order in which they were drawn, so that the first drawn may stand first upon the said roll, and the second may stand second, and so on. And the persons so drawn shall be notified of the same within ten days thereafter, by a written or printed notice, to be served personally or by leaving a copy at the last place of residence, requiring them to appear at a designated rendezvous to report for duty. In assigning to the districts the number of men to be furnished therefrom, the President shall take into consideration the number of volunteers and militia furnished by and from the several States in which said districts are situated, and the period of their service since the commencement of the present rebellion, and shall so make said assignment as to equalize the numbers among the districts of the several States, considering and allowing for the numbers already furnished as aforesaid and the time of their service.

SEC. 13. *And be it further enacted*, That any person drafted and notified to appear as aforesaid, may, on or before the day fixed for his appearance, furnish an acceptable substitute to take his place in the draft; or he may pay to such person as the Secretary of War may authorize to receive, such sum, not exceeding three hundred dollars, as the Secretary may determine, for the procuration of such substitute, which sum shall be fixed at a uniform rate by a general order made at the time of ordering a draft from any State or Territory; and thereupon such person so furnishing the substitute, or paying the money, shall be discharged from further liability under that draft. And any person failing to report after due service of notice, as herein prescribed, without furnishing a substitute, or paying the required sum therefor, shall be deemed a deserter, and shall be arrested by the provost marshal and sent to the nearest military post for trial by courtmartial, unless, upon proper showing that he is not liable to military duty, the board of enrollment shall relieve him from the draft.

SEC. 14. *And be it further enacted*, That all drafted persons shall, on arriving at the rendezvous, be carefully inspected by the surgeon of the board, who shall truly report to the board the physical condition of each one; and all persons drafted and claiming exemption from military duty on account of disability, or any other cause, shall present their claims to be exempted to the board, whose decision shall be final.

SEC. 15. *And be it further enacted*, That any surgeon charged with the duty of such inspection who shall receive from any person whomsoever any money or other valuable thing, or agree, directly or indirectly, to receive the same to his own or another's use for making an imperfect inspection or a false or incorrect report, or who shall willfully neglect to make a faithful inspection and true report, shall be tried by a court-martial, and, on conviction thereof, be punished by fine not exceeding five hundred dollars nor less than two hundred, and be imprisoned at the discretion of the court, and be cashiered and dismissed from the service.

SEC. 16. *And be it further enacted*, That as soon as the required number of able-bodied men liable to do military duty shall be obtained from the list of those drafted, the remainder shall be discharged. And all drafted persons reporting at the place of rendezvous shall be allowed traveling pay from their places of residence ; and all persons discharged at the place of rendezvous shall be allowed traveling pay to their places of residence; and all expenses connected with the en- rollment and draft, including subsistence while at the rendezvous, shall be paid from the appropriation for enrolling and drafting, under such regulation as the President of the United States shall prescribe; and all expenses connected with the arrest and return of deserters to their regiments, or such other duties as the provost marshals shall be called upon to perform, shall be paid from the appropriation for ar- resting deserters, under such regulations as the President of the United States shall prescribe : *Provided*, That provost marshals shall in no case receive commutation for transportation or for fuel and quarters, but only for forage, when not furnished by the Government, together with actual expenses of postage, stationery, and clerk hire authorized by the provost marshal general.

SEC. 17. *And be it further enacted*, That any person enrolled and drafted according to the provisions of this act who shall furnish an acceptable substitute, shall thereupon receive from the board of en- rollment a certificate of discharge from such draft, which shall exempt him from military duty during the time for which he was drafted ; and such substitute shall be entitled to the same pay and allowances pro- vided by law as if he had been originally drafted into the service of the United States.

SEC. 18. *And be it further enacted*, That such of the volunteers and militia now in the service of the United States as may re-enlist to serve one year, unless sooner discharged, after the expiration of their present term of service, shall be entitled to a bounty of fifty dollars, one half of which to be paid upon such re-enlistment, and the balance at the expiration of the term of re-enlistment. And such as may re-enlist to serve for two years, unless sooner discharged, after the expiration of their present term of enlistment, shall receive, upon such re-enlist- ment, twenty-five dollars of the one hundred dollars bounty for enlist- ment provided by the fifth section of the act approved twenty-second of July, eighteen hundred and sixty-one, entitled " An act to author- ize the employment of volunteers to aid in enforcing the laws and protecting public property."

SEC. 19. *And be it further enacted*, That whenever a regiment of volunteers of the same arm, from the same State, is reduced to one half of the maximum number prescribed by law, the President may direct the consolidation of the companies of such regiment : *Provided*, That no company so formed shall exceed the maximum number pre- scribed by law. When such consolidation is made, the regimental officers shall be reduced in proportion to the reduction in the number of companies.

SEC. 20. *And be it further enacted*, That whenever a regiment is reduced below the minimum number allowed by law, no officers shall be appointed in such regiment beyond those necessary for the com- mand of such reduced number.

SEC. 21. *And be it further enacted*, That so much of the fifth sec- tion of the act approved seventeenth July, eighteen hundred and sixty-two, entitled "An act to amend an act calling forth the militia to execute the laws of the Union," and so forth, as requires the approval of the President to carry into execution the sentence of a court-martial, be, and the same is hereby repealed, as far as relates to carrying into execution the sentence of any court-martial against any person convicted as a spy or deserter, or of mutiny or murder; and hereafter sentences in punishment of these offenses may be carried into execution upon the approval of the commanding general in the field.

SEC. 22. *And be it further enacted*, That courts-martial shall have power to sentence officers who shall absent themselves from their commands without leave, to be reduced to the ranks to serve three years or during the war.

SEC. 23. *And be it further enacted*, That the clothes, arms, military outfits, and accoutrements furnished by the United States to any soldier, shall not be sold, bartered, exchanged, pledged, loaned, or given away; and no person not a soldier, or duly authorized officer of the United States, who has possession of any such clothes, arms, military outfits, or accoutrements, furnished as aforesaid, which have been the subjects of any such sale, barter, exchange, pledge, loan, or gift, shall have any right, title, or interest therein, but the same may be seized and taken wherever found by any officer of the United States, civil or military, and shall thereupon be delivered to any quartermaster, or other officer authorized to receive the same; and the possession of any such clothes, arms, military outfits, or accoutrements, by any person not a soldier or officer of the United States shall be *prima facie* evidence of such a sale, barter, exchange, pledge, loan, or gift as aforesaid.

SEC. 24. *And be it further enacted*, That every person not subject to the rules and articles of war who shall procure or entice, or attempt to procure or entice, a soldier in the service of the United States to desert; or who shall harbor, conceal, or give employment to a deserter, or carry him away, or aid in carrying him away, knowing him to be such; or who shall purchase from any soldier his arms, equipments, ammunition, uniform, clothing, or any part thereof; and any captain or commanding officer of any ship or vessel, or any superintendent or conductor of any railroad, or any other public conveyance, carrying away any such soldier as one of his crew or otherwise, knowing him to have deserted, or shall refuse to deliver him up to the orders of his commanding officer, shall, upon legal conviction, be fined, at the discretion of any court having cognizance of the same, in any sum not exceeding five hundred dollars, and he shall be imprisoned not exceeding two years nor less than six months.

SEC. 25. *And be it further enacted*, That if any person shall resist any draft of men enrolled under this act into the service of the United States, or shall counsel or aid any person to resist any such draft; or shall assault or obstruct any officer in making such draft, or in the performance of any service in relation thereto; or shall counsel any person to assault or obstruct any such officer, or shall counsel any drafted men not to appear at the place of rendezvous; or willfully dissuade them from the performance of military duty as required by law, such person shall be subject to summary arrest by the provost marshal, and shall be forthwith delivered to the civil authorities, and, upon conviction thereof, be punished by a fine not exceeding five hundred dollars, or by imprisonment not exceeding two years, or by both of said punishments.

SEC. 26. *And be it further enacted*, That, immediately after the passage of this act, the President shall issue his proclamation declaring that all soldiers now absent from their regiments without leave may return within a time specified to such place or places as he may indicate in his proclamation, and be restored to their respective regiments without punishment, except the forfeiture of their pay and allowances during their absence; and all deserters who shall not return within the time so specified by the President shall, upon being arrested, be punished as the law provides.

SEC. 27. *And be it further enacted*, That depositions of witnesses residing beyond the limits of the State, Territory, or district in which military courts shall be ordered to sit, may be taken in cases not capital by either party, and read in evidence; provided the same shall be taken upon reasonable notice to the opposite party, and duly authenticated.

SEC. 28. *And be it further enacted*, That the judge advocate shall have power to appoint a reporter, whose duty it shall be to record the proceedings of and testimony taken before military courts instead of the judge advocate; and such reporter may take down such proceedings and testimony in the first instance in shorthand. The reporter shall be sworn or affirmed faithfully to perform his duty before entering upon it.

SEC. 29. *And be it further enacted*, That the court shall, for reasonable cause, grant a continuance to either party for such time and as often as shall appear to be just: *Provided*, That if the prisoner be in close confinement, the trial shall not be delayed for a period longer than sixty days.

SEC. 30. *And be it further enacted*, That in time of war, insurrection, or rebellion, murder, assault and battery with an intent to kill, manslaughter, mayhem, wounding by shooting or stabbing with an intent to commit murder, robbery, arson, burglary, rape, assault and battery with an intent to commit rape, and larceny, shall be punishable by the sentence of a general court-martial or military commission, when committed by persons who are in the military service of the United States, and subject to the articles of war; and the punishments of such offenses shall never be less than those inflicted by the laws of the State, Territory, or district in which they may have been committed.

SEC. 31. *And be it further enacted*, That any officer absent from duty with leave, except for sickness or wounds, shall, during his absence, receive half of the pay and allowances prescribed by law, and no more; and any officer absent without leave shall in addition to the penalties prescribed by law or a court-martial, forfeit all pay or allowances during such absence.

SEC. 32. *And be it further enacted*, That the commanders of regiments and of batteries in the field are hereby authorized and empowered to grant furloughs for a period not exceeding thirty days at any one time to five per centum of the non-commissioned officers and privates, for good conduct in the line of duty, etc., and subject to the approval of the commanders of the forces of which such non-commissioned officers and privates form a part.

SEC. 33. *And be it further enacted*, That the President of the United States is hereby authorized and empowered, during the present rebellion, to call forth the national forces, by draft, in the manner provided for in this act.

SEC. 34. *And be it further enacted*, That all persons drafted under the provisions of this act shall be assigned by the President to military duty in such corps, regiments, or other branches of the service as the exigencies of the service may require.

SEC. 35. *And be it further enacted*, That hereafter details to special service shall only be made with the consent of the commanding officer of forces in the field; and enlisted men, now or hereafter detailed to special service, shall not receive any extra pay for such services beyond that allowed to other enlisted men.

SEC. 36. *And be it further enacted*, That general orders of the War Department, numbered one hundred and fifty-four and one hundred and sixty-two, in reference to enlistments from the volunteers into the regular service, be, and the same are hereby rescinded; and hereafter no such enlistments shall be allowed.

SEC. 37. *And be it further enacted*, That the grades created in the cavalry forces of the United States by section eleven of the act approved seventeenth July, eighteen hundred and sixty-two, and for which no rate of compensation has been provided, shall be paid as follows, to wit: Regimental commissary the same as regimental quartermaster; chief trumpeter the same as chief bugler; the saddler sergeant the same as regimental commissary sergeant; company commissary sergeant the same as company quartermaster's sergeant: *Provided*, That the grade of supernumerary second lieutenant, and two teamsters for each company, and one chief farrier and blacksmith for each regiment, as allowed by said section of that act, be, and they are hereby abolished; and each cavalry company may have two trumpeters, to be paid as buglers; and each regiment shall have one veterinary surgeon, with the rank of a regimental sergeant-major, whose compensation shall be seventy-five dollars per month.

SEC. 38. *And be it further enacted*, That all persons who, in time of war or of rebellion against the supreme authority of the United States, shall be found lurking or acting as spies in or about any of the fortifications, posts, quarters, or encampments of any of the armies of the United States, or elsewhere, shall be triable by a general court-martial or military commission, and shall, upon conviction, suffer death.

THE INDEMNITY BILL.

AN act relating to habeas corpus, and regulating judicial proceedings in certain cases:

Be it enacted by the Senate and House of Representatives of the United States of America in Congress assembled, That during the present rebellion, the President of the United States, whenever in his judgment the public safety may require it, is authorized to suspend the privilege of the writ of habeas corpus in any case throughout the United States, or any part thereof. And whenever and wherever the said privilege shall be suspended as aforesaid, no military or other officer shall be compelled, in answer to any writ of habeas corpus, to return the body of any person or persons detained by him by authority of the President; but upon a certificate, under oath, of the officer having charge of any one so detained, that such person is detained by him as a prisoner, under authority of the President, further proceedings under the writ of habeas corpus shall be suspended by the judge or court having issued the said writ so long as said suspension by the President shall remain in force and said rebellion continue.

SEC. 2. *And be it further enacted,* That the Secretary of State and the Secretary of War be, and they are hereby directed, as soon as may be practicable, to furnish to the judges of the Circuit and District Courts of the United States and the District of Columbia a list of the names of all persons, citizens of States in which the administration of the laws has continued unimpaired in the said Federal courts, who are now, or may hereafter be, held as prisoners of the United States, by order or authority of the President of the United States or either of said secretaries, in any fort, arsenal, or other place, as state or political prisoners, or otherwise than as prisoners of war; the said list to contain the names of all those who reside in the respective jurisdictions of said judges, or who may be deemed by the said secretaries, or either of them, to have violated any law of the United States in any of said jurisdictions, and also the date of each arrest—the Secretary of State to furnish a list of such persons as are imprisoned by the order or authority of the President, acting through the State Department, and the Secretary of War a list of such as are imprisoned by the order or authority of the President, acting through the Department of War. And in all cases where a grand jury, having attended any of said courts having jurisdiction in the premises, after the passage of this act, and after the furnishing of said list, as aforesaid, has terminated its session without finding an indictment, or presentment, or other proceeding against any such person, it shall be the duty of the judge of said court forthwith to make an order that any such prisoner desiring a discharge from said imprisonment be brought before him to be discharged; and every officer of the United States having custody of such prisoner is hereby directed immediately to obey and execute said judge's order; and in case he shall delay or refuse so to do, he shall be subject to indictment for a misdemeanor, and be punished by a fine of not less than five hundred dollars and imprisonment in the common jail for a period not less than six months, in the discretion of the court: *Provided, however,* That no person shall be discharged by virtue of the provisions of this act until after he or she shall have taken an oath of allegiance to the Government of the United States, and to support the Constitution thereof; and that he or she will not hereafter, in any way, encourage or give aid and comfort to the present rebellion or the supporters thereof: *And provided, also,* That the judge or court before whom such person may be brought, before discharging him or her from imprisonment, shall have power, on examination of the case, and, if public safety shall require it, shall be required to cause him or her to enter into recognizance, with or without surety, in a sum to be fixed by said judge or court, to keep the peace and be of good behavior towards the United States and its citizens, and from time to time, and at such times as such judge or court may direct, appear before said judge or court to be further dealt with, according to law, as the circumstances may require. And it shall be the duty of the District Attorney of the United States to attend such examination before the judge.

SEC. 3. *And be it further enacted,* That in case any of such prisoners shall be under indictment or presentment for any offense against the laws of the United States, and by existing laws bail or a recognizance may be taken for the appearance for trial of such person, it shall be the duty of said judge at once to discharge such person upon bail or recognizance for trial as aforesaid. And in case the said Secretaries of State and War shall for any reason refuse or omit to furnish the said list of persons held as prisoners as aforesaid at the time of the passage of this act within twenty days thereafter, and of such persons as hereafter may be arrested within twenty days from the time of the arrest, any citizen may, after a grand jury shall have terminated its session without finding an indictment or presentment, as provided in the second section of this act, by a petition alleging the facts aforesaid touching any of the persons so as aforesaid imprisoned, supported by the oath of such petitioner or any other credible person, obtain and be entitled to have the said judge's order to discharge such prisoner on the same terms and conditions prescribed in the second section of this act: *Provided, however,* That the said judge shall be satisfied such allegations are true.

SEC. 4. *And be it further enacted,* That any order of the President, or under his authority, made at any time during the existence of the present rebellion, shall be a defense in all courts to any action or prosecution, civil or criminal, pending or to be commenced, for any search, seizure, arrest, or imprisonment, made, done, or committed, or acts omitted to be done, under and by virtue of such order, or under color of any law of Congress; and such defense may be made by special plea, or under the general issue.

SEC. 5. *And be it further enacted*, That if any suit or prosecution, civil or criminal, has been or shall be commenced in any State court against any officer, civil or military, or against any other person, for any arrest or imprisonment made, or other trespasses or wrongs done or committed, or any act omitted to be done, at any time during the present rebellion, by virtue or under color of any authority derived from or exercised by or under the President of the United States, or any act of Congress, and the defendant shall, at the time of entering his appearance in such court, or if such appearance shall have been entered before the passage of this act, then at the next session of the court in which such suit or prosecution is pending, file a petition, stating the facts and verified by affidavit, for the removal of the cause for trial at the next circuit court, of the United States, to be holden in the district where the suit is pending, and offer good and sufficient surety for his filing in such court, on the first day of its session, copies of such process and other proceedings against him, and also for his appearing in such court and entering special bail in the cause, if special bail was originally required therein, it shall then be the duty of the State court to accept the surety and proceed no further in the cause or prosecution; and the bail that shall have been originally taken shall be discharged. And such copies being filed as aforesaid in such court of the United States, the cause shall proceed therein in the same manner as if it had been brought in said court by original process, whatever may be the amount in dispute or the damages claimed, or whatever the citizenship of the parties, any former law to the contrary notwithstanding. And any attachment of the goods or estate of the defendant by the original process shall hold the goods or estate so attached to answer the final judgment in the same manner as by the laws of such State they would have been holden to answer final judgment had it been rendered in the court in which the suit or prosecution was commenced. And it shall be lawful in any such action or prosecution which may be now pending or hereafter commenced, before any State court whatever, for any cause aforesaid, after final judgment, for either party to remove and transfer, by appeal, such case during the session or term of said court at which the same shall have taken place, from such court to the next circuit court of the United States to be held in the district in which such appeal shall be taken, in manner aforesaid. And it shall be the duty of the person taking such appeal to produce and file in the said circuit court attested copies of the process, proceedings, and judgment in such cause; and it shall also be competent for either party, within six months after the rendition of a judgment in any such cause, by writ of error or other process, to remove the same to the circuit court of the United States of that district in which such judgment shall have been rendered; and the said circuit court shall thereupon proceed to try and determine the facts and the law in such action, in the same manner as if the same had been there originally commenced, the judgment in such case notwithstanding. And any bail which may have been taken, or property attached, shall be holden on the final judgment of the said circuit court in such action, in the same manner as if no such removal and transfer had been made, as aforesaid. And the State court from which any such action, civil or criminal, may be removed and transferred as aforesaid, upon the parties giving good and sufficient security for the prosecution thereof, shall allow the same to be removed and transferred, and proceed no further in the case: *Provided, however,* That if the party aforesaid shall fail daily to enter the removal and transfer, as aforesaid, in the circuit court of the United States, agreeably to this act, the State court, by which judgment shall have been rendered, and from which the transfer and removal shall have been made, as aforesaid, shall be authorized, on motion for that purpose, to issue execution, and to carry into effect any such judgment, the same as if no such removal and transfer had been made: *And provided, also,* That no such appeal or writ of error shall be allowed in any criminal action or prosecution where final judgment shall have been rendered in favor of the defendant or respondent by the State court. And if in any suit hereafter commenced the plaintiff is nonsuited or judgment pass against him, the defendant shall recover double costs.

SEC. 6. *And be it further enacted,* That any suit or prosecution described in this act, in which final judgment may be rendered in the Circuit Court, may be carried by writ of error to the Supreme Court, whatever may be the amount of said judgment.

SEC. 7. *And be it further enacted,* That no suit or prosecution, civil or criminal, shall be maintained for any arrest or imprisonment made, or other trespasses or wrongs done or committed, or act omitted to be done, at any time during the present rebellion, by virtue or color of any authority derived from or exercised by or under the President of the United States, or by or under any act of Congress, unless the same shall have been commenced within two years next after such arrest, imprisonment, trespass, or wrong may have been done or committed, or act may have been omitted to be done: *Provided,* That in no case shall the limitation herein provided commence to run until the passage of this act, so that no party shall, by virtue of this act, be debarred of his remedy by suit or prosecution until two years from and after the passage of this act.

ALPHABETICAL RECAPITULATION.

Advertisements inserted in newspapers, magazines, reviews, or any other
   publication, on gross receipts for............................... 3 per ct.
All receipts for, to the amount of $1,000........................... exempt.
   By papers whose circulation does not exceed 2,000 copies........... exempt.
Agents, insurance (see " Insurance Agents"), for license............... $10 00
Agreements, for each sheet or piece of paper on which written, stamp duty.   05
Agreements for the hire, use, or rent of any land, tenement, or portion
   thereof, if for a period of time not exceeding three years, stamp
   duty...................... 50
   If for a period of time exceeding three years, stamp duty............ 1 00
Alcohol, made or manufactured of spirits or materials upon which the duties
   imposed by this act shall have been paid, is not to be considered a
   manufacture.
Ale, per barrel of 31 gallons, fractional parts of a barrel to pay proportionately (see " Malt Liquors").
Animal oils, per gallon... 02
Anodynes, each package of the retail price or value of which does not ex-
   ceed 25 cents, stamp duty...................................... 01
   Each package of, the retail price or value of which exceeds 25 cents,
   and does not exceed 50 cents, stamp duty....................... 02
   Each package of, the retail price or value of which exceeds 50 cents,
   and does not exceed 75 cents, stamp duty....................... 03
   Exceeding 75 cents, and not exceeding $1....................... 04
   Each package of, the retail price or value of which exceeds $1, for each
   and every 50 cents, or fractional part thereof over and above $1, an
   additional stamp duty of.. 02
Apothecaries, under which term is included every person who keeps a shop
   or building where medicines are compounded or prepared according
   to prescriptions of physicians, and sold. Wholesale and retail dealers who have taken out a license therefor, shall not be required to
   take out a license as apothecary ; nor shall apothecaries who have
   taken out a license as such be required to take out a license as retail
   dealers in liquors, in consequence of selling alcohol, license tax.... 10 00
Applications for bounties, stamp duty............................... none.
   For arrears of pay, stamp duty............................. .... none.
   For pensions, stamp duty.. none.
Appraisements of value or damage, on each a stamp duty of............ 05
Architects and Civil Engineers, under which term is included every person
   whose business it is to plan, design, or superintend the construction
   of buildings or ships, or of roads, or bridges, or canals, or railroads,
   provided that this act shall not include a practical Carpenter who
   labors on a building, for license................................. $10 00
Arrears of pay, stamp duty.. none.
Assignment of mortgage, stamp duty same as on the original instrument.
   Of leases, do. do.
   Of policies of insurance, do. do.
Attorney—No license shall be required of an attorney, having taken out
   a license as such, in consequence of being employed to purchase,
   rent, or sell real estate, or to collect rent thereon for others in the
   ordinary course of business. See " Lawyers."
Auctioneers, under which term is included every person whose business it
   is to offer property for sale to the highest or best bidder, for license. 20 00

Auction sales of goods, merchandise, articles, and things, including all sales of stocks, bonds, and other securities, on gross amount of sales.1-10 to 1 per ct
Awnings, made of cotton, flax, or hemp, or part of either, or other material.. 3 per ct.
The sewing of, the material whereof belonged to the employer, shall be exempt from duty when the cloth or material from which made was imported or has been subject to and paid a duty.
Bags, made of cotton, flax, or hemp, or part of either, or other material... 3 per ct.
The sewing of, same as "Awnings."
Band Iron (see "Iron").
Banks—Every incorporated bank, or other bank legally authorized to issue notes as circulation, which shall neglect or omit to make dividends or additions to its surplus or contingent funds as often as once in six months, shall, in lieu thereof, make returns, under oath, to the Commissioner of Internal Revenue, on the 1st day of January and July in each year, or within 30 days thereafter, of the profits, etc. (see Section 14 Amendatory Act), and pay on such profits.......... 3 per ct.
Banks, on all dividends.. 3 per ct.
Bankers, under which term is included every person who keeps a place of business where credits are opened in favor of any person, firm, or corporation, by the deposit or collection of money or currency, and the same, or any part thereof, shall be paid or remitted upon the draft, check, or order of such creditor, but which does not include incorporated banks or other banks legally authorized to issue notes as circulation, for license..................................... $100 00
Bar Iron (see "Iron").
Barks, hereafter built... 2 per ct.
Barytes, sulphate of, 100 pounds....................................... 10
Beer, per barrel of 31 gallons, fractional parts of a barrel to pay proportionately (see "Malt Liqquors").
Bend leather, per pound..1 cent and 5 mills.
Benzine, per gallon..3 per ct. ad valorem.
Bicarbonate of soda, per pound.. 5 mills.
Billiard tables, kept for use, for each table............................. 10 00
Billiard rooms, for license, for each table............................. 5 00
Bill of exchange (Inland), draft, or order for the payment of any sum of money exceeding $20, otherwise than at sight or on demand, and any promissory note, shall have a stamp or stamps affixed thereon denoting a duty, upon every sum of $200 or any fractional part thereof, if payable on demand or at any time not exceeding 33 days, including the grace, from the date or sight....................... 01
If payable at any time not less than 33 days, as aforesaid, and not exceeding 63 days including the grace, from date or sight.......... 02
If payable at any time not less than 63 days, as aforesaid, and not exceeding 93 days, including the grace, from date or sight.......... 03
If payable at any time not less than 93 days, as aforesaid, and not exceeding 4 months from date, or sight and grace................. 04
If payable at any time not less than 4 months, as aforesaid, and not exceeding 6 months from date or sight and grace................. 06
If payable any time exceeding six months from date or sight and grace. 10
Bills of exchange (foreign) drawn in, but payable out of the United States, if drawn singly, or if drawn otherwise than in sets of more than one, according to the custom of merchants and bankers, same as bill of exchange (inland).
If drawn in sets of three or more, for every bill of each set, where the sum made payable shall not exceed $150, or the equivalent thereof in any foreign currency....................................... 03
Above $150 and not above $250............................... 05
Above $250 and not above $500.............................. 10
Above $500 and not above $1,000............................. 15
Above $1,000 and not above $1,500 20
Above $1,500 and not above $2,500........................... 30
Above $2,500 and not above $3,500 50

Bills of exchange, above $3,500 and not above $5,000 .... $0 70
Above $5,000 and not above $7,500 .... 1 00
For every $2,500, or part thereof, in excess of $7,500............ .. 30
Bills of lading for any goods, merchandise, or effects to be exported from a
port or place in the United States to any foreign port or place, a stamp
duty of.. 10
Bills of sale, by which any ship or vessel, or any part thereof, shall be con-
veyed to or vested in any other person or persons, when the consid-
eration shall not exceed $500, stamp duty..................... 25
When the consideration exceeds $500 and does not exceed $1,000,
stamp duty 50
For each and every additional amount of $1,000, or any fractional part
thereof in excess of $1,000..................................... 50
Bitters, same as "Medicines."
Boards are not to be considered as manufactures.
Bolts, iron, per tun 2 00
Bond or note secured by a mortgage, but one stamp shall be required on
such papers, provided that the stamp duty placed thereon is the
largest rate required for such instruments or either of them.
Bonds of canal companies............................•................. 3 per ct.
Bonds, auction sales of, on gross amounts of sales ....1-10 of 1 per ct.
Bonds indemnifying any person who shall have become bound or engaged
as surety for the payment of any sum of money, or for the due execution or performance of the duties of any office, and to administer
money received by virtue thereof, a stamp duty of............... 50
Of any description other than such as are required in legal proceedings
and such as are not otherwise charged, a stamp duty of............ 25
Bone, manufactures of, wholly or in part, if not otherwise specified, ad valorem... 3 per ct.
Books are not to be regarded as a manufacture, or submitted to a rate of
duty as a manufacture.
Bootmakers, making articles to order, as custom work, and not for sale generally, shall, to the amount of $1,000, be exempt from duty, and for
any excess beyond the amount of $1,000, shall pay a duty of ...... 1 per ct.
Bottles, containing medicines, etc., the retail price or value of which, contents included, does not exceed 25 cents, a stamp duty of 01
Containing medicines, etc., the retail price or value of which, contents
included, exceeds 25 cents, but does not exceed 50 cents, a stamp
duty of... 02
Containing medicines, etc., the retail price or value of which, contents
included, exceeds 50 cents, but does not exceed 75 cents 03
Containing medicines, etc., the value of which, contents included, shall
exceed 75 cents, and shall not exceed $1........................ 04
Containing medicines, etc., the value of which, contents included, ex-
ceeds $1, for each and every 50 cents or fractional part thereof over
and above $1, an additional stamp duty of...................... 02
Bounties, applications for, stamp duty............................... none.
Or indemnity awarded for depredations and injuries by certain bands
of Sioux Indians, applications for, stamp duty.................... none.
Bowling alleys, for each alley, duty for license...................... 5 00
Boxes, containing medicines, etc., same as " Bottles," which see.
Brass rolled, in rods or sheets .... 1 per ct.
Brass, manufacturers of, not otherwise specified..................... 3 per ct.
Brewers, under which term is included every person who manufactures fer-
mented liquors of any name or description for sale from malt, wholly
or in part, for license..................................... 50 00
Who manufacture less than 500 bbls. per year, for license.......... 25 00
Bricks are not to be considered a manufacture.
Bristles, manufactures of, not otherwise specified..................... 3 per ct.
Brokers, auction sales by, of goods, wares, merchandise, articles or things,
on gross amount of sale.................................1-10 of 1 per ct.
Brokers, under which term is included every person whose business it is to
purchase or sell stocks, coin, money, bank notes, drafts, promissory

notes, or other securities for the payment of money, for themselves
or others, or who deal in exchanges relating to money, for license.. $50 00

Brokers, commercial, under which term is included every person who purchases or sells goods or produce, or seeks orders therefor, in original
or unbroken packages, or manages business matters for the owners
of vessels, or the shippers or consignors of freight carried by vessels,
or purchases or sells real estate for others, for license 50 00

Brokers, land warrants (see "Land-warrant Brokers") 25 00

Brokers, Insurance (see " Insurance Agents"), for license 10 00

Bullion ; see " Coin."

Bullion, in the manufacture of silver-ware, is not to be considered a manufacture.

Burning fluid is not to be considered a manufacture.

Builders and contractors, under which term is included every person whose
business it is to construct buildings, or ships, or bridges, or canals,
or railroads by contract : *Provided*, That no license shall be required
from any persons whose building contracts do not exceed $2,500 in
any one year—for license 25 00

Butchers, under which term is included every person who shall sell
butchers' meat at retail : *Provided*, That no butcher having taken
out a license and paid $10 therefor, shall be required to take out a
license as retail dealer on account of selling other articles at the
same store, stall, or premises : *Provided, further*, That butchers who
retail butchers' meat exclusively from a cart or wagon, by themselves or agents, shall be required to pay $5 only for each license,
any existing law to the contrary notwithstanding, and having taken
out a license therefor, shall not be required to take out a license as
peddler for retailing butchers' meat as aforesaid : *Provided, further*,
that those whose annual sales do not exceed $1,000 shall be exempt—
for license 10 00

Calfskins, tanned, each 06

American patent. .... 5 per ct.

Calves, slaughtered, per head 05

Canal boats, hereafter built .... 2 per ct.

Canal Companies, Interest on bonds or dividends of .... 3 per ct.

Candles, tallow .... 3 per ct.

Lard .... 3 per ct.

Of whatever material made .... 3 per ct.

Candy, Sugar, see " Sugar Candy."

Cards, playing, per pack of whatever number, when the price per pack does
not exceed 18 cents 01

Over 18 and not over 25 cents per pack 02

Over 25 and not over 30 cents per pack 03

Over 30 and not over 36 cents 04

Over 36 cents 05

Carpets, the sewing of, same as " Awnings."

Carriages, etc , valued at $75 or over, drawn by one horse, including the
harness 1 00

Drawn by two horses, valued at $75 and not exceeding $200 .... 2 00

Exceeding in value $200 and not exceeding $600 .... 5 00

Exceeding $600 .... 10 00

Cars, railroad, see "Railroad Cars."

Cassia, ground, and all imitations of, per pound 01

Castile Soap, see " Soap."

Cattle, horned, slaughtered, for sale, each 20

Slaughtered by any person for his own consumption, not exceeding
six .... free.

Cattle Brokers, including every person whose business it is to buy and sell
and deal in cattle, hogs, or sheep, for license 10 00

Cavendish Tobacco—per pound 15

Cement, made wholly or in part of glue, to be sold in a liquid state, per
gallon 25

Certificates of stock in any incorporated company, stamp duty on each... 25

Certificate of profits, or any certificate or memorandums showing an interest in the property or accumulations of any incorporated company, if for not less than $10 and not exceeding $50, stamp duty.. $0 10
For a sum exceeding $50.............................. 25
Certificate—Any certificate of damage, and all other certificates or documents issued by any Port Warden, Marine Surveyor, or other person acting as such, stamp duty.............................. 25
Certificate of deposit of any sum of money in any bank or trust company, or with any banker or person acting as such, if for a sum not exceeding $100, a stamp duty.............................. 02
If for a sum exceeding $100, stamp duty.......................... 05
Certificates of measurement, stamp duty............................. none.
Certificates of profit, stamp duty... .... none.
Certificates of weight, stamp duty.................................. none.
Certificate of any other description than those specified in Schedule B, a stamp duty of... 05
Charcoal is not to be considered a manufacture.
Charter Party—Contract of agreement for the charter of any ship, or vessel, or steamer, or any letter, or memorandum, or other writing between the captain, master, or owner, or person acting as agent of any ship or vessel, or steamer, and any other person or persons, for or relating to the freight or charter of such ship, or vessel, or steamer, if the registered tunnage of such ship, or vessel, or steamer does not exceed 150 tuns, stamp duty.................... 1 00
Exceeding 150 tuns and not exceeding 300 tuns.................... 3 00
Exceeding 300 tuns and not exceeding 600 tuns, stamp duty........ 5 00
Exceeding 600 tuns, stamp duty.............................. 10 00
Charts are not to be considered a manufacture.
Checks drawn upon any bank, trust company, or any person or persons, companies or corporations. for the payment of money, exceeding $20, at sight or on demand................................... 02
Cheese is not to be considered a manufacture.
Chemical preparations same as "Medicines."
Chocolate, prepared, per pound.. 01
Circuses, under which term is included every building, tent, space, or area, where feats of horsemanship or acrobatic sports are exhibited, for license.. 50 00
Civil Engineers (see "Architect"), for license..................... 10 00
Claim Agents, under which term is included every person whose business it is to prosecute claims in any of the Executive Departments of the Federal Government, for each yearly license..................... 10 00
Clearance, same as manifest.
Clocks... 3 per ct.
Clock movements, sold without being cased.......................... 3 per ct.
Clocks—Any duties which may have been paid on Clock movements used for clocks or time-pieces upon which duties shall be assessed or paid shall be deducted from the three per cent. tax on clocks and time-pieces.
Cloth, before it has been dyed, printed, bleached, or prepared in any other manner... 3 per ct.
Cloths—On all cloths of silk, cotton, or other material dyed, printed, bleached, manufactured or prepared, which were removed from the place of manufacture prior to the 1st of September, 1862, or which have been or shall be imported, the duty or tax of 3 per centum shall be assessed only upon the increased value thereof; and where the dyeing, bleaching, printing, or finishing shall be done separately from the weaving, knitting, or felting, the increased value shall be, and hereby is, declared for dyeing, bleaching, printing, or finishing.
Coal, all mineral, except pea coal or dust coal, per ton................. 3½ cts.
Coal—All duties or taxes on coal mined and delivered by coal operators at the mines, on contracts made prior to July 1, 1862, shall be paid by the purchaser thereof.
Coal gas (see "Gas").

Coal oil, produced by the distillation of coal exclusively, refined, per gallon $0 08
Coal illuminating oil, refined, produced by the distillation of coal, asphaltum, shale, peat, petroleum or rock oil, and all other bituminous substances used for like purposes, per gallon........   10
Coal oil distillers, under which term is included any person who shall refine, produce, or distill crude petroleum or rock oil, or crude coal oil, or crude oil made of asphaltum, shale, peat, or other bituminous substances, for each license 50 00
Coal tar, produced in the manufacture of gas.......................... exempt.
Cocoa, prepared, per pound...   01
Coffee, ground, per pound.. 3 mills.
Coffee—All preparations of which coffee forms a part, or which is prepared for sale as a substitute for coffee, per pound.................... 3 mills.
Coin—All contracts for the purchase or sale of gold or silver coin or bullion, and all contracts for the loan of money or currency secured by pledge or deposit, or other disposition of gold or silver coin of the United States, if to be performed after a period exceeding three days, shall be in writing or printed, and signed by the parties, their agents or attorneys, and shall have one or more adhesive stamps, as provided in the Tax law, equal in amount to one half of one per centum, and interest at the rate of six per centum per annum on the amount so loaned, pledged, or deposited; and if any such loan, pledge, or deposit, made for a period not exceeding three days, shall be renewed, or in any way extended for any time whatever, said loan, pledge, or deposit shall be subject to the duty imposed on loans exceeding three days; and no loan of currency or money on the security of gold or silver coin of the United States as aforesaid, or of any certificate or other evidence of deposit payable in gold or silver coin, shall be made exceeding in amount the par value of the coin pledged or deposited as security, and any such loan so made, or attempted to be made, shall be utterly void.   If gold or silver coin be loaned at its par value, it shall be subject only to the duty imposed on other loans.   Nothing herein contained shall apply to any transaction by or with the Government of the United States.
Coin—All contracts, loans, or sales of bullion or gold and silver coin not made in accordance with this act, shall be wholly and absolutely void ; and in addition to the penalties provided in the act, any party to said contract may, at any time within one year from the date of the contract, bring suit before any court of competent jurisdiction to recover back, for his own use and benefit, the money paid on any contract not made in accordance with this act.
Commercial Brokers (see " Brokers").
Concentrated milk is not to be considered a manufacture.
Confectioners, under which term is included every person who sells or retails confectionary, sweetmeats, comfits, or other confects, in any building (confectioners who have taken out a license as wholesale or retail dealers are not required to take a separate license), for each license...   10 00
Confectionery, made wholly or in part of sugar, same as " Sugar Candy."
Consumption entry at any custom-house, not exceeding $100 in value, stamp duty...   25
    Exceeding $100 and not exceeding $500   50
    Exceeding $500 in value..   1 00
Contracts, for each sheet or piece of paper on which written, stamp duty..   05
    For the hire, use, or rent of any land, tenement, or portion thereof, under a period of time not exceeding three years, stamp duty......   50
    For a period of time exceeding three years.......................   1 00
Contracts, brokers' note, or memorandum of sale of any goods or merchandise, stocks, bonds, exchange, notes of hand, real estate, or property of any kind or description, issued by brokers, or persons acting as such, stamp duty...   10
Contractors, for license (see " Builders")............................   25 00
Conveyance—none to pay more than $1,000.

Conveyance, deed, instrument, or writing, whereby any lands, tenements, or other realty, sold, shall be granted, leased, assigned, transferred, or otherwise conveyed to or vested in the purchaser or purchasers, or to any person or persons, by his, her, or their direction, when the value exceeds $100 and does not exceed $500, stamp duty......... $0 50
Exceeding $500 and not exceeding $1,000......................... 1 00
Exceeding $1,000 and not exceeding $2,500...................... 2 00
Exceeding $2,500 and not exceeding $5,000 .... 2 00
Exceeding $5.000 and not exceeding $10,000..................... 10 00
Exceeding $10,000 and not exceeding $20,000.................... 20 00
For every additional $10,000, or fractional part in excess of $20,000.. 20 00
Copper, in rods or sheets... 1 per ct.
Copper, manufactures of, not otherwise provided for, ad valorem......... 3 per ct.
Cosmetics, same as " Medicines."
Cotton, raw, per pound... ½
Cotton, raw or manufactured, the growth or produce of countries beyond
    the Cape of Good Hope, when imported from this side the Cape, shall
    pay no greater duty than is imposed on the same article when im-
    ported directly from the places beyond the Cape.
Cotton, manufactures of, wholly or in part, not otherwise provided for... 3 per ct.
Cotton umbrellas... 3 per ct.
Coupons, railroad... 3 per ct.
Deeds, whereby any lands, tenements, or other things sold, shall be grant-
    ed, leased, assigned transferred, or otherwise conveyed to or vested
    in the purchaser or purchasers, or to any person or persons by his,
    her, or their direction, stamp duty, same as " Conveyance."
Deeds and other instruments in writing, having the fact of their acknowl-
    edgment, or any certificate showing that the acknowledgment has
    been made before the proper officer or in due form thereon certified,
    shall not, in consequence of such certificate, be subject to an addi-
    tional stamp duty.
Deed, none to pay a stamp duty of more than......................... 1,000 00
Deer skins, dressed and smoked, per pound........................... 02
Dentrifice, each package of, the retail price or value of which does not ex-
    ceed 25 cents, stamp duty...................................... 01
Exceeding 25 cents, but not exceeding 50 cents, stamp duty 02
Exceeding 50 cents, but not exceeding 75 cents.................... 03
Each package of, the value of which shall exceed 75 cents, and shall
    not exceed $1... 04
Exceeding $1, for each and every 50 cents, or fractional part thereof,
    over and above $1, an additional stamp duty of................. 02
Dentists, for license... 10 00
Deposit notes to mutual insurance companies, stamp duty............. none.
Deposits of banks doing a brokerage business ....¼ of 1 per ct.
Dispatch, telegraphic, when the charge of the first ten words does not ex-
    ceed 20 cents, stamp duty...................................... 01
When it exceeds 20 cents.. 03
Diamonds... 3 per ct.
Distilled spirits, first proof, per gallon............................ 20
Distilled Spirits.—The duty on spirituous liquors and all other spirituous
    beverages enumerated in the Tax Bill, is to be collected at no lower
    rate than the basis of first proof, and shall be increased in proportion
    for any greater strength than the strength of proof.
Distilled Spirits.—The term first proof is declared to mean that proof of a
    liquor which corresponds to 50 degrees of Tralles's centesimal hy-
    drometer, at the temperature of 60 degrees of Fahrenheit's thermom-
    eter ; and in reducing the temperature to the standard of 60, and in
    levying duties on liquors above and below proof. the table of com-
    mercial values contained in the Manual for Inspectors of Spirits, pre-
    pared by Prof. McCulloch, under the superintendence of Prof. Bache,
    and adopted by the Treasury Department, is to be used and taken
    as giving the proportions of absolute alcohol in the liquid guaged
    and proved, according to which duties shall be levied.

Distillers, under which term is included every person or copartnership who distills or manufactures spirituous liquors for sale, for license.. $50 00

Making less than 300 bbls. per year..............................   25 00

Of apples and peaches, making less than 150 bbls. per year.........   12 50

Dividends—Annual income from, when exceeding $600, and not exceeding $10,000, on the excess over $600 .... 3 per ct.

Exceeding $10,000, and not exceeding $50,000 on excess over $600.. 5 per ct.

Dividends, annual income from, when realized by any citizen of the United States residing abroad, and not in the employ of the United States, not otherwise provided for, when exceeding $600, on the excess over $600... 5 per ct.

Dividends of canal companies....................................... 3 per ct.

Documents made in foreign countries, same stamp duties as if made in the United States.

Draft, drawn upon any bank, trust company, or any person or persons, companies, or corporations, for the payment of money at sight or on demand, same as "Bill of Exchange."

Draining-tiles are not to be considered a manufacture.

Dressmakers, making articles to order, as custom work, and not for sale generally, shall, to the amount of $1,000 be exempt from duty, and for any excess beyond the amount of $1,000 shall pay a duty of 1 per ct.

Drops, medicinal, same as "Medicines."

Eating-houses, under which term is included every place where food or refreshments of any kind are provided for casual visitors and sold for consumption therein ; but the keeper of an eating-house, having taking out a license therefor, is not required to take out a license as confectioner, for license................................... 10 00

Emeralds.. 3 per ct.

Enameled leather, per square foot................................. 5 mills.

Enameled skirting leather, per square foot........................ 01½

Engines, marine.. 3 per ct.

Engineers, civil, for license, see "Architects."

Entry of any goods, wares, or merchandise, at any custom-house, for warehousing, see "Warehouse Entry."

Entry for the withdrawal of any goods, wares, or merchandise from bonded warehouse, stamp duty...................................... 50

Erasive soap, see "Soap."

Express companies, on gross receipts, instead of stamp duty............. 2 per ct.

Felloes.. free.

Ferry-boats, propelled by steam or horse power, on gross receipts........ 1½ per ct.

Fine cut tobacco, see "Tobacco."

Fire insurance companies, on all dividends......................... 3 per ct.

Fish, preserved, ad valorem....................................... 5 per ct.

Fish oil.. exempt.

Flax, manufacturers of, not otherwise specified.................... 3 per ct.

Prepared for textile or felting purposes, is not to be considered a manufacture until actually woven or felted into fabric for consumption.

Flour, made from grain, is not to be considered a manufacture.

Fruits, preserved... 5 per ct.

Gains, annual, of every person, when exceeding $600, and do not exceed $10,000 on the excess of gain over $600........................ 3 per ct.

Exceeding $10,000 and not exceeding $50,000, on excess over $600... 5 per ct.

Gains, on annual, from property of any kind in the United States, realized by any citizen of the United States residing abroad, and not in the employ of the United States, not otherwise provided for.......... 5 per ct.

Gains—rent of residence is to be deducted from the income taxed.

Gas, coal, when the product shall be not above 500,000 cubic feet per month, per 1,000 cubic feet................................. 5 per ct.

When the product shall be above 500,000 and not exceeding 5,000,000 cubic feet per month, per 1,000 cubic feet.................... 10 per ct.

When the product shall be above 5,000,000, per 1,000 cubic feet..... 15 per ct.

Gas, all illuminating, same as coal gas.

Gelatine, of all descriptions in solid state, per pound.................... 5 mills.
Ginger, ground, and all imitations of, per pound....................... $0 01
Glass, manufacturers of, not otherwise specified....................... 3 per ct.
Glue, in a liquid form, per gallon..................................... 25
   In a solid state, per pound....................................... 5 mills.
Goat skins, curried, manufactured, or finished........................ 4 per ct.
Gold, manufacturers of, not otherwise provided for..................... 3 per ct.
Gold Leaf, per pack, containing not more than 20 books of 25 leaves..... 15
Goods, made for the use or consumption of the maker.................. free.
   Except spirituous and malt liquors, and leaf, and stem, or manufactured tobacco, where the annual product does not exceed $600,
   provided that this shall not apply to any business or transaction
   where one party furnishes the materials, or any part thereof, and
   employs another party to manufacture, make, or finish the goods,
   wares, or merchandise, or articles paying or promising to pay therefor, and receiving the goods, wares, and merchandise, or articles;
   but, in all such cases the party furnishing the materials and receiving the goods, wares, and merchandise, or articles, shall be
   liable to and charged with all accruing duties thereon............ free.
Grindstones.. free.
Gunpowder, and all explosive substances used for mining, artillery, or
   sporting purposes, valued at 18 cents per pound or less, per pound.. 5 mills.
   When valued above 18 cents, and not exceeding 30 cents, per pound.. 01
   When valued above 30 cents per pound, per pound................. 06
Gutta percha, manufactures of, not otherwise provided for............. 3 per ct.
Gypsum is not to be considered a manufacture.
Harness leather, per pound...................................... 7 mills.
Harness leather, made of hides imported east of the Cape of Good Hope,
   per pound... 5 mills.
Headings are not to be considered a manufacture.
Hemp, manufactures of, when not otherwise specified.................. 3 per ct.
Hog skins, tanned or dressed.. 4 per ct.
Hogs, exceeding 100 pounds in weight, without reference to age, slaughtered,
   each, for sale 06
   Slaughtered, weighing less than 100 pounds, without reference to age. free.
   Slaughtered by any person for his own consumption, to a number not
   exceeding six... free.
Hollow ware, iron, per ton of 2,000 pounds......................... 1 50
Hoop iron ("see Iron").
Hoop skirts, material for the manufacture of, exclusively............. free.
Horn, manufactures of, not otherwise provided for..................... 3 per ct.
Horned cattle, slaughtered for sale, each............................. 20
Horse skins, tanned and dressed..................................... 4 per ct.
Horse shoes, per ton.... .... 2 00
Horse dealers, under which term is included every person whose business is
   to buy and sell horses and mules, for each license............... 10 00
   When they have taken out a license as livery-stable keepers, are not
   required to take out an additional one.
Hose, conducting... 3 per ct.
Hotels—under which term is included every place where food and lodgings
   are provided for and furnished to travelers and sojourners, in view
   of payment therefor, where the rent or the valuation of the yearly
   rental of the house and property occupied shall be $10,000 or more,
   for each yearly license.. 200 00
   Where the rent or the valuation of the yearly rental shall be $5,000
   and less than $10,000, for each yearly license.................. 100 00
   Where the rent or the valuation of the yearly rental shall be $2,500
   and less than $5,000, for each yearly license................... 75 00
   Where the rent or the valuation of the yearly rental shall be $1,000
   and less than $2,500, for each yearly license................... 50 00
   Where the rent or the valuation of the yearly rental shall be $500 and
   less than $1,000, for each yearly license...................... 25 00
   Where the rent or the valuation of the yearly rental shall be $300 and
   less than $500, for each yearly license........................ 15 00

Hotels—Where the rent or the valuation of the yearly rental shall be $100 and less than $300, for each yearly license............. .... $10 00
Where the rent or the valuation of the yearly rental shall be less than $100, for each yearly license................................... 5 00
Steamers and vessels upon waters of the United States, on board of which passengers or travelers are provided with food or lodging, shall be required to take out a license of the fifth class, viz., at.... 25 00
Illuminating oil, coal, proved to have been manufactured before Sept. 1, '62. free.
Income, annual, of every person, when exceeding $600 and not exceeding $10,000, on the excess over $600.............................. 3 per ct.
Exceeding $10,000 and not exceeding $50,000, on excess over $600... 5 per ct.
Annual, from property of any kind in the United States, realized by any citizen of the United States residing abroad, and not in the employment of the U. S. Government, not otherwise provided for.... 5 per ct.
Indemnity—Papers relating to indemnity awarded for depredations and injuries by certain bands of Sioux Indians
India-rubber, manufacture of, not otherwise specified.................. 3 per ct.
Inns, same as "Hotels."
Instruments of attorney, made in foreign countries, same stamp duty as if made in the United States.
Insurance Companies, Mutual, deposit notes to, stamp duty............. none.
Insurance policies of any kind, on which there is a premium not exceeding $10, stamp duty.... 10
Insurance Companies, all, on dividends.............................. 3 per ct.
Insurance Companies, inland or marine, upon gross receipts for premiums and assessments... 1 per ct.
Insurance (life)—Policy of insurance, or other instrument by whatever name the same shall be called, whereby any insurance shall be made or renewed, marine or inland, upon property of any description, made by any insurance company or its agents or by any other company or persons.. 25
Insurance agents, under which term is included every person who shall act as agent of any fire, marine, life, mutual or other insurance company or companies ; *Provided*, That no license shall be required of any insurance agent or broker, whose receipts, as such agent, are less than the sum of $600 in any one year, for license............... 10 00
Insurance, tickets or contracts of, when limited to fatal or non-fatal injury to persons while traveling, are not required to pay a stamp duty.
Insurance, persons insuring against injury to travelers, on gross receipts.. 1 per ct.
Interest, income from, when exceeding the sum of $600 per annum, and not exceeding $10,000 on the excess of income over $600........ 3 per ct.
Exceeding $10,000, and not exceeding $50,000, on the excess over $600...................................... 5 per ct.
Incomes from, when realized by any citizen of the United States residing abroad, and not in the employ of the United States Government, not otherwise provided for.......................... 5 per ct.
Interest on bonds and dividends of canal companies.................. 3 per ct.
Iron, manufactures of, if not otherwise specified..................... 3 per ct.
Cast, used for bridges, buildings, or other permanent structures, per tun... 1 00
Casting, exceeding ten pounds in weight, not otherwise provided for in the Tax law (see "Railroad Cars") per tun.................. 1 50
Railroad, per tun.. 1 50
Re-rolled, per tun... 75
Advanced beyond slabs, blooms, or hoops, and not advanced beyond bars or rods, per tun...................................... 1 50
Band, hoop, and sheet, not thinner than No. 18 wire-gauge, per tun. 1 50
Plate not less than one eighth of an inch in thickness, per tun..... 1 50
Band, hoop, or sheet, thinner than No. 18 wire-gauge, per tun...... 2 00
Plate, less than one eighth of an inch in thickness, per tun........ 2 00
Nails, cut, and spikes, per tun.................................. 2 00
Bars, rods, bands, hoops, sheets, plates, nails, and spikes, upon which the duty of $1 50 has been levied and paid, are only subject to an additional duty of, per tun.... 50

Iron—Marine engines.. 3 per ct.
   Rivets, exceeding one fourth of an inch in diameter, per tun........ $2 00
   Nuts, per tun.. 2 00
   Railroad chairs, per tun... 2 00
   Bolts, per tun.. 2 00
   Horse-shoes, per tun.. 2 00
Iron, rivets, nuts, railroad chairs, bolts, and horse-shoes, where the duty
   upon the iron from which said articles shall have been made has
   been actually paid, only an additional duty of, per tun 50
Iron, pig, is not to be considered a manufacture.
Ivory, manufacture of, if not otherwise specified.................. 3 per ct.
Jacks and stallions, for license, see "Stallions"................... 10 00
Jewelry... 3 per ct.
Jute, manufacture of, if not otherwise specified................... 3 per ct.
Jugglers, including every person who performs by sleight of hand, for
   each license.. 20 00
The proprietors or agents of all other public exhibitions or shows for
   money, not enumerated in this section, shall pay for each license... 10 00
Kid skins, curried, manufactured, or unfinished................... 5 per ct.
Lager beer, per barrel, containing 31 gallons (fractional parts of a barrel
   to pay proportionately), see "Malt Liquors."
Lambs, slaughtered for sale, each.................................. 03
Land warrant brokers, under which term is included every person who
   makes a business of buying and selling land warrants and furnishing them to settlers or other persons, under contracts that the lands
   procured by means of them shall be bound for the prices agreed on
   for the warrants, for each license............................... 25 00
Lard oil, per gallon.. 02
Lawyers, under which term is included every person whose business it is,
   for fee or reward, to prosecute or defend any cause in any court of
   record or other judicial tribunal of the United States, or of any of
   the States, or give advice in relation to any cause or matter pending
   therein for each license, see ("Attorney.")...................... 10 00
Lead, manufactures of, if not otherwise specified................. 3 per ct.
Lead, white, per hundred.. 25
Leaf, gold, per package containing not more than 20 books of 25 leaves
   each.. 15
Lease, for the hire, use, or rent of any land, tenement, or portion
   thereof, if for a period not exceeding three years, stamp duty...... 50
   For a period of time exceeding three years, stamp duty............ 1 00
Leases, assignment of, see "Assignment."
Leather, bend or butt, per pound.................................. 01½
   Damaged, per pound... 5 mills.
   Enameled, per square foot...................................... 5 mills.
   Enameled skirting, per square foot............................. 01½
   Harness, per pound.. 7 mills.
   Harness, made from hides imported east of the Cape of Good Hope,
   per pound.. 5 mills.
   Offal, per pound.. 5 mills.
   Oil dressed, per pound.. 02
   Patent, per square foot....................................... 5 mills.
   Patent japanned splits, used for dasher leather, square foot......... 4 mills.
   Patent enameled skirting, per square foot..................... 01½
   Rough, made from hides imported east of the Cape of Good Hope,
   per pound... 5 mills.
   Rough, all other hemlock tanned, per pound.................... 7 mills.
   Rough, tanned in whole or in part with oak, per pound......... 01
   Sole, made from hides imported east of the Cape of Good Hope, per pound 5 mills.
   Sole, all other hemlock tanned, per pound..................... 7 mills.
   Sole, tanned in whole or in part with oak, per pound.......... 01
   Tanned calfskins, each.. 06
   Upper finished or curried, made from leather tanned in the interest
   of the parties currying such leather, not previously taxed in the
   rough, per pound.. 01

Leather, manufactures of, when not otherwise specified.................. 3 per ct.

Legacies—Any person or persons having charge or trust as administrators, executors, or trustees, of any legacies or distributive shares arising from personal property, of any kind whatever, where the whole amount of such personal property, as aforesaid, shall exceed the sum of $1,000 in actual value, passing from any person who may die after the passage of this act, possessed of such property either by will or by the intestate laws of any State or Territory, or any part of such property or interest therein, transferred by deed, grant, bargain, sale, or gift, made or intended to take effect in possession or enjoyment after the death of the grantor or bargainer, to any person or persons, or to any body or bodies, politic or corporate, in trust or otherwise, are subject to the following taxes : Where the person or persons entitled to any beneficial interest in such property shall be the lineal issue or lineal ancestor, brother or sister, to the person who died possessed of such property, for each and every $100 of the clear value of such interest in such property.......... $0 75

When the person or persons entitled to any beneficial interest in such property shall be a descendant of a brother or sister of the person who died possessed of such property, for each and every $100 of the clear value of such interest............................... 1 50

When the person or persons entitled to any beneficial interest in such property shall be a brother or sister of the father or mother, or a descendant of a brother or sister of the father or mother of the person who died possessed of such property, for each and every $100 of the clear value of such interest............................... 3 00

Where the person or persons entitled to any beneficial interest in such property shall be a brother or sister of the grandfather or grandmother, or a descendant of the brother or sister of the grandfather or grandmother of the person who died possessed of such property, for each and every $100 of the clear value of such interest.......... 4 00

Where the person or persons entitled to any beneficial interest in such property shall be in any other degree of collateral consanguinity than is stated above, or shall be a stranger in blood to the person who died possessed, as aforesaid, or shall be a body politic or corporate, for each and every $100 of the clear value of such interest........ 5 00

Passing by will or by the laws of any State or Territory, to husband or wife of the person who died possessed of the property .... free.

Legal documents, writ, or other original process commenced in any court of law or equity, stamp duty................................... 50

Letters of credit, see " Bills of Exchange (Foreign)."

Letters of Administration—Where the estate and effects for or in respect of which such letters of administration applied for shall be sworn or declared not to exceed the value of $2,500, stamp duty......... 50
To exceed $2,500, and not exceeding $5,000...................... 1 00
To exceed $5,000, and not exceeding $20,000...................... 3 00
To exceed $20,000, and not exceeding $50,000 .... 5 00
Letters of Administration—To exceed $50,000, and not exceeding $100,000   10 00
Exceeding $100,000, and not exceeding $150,000.................. 20 00
For every additional $50,000 or part thereof...................... 10 00

Licenses must be taken out each year by the following-named persons, for which they are to pay the sum placed opposite their names, viz. :

Agents, insurance	$10 00	Cattle brokers...............	$10 00
Apothecaries................	10 00	Circuses....................	50 00
Architects	10 00	Civil engineers...............	10 00
Auctioneers.................	20 00	Claim agents................	10 00
Bankers	100 00	Coal oil distillers...........	50 00
Billiard tables, each	5 00	Commercial brokers..........	50 00
Brewers, see " Brewers"......25 and 50		Confectioners..............	10 00
Brokers....................	50 00	Contractors.................	25 00
Brokers, Insurance..........	10 00	Dentists....................	10 00
Bowling alleys, for each alley.	5 00	Distillers, see " Distillers."	
Builders	25 00	Eating houses...............	10 00
Butchers, see "Butchers"....	10 00	Horse dealers...............	10 00

Hotels, see "Hotels," from $5 to 200 00	Physicians		$10 00
Jacks	10 00	Retail dealers	10 00
Jugglers	20 00	Retail dealers in liquors	20 00
Lawyers	10 00	Rectifiers, see "Rectifiers."	
Livery stable keepers	10 00	Surgeons	10 00
Lottery ticket dealers	1,000 00	Tobacconists	10 00
Manufacturers	10 00	Theaters	100 00
Peddlers, see "Peddlers".from 5 to 20 00	Tallow chandlers		10 00
Photographers	10 00	Soap makers	10 00
Pawnbrokers	50 00	Stallions. owners of	10 00

Wholesale dealers, whose sales do not exceed $50,000, for each license.... 25 00
Exceeding $50,000 and not exceeding $100,000, for each license..... 50 00
Exceeding $100,000 and not exceeding $250,000, for each licenses.... 100 00
Exceeding $250,000 and not exceeding $500,000, for each license.... 200 00
Exceeding $500,000 and not exceeding $1,000 000, for each license.. 300 00
Exceeding $1,000,000 and not exceeding $2,000,000, for each license. 500 00
Exceeding $2,000,000, for each $1,000,000 in excess of $2,000,000, for
each license.. 250 00
Wholesale dealers in liquors, same as "Wholesale Dealers."
Life insurance companies, see "Insurance."
Lime is not to be regarded as a manufacture.
Liniments, same as "Dentrifice."
Linseed oil, per gallon.. 02
Liquors, malt, until April 1, 1864, duty, per bbl. containing not more than
31 gallons... 60
Liquors, malt, proved to have been manufactured before Sept. 1, 1862.... free.
Livery stable keepers, under which term is included every person whose
occupation is to keep horses for hire or to let, for license, ... 10 00
Lottery tickets, on each offered for sale without a stamp, penalty........ 50 00
Lottery tickets, when they, or any fraction of them, shall not exceed the
retail price of $1... 50
Exceeding $1, for every dollar or fraction........................ 50
Lottery ticket dealers, under which term is included every person, association, firm, or corporation, who shall make, sell, or offer to sell
lottery tickets or fractional parts thereof, or any token, certificate,
or device representing or intended to represent a lottery ticket, or
any fractional part thereof, or any policy of numbers in any lottery,
or shall manage any lottery or prepare schemes of lotteries, or superintend the drawing of any lottery, for license.................. 1,000 00
Lumber is not to be considered a manufacture.
Magazines are not to be regarded as a manufacture of paper, or submitted
to a rate of duty as a manufacture.
For all advertisements, on gross receipts......................... 3 per ct.
Malt is not to be considered a manufacture.
Malt liquors, until April 1, 1864, duty, per bbl, containing not more than
31 gallons... 60
Proved to have been manufactured before September 1, 1862........ free.
Manifest of the cargo of any ship, vessel, or steamer, for a foreign port, if
the registered tonnage of such ship, vessel, or steamer does not ex-
ceed 300 tuns, stamp duty.. 1 00
Exceeding 300 tuns, and not exceeding 600 tuns.................... 3 00
Exceeding 600 tuns... 5 00
Manufacturers, under which term is included any person or persons, firms,
corporations or companies, who shall manufacture by hand or machinery and offer for sale any goods, wares, or merchandise, or who
shall manufacture by hand or machinery for any other person or
persons, goods, wares, or merchandise, exceeding annually the sum
of $1,000, for license.. 10 00
Manufactures not otherwise specified :

Of bone	3 per ct.	Of flax	3 per ct.
Of brass	3 per ct.	Of glass	3 per ct.
Of bristles	3 per ct.	Of gold	3 per ct.
Of copper	3 per ct.	Of gutta percha	3 per ct.
Of cotton	3 per ct.	Of hemp	3 per ct.

Of horn	3 per ct.	Of silk	3 per ct.
Of India-rubber	3 per ct.	Of silver	3 per ct.
Of iron	3 per ct.	Of steel	3 per ct.
Of ivory	3 per ct.	Of tin	3 per ct.
Of jute	3 per ct	Of willow	3 per ct.
Of lead	3 per ct.	Of wood	3 per ct.
Of leather	3 per ct.	Of wool	3 per ct.
Of paper	3 per ct.	Of worsted	3 per ct.
Of pottery	3 per ct.	Of other materials	3 per ct.

Maps are not to be considered a manufacture.

Marine Engines... 3 per ct.

Marine Insurance Companies, see "Insurance."

Marine protest... $0 25

Measurement, Certificates of, stamp duty............................... none.

Meats preserved... 5 per ct.

Medicines, see when the value of the package containing the same shall not
  exceed, at the retail price or value, the sum of 25 cents.......... 01
  Exceeding 25 cents, and not exceeding 50 cents................... 02
  Exceeding 50 cents, and not exceeding 75 cents................... 03
  Exceeding 75 cents, and not exceeding $1......................... 04
  Exceeding $1, for each and every 50 cents, or fractional part thereof
  over and above $1, an additional............................... 02

Metal, yellow sheathing, in rod or sheets............................. 1 per ct.

Milliners, making articles to order as custom work and not for sale generally, shall to the amount of $1,000 be exempt from duty, and for
  any excess beyond the amount of $1,000 shall pay a duty of....... 1 per ct.

Mineral coal, except pea coal, per ton................................ 0 3½

Mineral water, per quart bottle....................................... 01
  For bottles holding more than a quart........................... 02

Morocco, skins, cured, manufactured, or finished..................... 4 per ct.

Mortgage—Any, or personal bond for the payment of money, or as security
  for the payment of any definite or certain sum of money, shall have
  a stamp or stamps affixed thereon denoting a duty upon every sum
  of $200, or any fractional part thereof, of....................... 10

Mortgage—Not required to pay a stamp duty of more than $1,000.

Movements, clock, made to run one day each.......................... 05
  Made to run over one day, each................................. 10

Mustard. ground, per pound.. 01
  Mustard-seed oil, per gallon................................... 02

Mutual insurance companies ; see "Insurance."

Nails, cut, per ton... 2 00

Naphtha, per gallon...3 per ct. ad valorem.

Newspapers are not to be regarded as a manufacture, or submitted to a rate
  of duty as a manufacture.

Newspapers, for all advertisements, on gross receipts, see "Advertisements" 3 per ct.

Notarial act, see "Protest."

Note, see "Promissory Note."

Nuts, iron, per ton... 2 00
  Where the duty has been paid on the material of which made, only an
  addition of, per ton.. 50

Oils, animal all, pure or unadulterated, if not otherwise provided for, per
  gallon.. 02
  Illuminating, refined, produced by the distillation of coal, asphaltum,
  shale, peat. petroleum or rock, oil, and all other bituminous substances
  used for like purposes, per gallon.............................. 10
  Proved to have been manufactured before Sept. 1, 1862............ free.
  Lard, pure or unadulterated, if not otherwise provided for, per gallon. 02
  Linseed, mustard seed, and all vegetable do., per gallon.......... 02

Oils, refined, produced by distillation of coal exclusively, per gallon...... 08

Oleic acid, produced in the manufacture of candles, and used in the manufacture of soap... free.

Order for the payment of any sum of money drawn upon any bank, trust
  company, or any person or persons, companies or corporations, at
  sight or on demand, stamp duty same as "Bill of Exchange."

Oxide of zinc, per 100 pounds.. $0 25
Packet, containing medicines, etc., see "Bottles."
Paints, dry or ground in oil or in paste, with water, not otherwise provided
    for... 5 per ct.
Paints shall not be subject to any additional duty in consequence of being
    mixed or ground in oil, when the duties upon all the materials so
    mixed and ground shall have been previously actually paid.
Painters' colors, same as "Paints."
Pamphlets are not to be regarded as a manufacture, or submitted to a rate
    of duty as a manufacture.
    On gross receipts for advertisements............................. 3 per ct.
Paper of all descriptions... 3 per ct.
Paraffine oil.. exempt.
Parasols of any material.. 3 per ct.
Passport, on each issued from the office of the Secretary of State......... 3 00
    On each issued by Ministers or Consuls of the United States........ 3 00
Passage ticket, by any vessel from a port in the United States to a foreign
    port, of $30 or less... 50
    Exceeding $30... 1 00
Pasteboard, made of junk, straw, or other material..................... 3 per ct.
Patent leather (see "Leather"), per square foot....................... 5 mills.
Pawnbrokers, under which term is included every person whose business
    or occupation is to take or receive, by way of pledge, pawn, or ex-
    change, any goods, wares, or merchandise, or any kind of personal
    property whatever, for the repayment or security of money lent
    thereon, for license... 50 00
Pearl barley is not to be considered a manufacture.
Peddlers, under which term is included every person who sells, or offers to
    sell, at retail, goods, wares, or other commodities, traveling from
    place to place, in the street, or through different parts of the
    country, when traveling with more than two horses, for each license 20 00
    When traveling with two horses, for each license................. 15 00
    When traveling with one horse, for each license.................. 10 00
    When traveling on foot, for each license........................ 5 00
    Who sell newspapers, Bibles, or religious tracts................... exempt.
    Who sell, or offer to sell, dry goods, foreign or domestic, by one or
    more original packages or pieces at one time to the same person,
    for each license.. 50 00
Peddlers, who peddle jewelry, for each license......................... 25 00
Pensions, applications for, stamp duty .... none.
Pepper, ground, and all imitations of, per pound...................... 1
Perfumery, same as "Medicines."
Petroleum, refined, per gallon.. 10
Phial, containing medicines, etc., same as "Bottles," which see.
Photographers, under which term is included every person who makes for
    sale photographs, ambrotypes, or pictures on glass, metal, or paper,
    by the action of light, for each license, when the receipts do not
    exceed $500.. 10 00
    When the receipts are over $500, and under $1,000, for license...... 15 00
    When the receipts are over $1,000, for license................... 25 00
Physicians, under which term is included every person (except apothe-
    caries) whose business it is to, for fee or reward, prescribe medicine or
    perform any surgical operation for the cure of any bodily disease
    or ailing, dentists included, for each license................... 10 00
Pickles .... 5 per ct.
Pig iron is not to be considered a manufacture.
Pills, same as "Dentifrice."
Pimento, ground, and all imitation of, per pound...................... 1
Pins, solid head or other, in boxes, packets, bundles, or other form....... 5 per ct.
Plaster is not to be considered a manufacture.
Plate of gold, kept for use, per oz. troy.............................. 50
Plate of silver, do., per oz. troy..................................... 3
Plate, silver, as above, to the extent of 40 ozs....................... free.
Plate, belonging to religious societies............................... free.

Plate iron, see "Iron."

Playing cards, see "Cards."

Policy of insurance (life, marine or inland, or fire), see "Insurance."

Porter, per barrel of 31 gallons, fractional parts in proportion, see "Malt Liquors."

Pot, containing medicine, etc., same as "Bottles."

Pottery ware, if not otherwise specified.............................. 3 per ct.

Power of attorney for the sale or transfer of any scrip, or certificate of profits, or memorandum, showing an interest in the profits or accumulation of any corporation or association, for a sum less than $50.. $0 10

Power of attorney for the sale or transfer of any stock, bonds, or scrip, or for the collection of any dividend, or interest thereon, stamp duty   25

Power of attorney or proxy for voting at any election for officers of any incorporated company or society, except charitable, religious, literary, and cemetery societies, stamp duty...................   10

Power of attorney to sell and convey real estate, or to rent or lease the same, or to perform any and all other acts not specified, stamp duty   1 00

Power of attorney to receive or collect rents, stamp duty..............   25

Power of attorney made in any foreign country, same stamp duty as if made in the United States.

Preparations of which coffee forms a part, or which are prepared for sale as a substitute for coffee, per pound........................... 3 mills.

Preserved fish... 5 per ct.

Preserved fruit or meats.. 5 per ct.

Printed books are not regarded as a manufacture, or submitted to a rate of duty as a manufacture.

On all advertisements on gross receipts, for...................... 3 per ct.

Printers' ink is not to be considered a manufacture.

Probate of will, where the estate and effects for or in respect of which such probate applied for shall be sworn or declared not to exceed the value of $2,500, stamp duty....................................   0 50

To exceed $2,500 and not exceeding $5,000........................   1 00

To exceed $5,000 and not exceeding $20,000.......................   2 00

To exceed $20,000 and not exceeding $50,000......................   5 00

To exceed $50,000 and not exceeding $100,000.....................   10 00

Exceeding $100,000 and not exceeding $150,000....................   20 00

For every additional $50,000, or fractional part thereof............   10 00

Profits, annual, of every person when exceeding $600, and not exceeding $10,000 on the excess over $600............................... 3 per ct.

Exceeding $10,000, and not exceeding $50,000 on the excess over $600.. 5 per ct.

Annual, when received by any citizen of the United States resident abroad, and not in employ of the U. S., not otherwise provided for. 5 per ct.

Promissory note—Any memorandum, check, receipt, or other written or printed evidence of an amount of money to be paid on demand, or at a time designated, shall be considered as a "Promissory Note," and re-stamped accordingly. See "Bill of Exchange (Inland)."

Property, annual income from, same as profits.

Property left by legacy, see "Legacies."

Protest of every note, bill of exchange, acceptance, check, or draft.......   25

Publications, same as "Printed Books."

Railroads—On gross receipts from carrying passengers.................. 3 per ct.

The motive power of which is not steam, on gross receipts from carrying passengers... 1½ per ct.

Railroads—On bonds or other evidence of indebtedness upon which interest is stipulated to be paid, on the amount of interest............. 3 per ct.

Railroad cars—There shall be deducted from duties assessed upon railroad cars any duties which may have been assessed and paid upon car wheels.

Railroad chairs, per tun..   2 00

Where the duty has been paid on the material of which made, only an additional duty, of per tun...............................   50

Railroad iron, per tun..   1 50

Railroad iron, re-rolled per tun $0 75
Receipt, warehouse, stamp duty....................................... 25
Receipt (other than charter party) for any goods, merchandise, or effects
    to be exported from a port or place in the United States to any for-
    eign port or place, stamp duty.............................. 10
    For any goods, merchandise, or effects to be carried from one port or
    place in the United States to any other port or place in the United
    States, either by land or water, except when carried by an express
    company or carrier. *Stamp duty repealed.*
Receipts of express companies, gross................................ 2 per ct.
Receipts, gross, of ferry-boat companies............................1½ per ct.
Rectifiers, under which term is included every person who rectifies, puri-
    fies, or refines spirituous liquors or wines by any process, or mixes
    distilled spirits, whisky, brandy, gin, or wine with any other mate-
    rials for sale under the name of rum, whisky, brandy, gin, wine, or
    any other name or names, for each license to rectify any quantity of
    spirituous liquors not exceeding 500 barrels, containing not more
    than forty gallons to each 25 00
    For each additional 500 barrels, or any fraction thereof............. 25 00
Red oil, used as material in the manufacture of soap .... free.
Renewal of insurance,·see "Policy of Insurance."
Rents, annual income from, when exceeding $600, on the excess over $600
    (see "Incomes"·).. 3 per ct.
Rents, annual income from, when realized by a citizen of the U. S. resid-
    ing in a foreign country and not in the employ of the U. S........ 5 per ct.
Rent of residence deducted from income before levying tax thereon.
Retail dealers, under which term is included every person whose business
    or occupation it is to sell or offer for sale any goods, wares, or mer-
    chandise of foreign or domestic production not including wines,
    spirituous or malt liquors, but not excluding drugs, medicines, ci-
    gars, snuff, or tobacco, and whose annual sales exceed $1,000 and do
    not exceed $25,000, for license.................................. 10 00
Retail liquor dealers, under which term is included every person other
    than a distiller or brewer who shall sell or offer for sale any dis-
    tilled spirits, fermented liquors, or wine of any description in quan-
    tities of three gallons or less, and whose annual sales do not exceed
    $25,000 ; but nothing herein contained shall authorize the sale of
    any spirits, liquors, wines, or malt liquors to be drank on the
    premises : *Provided,* That no person licensed to keep an hotel, inn,
    or tavern shall be allowed to sell any liquors to be taken off the
    premises, and no person licensed to keep an eating-house shall be
    allowed to sell spirituous or vinous liquors, and no person who has
    taken out a license to keep an hotel, inn, tavern or eating-house shall
    be required to take out a license as a tobacconist because of any to-
    bacco or cigars furnished in the usual course of business as a keeper
    of an hotel, inn, tavern or eating-house...................... 20 00
Reviews, same as "Pamphlets."
Rivets, exceeding one fourth of an inch in diameter, per tun........... 2 00
Rivets, exceeding one fourth of one inch in diameter, iron, where the duty
    has been paid on the material of which made, only an additional
    duty, per tun...,.. 50
Rock oil, refined, see "Oils."
Roman cement is not to be regarded as a manufacture.
Sail boats, hereafter built... 2 per ct.
Sails made of cotton, flax, or hemp, or parts of either, or other material.. 3 per ct.
Sails, see "Awnings."
Salaries, annual income from, when exceeding $600, on the excess over
    $600.. 3 per ct.
    All, of persons in employ of the United States, when exceeding the
    rate of $600 per year, on the excess above $600.................. 3 per ct.
Saleratus, per pound.. 5 mills.
Sales, auction, of goods, stocks, etc., on gross amount of sales.....1-10 of 1 per ct.
Sales made by public officers, etc................................... exempt.
Salt, per hundred pounds.. 04

Savings institutions, on all dividends............................... 3 per ct.
Schooners, hereafter built.. 2 per ct.
Screws called wood screws, per pound................................. $0 01½
Scrip, paper for the sale or transfer of, stamp duty.................... 10
Segars, valued at not over $5 per 1,000, per 1,000................... 1 50
    Valued at over $5 per 1,000 and not over $10 per 1,000............ 2 00
    Valued at over $10 and not over $20 per 1,000, per 1,000.......... 2 50
    Valued at over $20 per 1,000, per 1,000......................... 3 50
Shades, same as "Awnings."
Sheathing metal, yellow.. 1 per ct.
Shell-fish, in cans or air-tight packages............................ 5 per ct.
Sheep, slaughtered for sale, per head............................... 03
Sheep, slaughtered by any person for his own consumption, to a number
    not exceeding six.. free.
Sheep skins, tanned, curried, and finished.......................... 4 per ct.
Shingles are not to be considered a manufacture.
Ships, hereafter built.. 2 per ct.
Shoemakers, see "Bootmakers."
Silk parasols and umbrellas... 3 per ct.
Silk, manufactures of, not otherwise specified...................... 3 per ct.
Silver bullion, rolled or prepared for platers' use exclusively......... free.
Silver, manufactures of, when not otherwise specified................ 3 per ct.
Skins, calf, tanned, each... 06
    American patent... 5 per ct.
    Goat, curried, manufactured, or finished....................... 4 per ct.
    Kid, do... 4 per ct.
    Morocco, do... 4 per ct.
    Sheep, tanned, curried, or finished............................ 4 per ct.
    Deer, dressed and smoked, per pound. 02
    Hog and horse, tanned and dressed............................. 4 per ct.
Skirts, hoop, materials for the manufacture of, exclusively.......... free.
Slates are not to be considered a manufacture.
Slaughtered cattle, see "Cattle."
Sloops, hereafter built... 2 per ct.
Snuff, manufactured of tobacco, or stems, or of any substitute for tobacco,
    ground, dry or damp, of all descriptions, per pound............. 20
Soap, castile or erasive, valued not above 3½ cents per pound, per pound.. 1 mill.
    Castile, valued above 3½ cents per pound, per pound............. 5 mills.
    Cream, per pound... 02
    Erasive, valued above 3½ cents per pound, per pound............ 5 mills.
    Fancy and honey, per pound................................... 02
    Palm oil, valued not above 3½ cents per pound, per pound........ 1 mill.
    Palm oil, valued above 3½ cents per pound, per pound........... 5 mills.
    Scented, shaving, toilet, and transparent, per pound............ 02
    Of all other descriptions, white or colored, except soft soap, and soap
    otherwise provided for, valued not above 3½ cents per pound, per
    pound.. 1 mill.
    Valued above 3½ cents per pound, per pound.................... 5 mills.
Soapmakers, under which is included every person whose business is to
    make or manufacture soap, for each license.................... 10 00
Soda, bi-carbonate of, per pound................................... 5 mills.
Spikes, per tun.. 2 00
Spindles, exclusively for articles on which duties are paid, and articles
    manufactured from material already taxed, where the increased
    value does not exceed 5 per cent.............................. free.
Spirits, distilled, per gallon.. 20
Split peas are not to be considered a manufacture.
Spokes.. free.
Stallions and jacks, owners of, under which term is included every person
    who keeps a male horse or a jackass for the use of mares, requiring
    or receiving pay therefor, shall be required to take out a license
    under this act, which shall contain a brief description of the an-
    imal, its age, and place or places where used or to be used ; *Provided*,
    that all accounts, notes, or demand for the use of any such horse or

jack without a license, as aforesaid, shall be invalid, and of no force in any court of law or equity, for license $10 00
Starch, made of corn or wheat, per pound .... 1½ mills.
Made of potatoes, per pound .... 1 mill.
Made of rice, per pound .... 4 mills.
Made of any other material, per pound .... 4 mills.
Steamboats, except ferry-boats, on gross receipts .... 3 per ct.
Hereafter built, not including the engines .... 2 per ct.
Steel, manufactures of, when not otherwise specified.................. 3 per ct.
Steel, in ingots, bars, sheets, or wire, not less than one quarter of an inch
in thickness, valued at 7 cents per pound or less, per tun.......... 4 00
Valued above 7 cents, and not above 11 cents per pound, per tun.... 8 00
Valued above 11 cents per pound, per tun........................ 10 00
Stills, used in distilling spirituous liquors, for each yearly license........ 50 00
Used in distilling spirituous liquors, for each half-yearly license 25 00
Used by distillers of apples and peaches, may be licensed for the space
of three months, upon payment for each license for such time 12 50
Stoves, per tun of 2,000 pounds.................................. 1 50
Sugar refiners, under which term is included every person whose business
it is to advance the quality and value of sugar by melting and recrystallization, or by liquoring, claying, or any other washing process, or by any other chemical or mechanical means, or who shall
advance the quality or value of molasses and concentrated molasses, melado or concentrated melado, by boiling or other process,
on the gross amount of the sales of all the products of their manufactories .... 1½ per ct.
Sugar, brown, Muscovado or clarified, produced directly from the sugar-cane,
and not from sorghum and imphee cane, per pound.............. 01
Sugar candy, made wholly or in part of sugar valued at 14 cents per pound
or less, per pound... 02
Valued at exceeding 14 cents per pound and not exceeding 40 cents
per pound, per pound...................................... 03
Valued at exceeding 40 cents per pound, or when sold otherwise than
by the pound... 5 per ct.
Sulphate of barytes, per 100 pounds.............................. 10
Surgeons, for each license....................................... 10 00
Tailors, same as "Milliners."
Tallow chandlers, under which term is included every person whose busi-
ness it is to make or manufacture candles, for each license......... 10 00
Tar, coal, produced in the manufacture of gas..................... exempt.
Taverns, same as "Hotels."
Telegraphic dispatches, see "Dispatch."
Tents, same as "Awnings."
Theaters, under which term is included every place or edifice erected for
the purpose of dramatic or operatic representation, plays or perform-
ances, and not including halls rented or used occasionally for con-
certs or theatrical representations, for each license 100 00
Ticket, passage, by any vessel from any port in the United States to a for-
eign port, if less than $30 50
Exceeding $30... 1 00
Timber is not to be considered a manufacture.
Tin, manufactures of, when not otherwise specified.................. 3 per ct.
Tobacconists, under which term is included every person who shall offer
for sale, at retail, cigars, snuff, or tobacco in any form (wholesale
and retail dealers, keepers of hotels, inns, and taverns, or eating-
houses having taken out a license, are not required to take out a li-
cense as tobacconists), for each license......................... 10 00
Tobacco, cavendish, per pound 15
Fine cut, per pound.. 15
Ground, dry or damp of all descriptions (except aromatic or medicinal
snuff in vials, pots, boxes, or packets), per pound................. 03
Manufactured, of all kinds, not including snuff, cigars, or smoking
tobacco, prepared with all the stems, or made exclusively of stems,
per pound... 15

Tobacco, smoking, prepared with all the stems in, or made exclusively
of stems, per pound... $0 05
Plug, same as "Tobacco, cavendish."
Twist, same as "Tobacco, cavendish."
Trust companies, on dividends, etc................................. 3 per ct.
Umbrellas, made of cotton..................................... 3 per ct.
Made of any other material .... 3 per ct.
Umbrella stretchers are not to be considered a manufacture.
Varnish, made wholly or in part of gum copal, or of other substances.... 5 per ct.
Made of other gums or substances............................... 5 per ct.
Vegetable oils, per gallon....................................... 02
Vessels, hereafter built.. 2 per ct.
Warehouse entry, at custom-houses, not exceeding $100 in value, stamp
duty... 25
Exceeding $100 and not exceeding $500...................... 50
Exceeding $500 in value..................................... 1 00
Warehouse receipts, stamp duty.................................. 25
Whale oil.. exempt.
Whisky, per gallon... 20
Rectified, is not to pay an additional duty.
Wholesale dealers under which term is included every person whose busi-
ness or occupation it is to sell or offer to sell any goods, wares, or
merchandise of foreign or domestic production, not including dis-
tilled spirits, fermented liquors, or wines, but not excluding drugs,
medicines, cigars, snuff, or tobacco), whose annual sales exceed
$25,000, and do not exceed $50,000, for each license.............. 25 00
If exceeding $50,000, and not exceeding $100,000, for each license... 50 00
Exceeding $100,000 and not exceeding $250,000, for each license.... 100 00
Exceeding $250,000 and not exceeding $500,000, for each license.... 200 00
Exceeding $500,000 and not exceeding $1,000,000, for each license.. 300 00
Exceeding $1,000,000 and not exceeding $2,000,000, for each license. 500 00
Exceeding $2,000,000, for every $1,000,000 in excess of $2,000,000,
in addition to the $500....................................... 250 00
Wholesale dealers—The license required by any wholesale dealer shall
not be for a less amount than his sales for the previous year, unless
he has made or proposes to make some change in his business that
will obviously reduce the amount of his annual sales, nor shall any
licensed or wholesale dealer allow any such persons to act as commercial broker : Provided, That any license understated may be ·
again assessed.
Wholesale dealers in liquors—under which term is included every person
other than the distiller or brewer who shall sell, or offer for sale, any
distilled spirits, fermented liquors, and wines of all kinds, in
quantities of more than three gallons at one time, or whose annual
sales shall exceed $25,000—shall pay for each license the amount
required for license to "wholesale dealers."
Willow, manufactures of.. 3 per ct
Wine made of grapes, per gallon................................. 05
Withdrawal entry, at custom-house, stamp duty..................... 50
Wood, manufactures of, if not otherwise provided for................ 3 per ct.
Wood screws.. 01½
Wool, manufactures of, not otherwise specified..................... 3 per ct.
Worsted, manufactures of, not otherwise specified.................. 3 per ct.
Writ, stamp duty.. 50
Yachts, under the value of $600................................. 5 00
Value above $600, and not above $1,000....................... 10 00
For each additional $1,000 in value.......................... 10 00
Yellow sheathing metal... 1 per ct.
Zinc, manufactures of, not otherwise specified..................... 3 per ct.
Oxide of, per 100 pounds..................................... 25

www.ingramcontent.com/pod-product-compliance
Lightning Source LLC
Chambersburg PA
CBHW020554270326
41927CB00006B/843